THE PRINCETON REVIEW

READING
SMART

ADVANCED TECHNIQUES
FOR IMPROVED READING

THE PRINCETON REVIEW

READING
SMART

ADVANCED TECHNIQUES
FOR IMPROVED READING

By Nicholas Reid Schaffzin

Random House, Inc.
New York 1998
www.randomhouse.com

Acknowledgments for previously published material
can be found on pages 269–270.

Schaffzin, Nicholas Reid.
    Reading smart: advanced techniques for average readers/
Nicholas Reid Schaffzin—1st ed.
        p.   cm.
    ISBN 0-679-75361-3 (acid-free paper) : $12.00
    1. Reading.   2. Rapid reading.   3. Reading comprehension.
    I. Title.
    LB1050.54.S33   1994   428.4'3—dc20   94-20594 CIP

Manufactured in the United States of America
9 8 7

"I took a speed reading course once. We read *War and Peace* in twenty minutes. It was about Russia."

—Woody Allen

ACKNOWLEDGMENTS

I would like to acknowledge the help and patience of Cynthia Brantley, Andy Dunn, Leland Elliott, Nell Goddin, Julian Ham, Chris Kensler, Marcia Lerner, Kristin Fayne-Mulroy, Laurice Pearson, Tracy Schaffzin, and Beth Young in the creation of this book. I would especially like to thank Tom Polley, without whom this book would not exist. And, of course, my father, without whom I would not exist.

CONTENTS

INTRODUCTION

IT'S JUST NOT FAIR

Have you ever known people for whom reading seems effortless? You know, those people who casually say, "Oh, that book? Took me three hours, man," while you are on your third week of grinding through the same title? Don't you just want to smack them?

These people aren't born different. They don't have a different type of brain. They just learned to read differently. Is this difference taught so young that there is no hope for the reader for whom reading is a chore?

Absolutely not. And being able to read quickly and efficiently doesn't mean that you have to become a complete nerd—it only means you have to figure out how these people do it, then steal from them.

The good news is we've done that for you.

DON'T KEEP ME IN SUSPENSE—HOW DO THEY DO IT?

These people read well, but very few of them know how they do it. Reading is, for most of them, second nature. They have integrated their reading skills seamlessly into how they handle all information; they read unconsciously, applying techniques they are not even aware of.

We've taken the best of what they do, added a few other tips, and summarized it here. By the end of this book, you *will* be a better reader.

Reading Smart is about breaking the barriers which make reading a chore. *It's not just about reading faster; it's about reading smarter.* Necessarily, reading smarter will improve both speed and comprehension. Increasing your reading speed without increasing your comprehension is like increasing the speed of a car without increasing the traction in the tires or the precision of the steering wheel. Sooner or later, that car's going to crash.

I'd Like To Read Faster, But I Don't Really Need To

Drop this idea out of your mind—quickly. Sure, if you read smarter, it won't change where you live, what you wear, or how your breath smells. But try to think of it this way: if you walked past a table of money every day of your life, stacked to the ceiling with hundred-dollar bills all of which were free for the taking, and you only swept the loose change from the corner of the table into your palm, would you say that you were making your life as good as it could be? Well, learning to read faster won't make you rich (necessarily), but it will help you increase your wealth of knowledge. Which, come to think of it, may have an effect on where you live, what you wear, and yes, even how your breath smells.

Now wait a minute, you say. Reading smarter would be nice but it can't change my life.

Can't it?

In school, the difference between an F and a C is remembering the facts from a given piece of reading, whether it is Chemistry, History or English. The difference between a C and an A is being able to bring other ideas, other ideas you have read, into your analysis of a situation. If you had only As on your transcript, could that change your life?

Have you ever seen a co-worker discussing a common interest, or a popular book, with the boss? It sounds small-minded, but right there the co-worker has gained an edge on you, because the boss thinks they have more in common. Perhaps if you read more efficiently, that promotion could have been yours.

Drop the change and grab some hundreds. No matter what you do, you'll be doing a lot of reading for the rest of your life. *Reading Smart* trains you for all the reading ahead and gives you that leg up that others have enjoyed for so long.

THEN WHAT THE HECK DO I DO?

This book breaks up the reading you do into three types:

1. **Textbook reading**
2. **Journalistic reading**
3. **Narrative reading**

Don't worry if you don't know what this means yet. The following chapters will lay it all out for you.

You are going to learn to go into each piece of reading with an approach, a specific strategy, depending on what you need. Some of the techniques here may seem unusual. Try them. They work. If you become frustrated with a technique, stop reading the book at that point. Take a walk to the video store and rent a movie. We recommend *Roadhouse*: it's not too demanding. Then come back and try it again. Everything in this book has a point. We have no reason to steer you in the wrong direction.

You're not in school. No one is going to send you to detention if you get tired and nod off. The more you push yourself, the better you'll get, but if you have something better to do on a Saturday night, we recommend you have a good time. When you come back, however, be focused and careful. We've cut all extraneous material out of this book—which means that everything in it is important. You can't skip a few pages and expect to get better. You'll have missed something.

HOW TO USE THIS BOOK

Don't try to memorize every word in this book. *Reading Smart* is designed to demystify the reading process and show you what the best readers do. There will be many small techniques that will help, but examining and relearning the basic elements of reading is more important. For example, when you learned that electrical sockets were dangerous, did you memorize a list of things not to do to the electrical socket? Did you write:

1. Don't stick finger in socket.
2. Don't lick socket.
3. Don't stick toe in socket.

No, you got the general idea, and when the situation arose, you used logic to decide what to do. You should do the same with reading. We'll show you the larger idea, and you'll apply it to the reading. (By the way, don't stick a paper clip in an electrical socket. It can short out a whole power line.)

If you find yourself memorizing without understanding, or doing things that confuse you, you're doing the opposite of what we want you to do. **Mark up this book as you read.** Write questions in the margin. They should be answered by the end of each chapter.

Trying new techniques in reading is difficult, and it will seem awkward at first. Do all of the **Exercises** and the **Reading Racetracks**—they are designed to get you used to approaching reading in a specific way. The Exercises immediately follow each technique, so use them as an accurate gauge of how clear the techniques are to you. The Reading Racetracks are only a part of trying out your new techniques. If when you put down this book you don't try to use the techniques on everything you read (from the newspaper to *War and Peace*), then you won't improve at all. This is a practical manual on how to be a better reader. This is not theory. It is designed for real life.

WHAT DO I NEED?

What do you need to read smart? Vision helps. So does a brain. Bring a pen and paper (yes—even though this is reading you need a pen), and some desire to improve your reading. This is all you need.

Change will not happen overnight. Don't expect to go to bed a caterpillar and wake up a butterfly (if you wake up and you are a butterfly, you've got bigger problems). But you can expect improvement, and the more time and effort you put into learning the techniques, and the more confidence you have in the approach, the more improvement you can expect.

Most of all, if you view this as a chore, as a horrible task you have to go through, you can expect only limited success. This book is designed to be non-horrible. In fact, it should be fun sometimes, and there is nothing more fun than succeeding at something you set your mind to doing.

So have fun with this book, and when you're done you can try reading it again, this time using our techniques. We'll bet it takes you less time and you'll remember more! Enjoy.

THE PRINCETON REVIEW

READING SMART

ADVANCED TECHNIQUES FOR IMPROVED READING

CHAPTER 1

Why Doesn't Everyone Read Well?

"Men should use common words to say uncommon things, but they do the opposite."

—Schopenhauer

W e all learn to read in basically the same way. We're shown symbols and taught to associate those symbols with sounds and meanings. The rest is reinforcement and repetition: See Jane run. Run, Jane, run. Sleep, student, sleep.

How could your teachers tell you were learning to read? By listening to you reading out loud. How fast can you read out loud? About 150 words per minute. How fast does the average person read? About 150 words per minute. Hmm.

YOU ARE ON YOUR OWN

Through the rest of your life, you're on your own as far as reading goes. You will be inundated with different types of reading: newspapers, textbooks, essays, fiction, memos, and magazines. You're expected to wade through this ocean of information with no further guidance.

WERE YOUR TEACHERS INSANE?

After you learned how to count, did your teachers expect you to figure out everything up through calculus by yourself? No, they taught you. After you realized a ball dropped from your hand falls to the floor, did they expect you to derive the laws of physics? Of course not. They taught you.

So why did they abandon you in reading? Frankly, it beats us. There is no single more important skill in school, work, and life than reading. The best we can figure is that the same people who set the curriculum in schools, who teach and train you for the future, read well all by themselves. No one taught them, so they feel no need to teach you.

PRETTY NICE OF THEM, HUH?

Even if you were to ask them to teach you, your teachers would be hard-pressed to explain how they themselves read well. Reading is an internal process, ingrained so deeply that people are barely aware of the act of reading. It's an automatic response, like the way you raise your hands when a snowball comes flying at your face.

What we have done in this book is drag that process into the open, to make it visible for you. Once you realize that there is no genetic difference between people who read well and you—only that they unconsciously use certain approaches that work well—the sooner you can realize your potential as a reader.

OFF TO THE RACES

To help you achieve your reading potential, we have included throughout the book a bunch of short passages we call Reading Racetracks. The Reading Racetracks include a variety of writing styles and forms: short stories, textbook passages, magazine articles—even a couple of poems. Some of the stuff will be hard, some will be fun; all of the passages will help you improve your reading skills.

READING RACETRACK #1

Read the following passage and answer the questions after it to find your speed and comprehension levels. Time yourself on a watch with a second hand. Time only the reading portion of the exercise, not the question portion. Then calculate your reading speed and comprehension level, using the formulas following the questions.

> Although the conventional American view has been that parties would perform better if they were internally democratic, the question is by no means as simple as the standard view suggests. Our starting point must be the functions we want parties to perform, and to perform well. If one of these is to facilitate popular control over elected officials—as it surely is—then it does not follow that this result is to be obtained only, or even best, by internal party democracy.
>
> An analogy may help to clarify the point. Political parties are sometimes likened to business firms competing for customers—the customers being in this case the voters. And just as business firms are driven by competition to satisfy consumers, even if they are *internally* not governed by consumers in the way that a consumers' cooperative is, so, it is sometimes argued, competitive parties will fulfill all of the essential functions of democratic control listed earlier, even though each party is internally controlled by its leaders. If the main function of competing parties is to insure that the views of voters are translated into government policies, then it is less important that parties be internally democratic than they be responsive to the view of the voters.
>
> Would greater internal democracy insure that the parties would be more responsive to the voters? If we take presidential nominations as the most crucial test case, the answer is not as clear as one might hope.
>
> For one thing, changes in procedures intended to insure greater internal democracy may only shift control from one set of political activists to another. Political activists are, roughly speaking, of two kinds. One is the familiar party

"regular," party leaders who over a considerable period of time occupy positions of influence in the party and regularly devote a large share of their time, energy, and resources to party activities. The others are the "irregulars," insurgents and amateurs who become active in behalf of a particular cause or candidate. Having been drawn into a campaign, some of the irregulars may later become regulars, but many drop out after the campaign is over, or bide their time until another attractive cause or candidate comes along.

The difficulty is that the insurgents may be no more representative of the opinions of a majority of voters than the regulars—and quite possibly they may be less so. Both parties provide evidence on this point. In 1964, the most ideologically conservative activists in the Republican party, a group of insurgents whose views probably represented only a minority among Republican voters and an even smaller minority in the electorate as a whole, seized control of the nominating convention from the Republican "establishment," nominated Senator Barry Goldwater and suffered one of the three or four worst defeats in the entire history of the party.

The Goldwater insurgency in the Republican party was duplicated in the Democratic party by the nomination of George McGovern in 1972. McGovern was an insurgent candidate who gathered around him an enthusiastic core of activists, most of whom were irregulars without prior political experience and his candidacy was probably aided somewhat—though not decisively—by a change in party rules intended to make the Democratic convention more representative of previously underrepresented groups—specifically blacks, women, and youth. The McGovern forces won a majority of delegates elected in the primaries and then went on to victory in the Democratic convention. In the election, McGovern suffered the worst defeat of any Democratic candidate in fifty years.

The delegates to the Democratic convention, it turned out, were highly unrepresentative of Democratic supporters. Of all the groups at the convention, the insurgent McGovern delegates deviated most from the views of rank-and-file Democrats. The women delegates chosen under the new rules were not at all representative of rank-and-file Democratic women, nor the youth of rank-and-file young people. Even the black delegates were rather unrepresentative of attitudes among the black population at large and among black Democratic supporters. Ironically, in 1972, the delegates to the Republican convention were much closer to the views of rank-and-file Democrats in the country at large than were the delegates to the Democratic convention.

In the face of experiences like these, some people concluded that the parties were still not democratic enough in their internal organization since in both cases the insurgents proved to be unrepresentative of broader opinion. It was thought necessary to bring about even more control by rank-and-file party followers, reducing even further the influence of party leaders and activists. From this perspective, the rapidly expanding participation in presidential primaries noted above is a sign of health in the political parties.

Write your time down and answer the following questions based on the information contained in the previous passage:

1. According to the passage, what does "internally democratic" mean?

   (A) Only Democrats are members.
   (B) Both Democrats and Republicans can be members.
   (C) The organization obeys the wishes of all people.
   (D) The election of delegates is done democratically.
   (E) It was founded by Democrats.

2. The main point of the passage is to

   (A) show the health and the internal voting process of the Republican party in the 1960s and 1970s
   (B) show the abundance of internal democracy in the two-party system
   (C) illuminate the internal voting process
   (D) show that internal democracy does not necessarily ensure accurate representation
   (E) show the health of the Democratic party

3. Which example most supports the author's premise?

   (A) Goldwater's candidacy
   (B) McGovern's candidacy
   (C) Both
   (D) Neither

4. Barry Goldwater's defeat can be ascribed to

(A) a small but vocal minority within the Democratic party
(B) competition from George McGovern
(C) excessive conservatism among mainstream Republicans
(D) the inexperience of his party's "regulars"
(E) the capture of the Republican platform by extremists

5. Which, if any, party benefited from the change in rules that assisted McGovern's candidacy?

(A) The Republican Party
(B) The Democratic Party
(C) Both
(D) Neither

6. Which statement would the author most likely <u>agree</u> with?

(A) Political parties are run like businesses.
(B) Political parties should be run like businesses.
(C) Businesses should be run more democratically.
(D) Political parties can be likened to businesses in their organization.
(E) Business and politics don't mix.

7. The author uses the term "rank-and-file" to mean

(A) extremist
(B) military
(C) civil servants
(D) party "regulars"
(E) ordinary

8. According to the passage, what must be the "starting point" for any discussion about making a party function efficiently?

(A) What party a person belongs to
(B) What political agenda the party maintains
(C) What functions the party should perform
(D) What form the party should take
(E) A common definition of efficiency

9. Changes in procedure intended to ensure greater democracy

(A) are unusual and difficult to enforce
(B) may remove any hope of extremist issues being discussed
(C) may not result in agreed-upon change
(D) aren't necessarily beneficial to extremist groups
(E) may only shift control from one unrepresentative group to another

10. According to the passage, a sign of health in the political parties is

(A) the expanding participation in presidential primaries
(B) the expanding membership of both major political parties
(C) the declining number of rule changes since 1974
(D) the declining number of party "irregulars" in both major political parties
(E) the expanding participation in the presidential elections

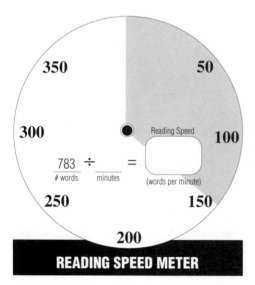

Calculate your reading speed using the following formula. First, mark down how long it took you, in minutes, to read the passage (if it took you 2 minutes, 15 seconds, then it took you 2.25 minutes). Divide the number of words in the passage by that number. This is your reading speed in words per minute. For example, there are 783 words in this passage. If it took you 4 minutes to read the entire selection, then divide 783 by 4. This would result in a reading speed of 196 w.p.m.

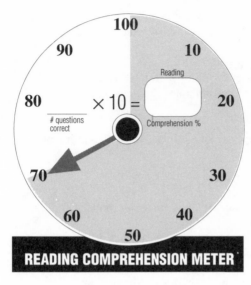

Calculate your comprehension rate using the following formula. Multiply the number of questions you answered correctly by 10. That is your comprehension percentage. You want to keep your percentage above 70 percent for any type of reading. Below that, you start losing important information presented in the passages.

Don't Drive 55

Federal funding for transportation depends on each state mandating a speed limit of 55 miles per hour on highways (except for where it's 65—but you know what we mean). The campaign—which has littered the landscape on television, in newspapers, on large signs blocking scenic views, that informed people of the law—was the genius phrase "Drive 55." It rhymed, was memorable and had the proper effect. Most drivers knew about and obeyed the 55-mile-per-hour speed limit.

But do you want to drive 55 all the time? What if you were in a hospital zone? What if you were looking for a parking space in a crowded city? The autobahn in Germany? On roads slick with rain or snow? Driving 55 in these places would be dangerous and irresponsible. People who know tell you. Your own common sense tells you. You drive differently depending on the circumstances.

Drawing by John O'Brien; © 1993 The New Yorker Magazine, Inc.

THIS APPLIES TO READING AS WELL

How you are going to read is fundamentally linked to what you are reading, just as the speed at which you are driving is fundamentally linked to the road conditions. Should you read a textbook the same way you read a novel? No way. The better you understand that your reading approach depends on *what* you are reading, the more your reading skills will improve.

In other words, don't always drive 55. If you use the same approach for every type of reading you have to do, sometimes you will be right on track. Other times you will be reading too fast or too slow, missing important information, and wondering why you had to read the same sentence three or four times. If you listen to your common sense, you'll never be far off from the best path. Keep your common sense with you at all times; it's your best ally against reading inefficiently.

Oh Yeah? Prove It

Adjusting your speed is critical to reading smart, and easier than you would imagine. Read the following passages, and mark next to them what speed you would read them: fast, medium, or slow.

1. Measurements of net income *for the period* and of financial position *at the end of the period* are inter-related. Revenues result from selling goods or rendering services to customers and lead to increases in assets or decreases in liabilities. Expenses indicate the services have been used in generating revenue and result in decreases in assets or increases in liabilities. Because revenues represent increases in shareholders' equity, revenues are recorded by crediting (increasing) a shareholder's equity account for the specific type of revenue and debiting either an assets or liability account.

2. Riefenstahl tells her story in a clean, well-lighted prose, interrupted by occasional purple passages, with here and there an intensely personal touch to remind us that this is a memoir, not just a set of memos. (The uncredited translation is fluent and generally satisfactory, but does not avoid some common errors.) How truthful is it? How does one assess the veracity of any memoir?

3. Herb's house is on curvy little Glacier Way, a hundred yards from Walled Lake itself and not far from the amusement park that operates summers only. I came here long ago, when I was in college, to a dense festering old barrelly dance hall called the Walled Lake Casino. It was at the time when line dances were popular in Michigan, and my two friends and I drove over from Ann Arbor with the thought of picking up some women, though of course we knew no one for forty miles and ended up standing against the firred, scarred old walls being wry and sarcastic

about everyone and drinking Cokes spiked with whiskey. Since then, Mr. Smallwood has informed me, the Casino has burned down.

These three passages are different in tone, style, vocabulary and pace. Each one has ways into it, and how much you get out of the passage depends on you identifying the best way to read it. The main idea is that writers writing on different topics use different approaches to get their point across. If you read the first and third passages at the same speed, you're going to miss a lot from both. Identifying what you are reading and why you are reading it is the first step in becoming a smarter reader. Let's look at the passages one by one and see what clues each passage has as to how you should read it.

PASSAGE 1: TEXTBOOK READING

If you made it through without falling asleep, and if you were able to decipher the academic prose, give yourself a pat on the back. Do you remember what to do to an account ledger when you sell goods? How are the measurements of net income related on the two statements? You can expect to retain very little from this passage if you don't adjust your speed.

There are many tip-offs which tell you that you should read this slowly. Words are repeated in a way that drones you to sleep, it is filled with specific, inaccessible, unexplained terminology, and there is no reference to anything other than itself (it is self-contained). This is a textbook selection. It is very easy to stop and find yourself lost in this kind of passage, having read words with no idea what they mean. In chapter five, we'll look at specific techniques to keep your head in the page, but for now, be concerned with pacing. You should read this passage slowly. *Any time you need to learn specific facts, particularly when technical jargon is involved, slow down and learn more.* If you have to read a passage three or four times to decipher it, then it's better to slow down and get it right the first or second time.

PASSAGE 2: JOURNALISTIC READING

The second passage reads as if someone were lecturing to you. Newspapers and magazines take this informational tone. Most news stories have an opinion, and present information in that light. This kind of passage is journalistic, and will cross some of the academic tone of the first with the conversational tone of the third (notice that instead of saying "How do we know if she's lying?" he says "How do we assess the veracity of any memoir?" One question is easier to understand; the other is unnecessarily pompous, but that discussion should be saved for *Writing Smart*).

This passage should be read at a moderate speed and with a quick identification of what's going on. What is the author talking about? Does he like this Riefenstahl? What's his opinion? Chapter six will take this on. This is the most difficult type of material to approach. It's the most difficult type of material because you don't know exactly what information you are going to need from it.

PASSAGE 3: NARRATIVE READING

The third passage tells a story. The retention level for most people is highest on this kind of passage. Passages with physical images, with dialogue, and with clearly identified characters and actions allow the reader to achieve the fastest speed and the highest retention. Do you remember the name of the lake? Anything they did? Fiction, narrative discourse, writing that sounds like talking or describing, is the easiest to deal with. In chapter seven you'll find out how to read these passages even faster with higher retention levels.

What You Need to Remember

Once you can identify the type of passage you have to read, you should go into it with expectations. What do we mean by expectations? Ask yourself these questions:

- What do I need to get out of this piece?
- Do I need to memorize a bunch of facts?
- Do I just need an overview?
- Will I be tested on this stuff?
- What can I expect from a passage like this?

One thing you should notice is that *your approach to reading is affected not only by the type of passage, but also by your purpose for reading it.* For example, you'll read a biography of Andy Warhol one way on the beach and another for a modern art class. If you are going to be tested on material, or need to master information, you are going to go slower, read with a pen in your hand, take notes in the margin, and use other techniques to reinforce comprehension. If you are going to read a paper or magazine where the information may or may not be useful, you want to use different techniques, increasing your pace with a corresponding decrease in retention. If you are reading a work of fiction (something you should read but from which you don't have to remember the details—just the plot, situations and tone) you should read faster and approach it as a completely different situation. The following chart is a general guideline for deciding what pace you will need to read different types of writing. Most of all, make sure you're comfortable with that reading speed. The idea is to strike the right balance between speed and comprehension.

PACING CHART

TYPE OF WRITING	REQUIREMENT	PACE
Textbook • English • History • Math • Sciences	• Memorization • Overall Mastery • Tested	Slow
Journalistic • Newspapers • Magazines • Memos • Essays	• Overall Understanding • Solid Familiarity • Important to know, but most likely never tested	Medium
Other Writing • Fiction • Personal Histories • Narrative Discourse	• Basic Understanding • Basic Familiarity • Not Tested	Fast

Remember, this list is useful as a guideline, but if you're going to use it as a rulebook, without using common sense, you're no better off than when you started this chapter. Never, never forsake your common sense!

THINGS TO TAKE WITH YOU

Good readers tailor their approach. They decide what type of book they're reading and why they're reading it. Reading isn't one thing, it's many things. It's a tool and, like any tool, you have to know how to use it effectively. Whenever you sit down to read a book, have a plan ready. Ask yourself the questions:

- What kind of reading is it?
- What do I need to get out of it?
- What pace should I be using?
- What techniques should I be using?

We haven't told you how to answer these questions yet, so don't worry, you haven't missed anything. We'll get to that in the chapters to come. Once you have gotten the hang of the techniques in the following chapters, you'll be reading not only faster, but smarter, and remembering more.

EXERCISE #1

Read the following sentences. Mark next to each how you would read the passage: Fast, Medium, or Slow.

1. Boris looked at his gun, and it was empty. He knew the end was near. He closed his eyes and saw only darkness.

2. The reforms in Russia continue in a "herky-jerky" fashion and, therefore, so does the economic growth of the former Soviet state. The capricious attitude of the Russian leadership to questions of finance has unnerved the watching world.

3. Mary closed her eyes and saw stars exploding in brilliant flowers of light. It was the Fourth of July in her head, an orchestra of pleasure.

4. If e.e. cummings is considered a genius, then too must William Carlos Williams, for his poetry most closely approximates the shape of what cummings attempted to explore. Both took advantage of spatial constructs to open doorways to interpretive possibility.

5. Fasten the tube with the E-Bar connector, making sure to seal both ends with bonding glue, scoring the edges first to ensure a snug fit. Test for leakage by running warm water through the tube.

6. Maria poked her head from behind the door and called, "If you knew anything you would know I can never love a person like you!" She stomped upstairs, leaving little bits of Vladimir's heart in shreds on the living room floor.

7. The regression is valid for the first, second, and third tenths of the population, but once the fourth and fifth are included, the error factor (t-regression) retreats to a degree of 20%. With inconsistencies in the regression apparent, the entire study must be reconsidered.

8. A person's worth cannot be judged solely by his actions; his intentions must also be taken into account. In acting rashly, my client committed a crime. In rushing to help a friend, he hurt someone else. At all times, only the possible positive effects of his action were on his mind.

9. "He needs me like he needs a head cold," quipped Martin, sipping his Margarita. Quickly, he spit the frothy beverage, two parts lime juice, two parts triple sec, three parts tequila, on the Oriental rug. Someone had replaced the lime juice with Valvoline.

10. The twenty-four vertebrae in the spinal column are divided into three parts; the cervical, the thoracic, and the lumbar, of which the first two cervical vertebrae are known as the Atlas (C-1) and the Axis (C-2).

11. Did madness take over Genet in his final days, as the passion of his life had been spent? None but his lover shall ever know. His lover took the secrets of Genet's final days to the grave. Buried in a layer of mystery, Genet's ending is extended into all of our futures.

12. Raising temperature is simple: first, seal off all possible manner of perspiration. This reduces the body's natural cooling efficiency by up to 80%. Then, provide the subject with large quantities of food and water. This will stimulate internal processes which cause the temperature to rise dramatically. The harder the body works, the more energy it produces.

13. Elizabeth Montgomery played Samantha on the hit 1960s television show "Bewitched." A number of actors, however, played her witchlet daughter, Tabitha. Regardless of the changing cast, the show enjoyed years of ratings prosperity until Elizabeth Montgomery's retirement seven years after the show's inception.

14. Darryl stood face to face with the moose. The moose pawed at the ground. Darryl lowered to a three-point-stance. The moose bellowed. Darryl yelled something about the moose's mother. The moose charged, antlers low. Darryl darted forward, using exceptional blocking technique. If he were facing a human opponent, that is.

15. Up at Altamont, 1,500 windmills stand, braced against the wind. They are situated on the crests of 700 small natural inclines, and their arms pinwheel in crazy circles at up to 120 miles per hour. They form a church, of sorts; a church dedicated to the proposition that natural energies can be harnessed, and used, without destroying fossil fuels and creating pollution. Professor Jonathan Davis, who runs the institute, is the pastor at this church, and makes it known that he will accept all comers into his fold.

CHAPTER 2

The Approach

"Zounds! I was never so bethumped with words!"

—William Shakespeare

On the next bright summer day, as people step outside and decide to enjoy the sun and read a little, go to your local park or picnic area and watch them. They will recline, holding a book in one hand, occasionally putting the book down or looking around at the other people. They will remember the day as pleasant, the people as relaxed, and very little about the book they brought. It's the truth. Completely relaxed approaches and environments just don't lead to high levels of reading retention. So if your friends tell you that listening to great music on your comfortable couch with the television remote and telephone near you is the best way to read, don't listen to them. That is, if reading smarter is your goal.

On the other hand, sitting in a perfectly silent room with flickering flourescent lights while a dozen people furiously scribble notes and tear out their hair is not any better. At best, you will read at the same levels of speed and retention as before and give yourself a headache. Very few of your friends will recommend this as an optimal way to study.

Where, then, is a person to read efficiently?

FIND THE RIGHT PLACE

Find a place both comfortable and quiet, with few distractions and little noise. This is not always possible, but if you can find such a spot, your reading efficiency (particularly your comprehension) can improve dramatically. Choose a place where the lighting is bright but not overly so. Indirect lighting is best. Your eyes are the workhorse of reading, and treating them poorly is the surest way to give yourself eyestrain, headaches, and a good excuse to stop reading. Do not have distractions available. A ringing phone, a television with remote control, or a video game can all call to you, saying "Don't read—I need some attention!" and drag you away from the task at hand. If you have music playing, try to make it music with no words. Even if you concentrate very well, words tend to seep into your ears and mix with words you read. If you don't like classical, new age, or folk guitar, there are many Jimmy Hendrix, Metallica, and Anthrax jams which will satisfy the no-word convention. If this sounds too demanding, you'll find that as you begin to read smarter, your concentration will improve, and all this location scouting will be less necessary.

If you cannot find the perfect place to read, don't despair. Reading can be done anywhere—but you have to increase the intensity of your concentration in proportion to the number of distractions around you. A student of ours once failed a European history exam because she was living in a house with a nest of wasps outside the window. She would sit down to read the textbook, but every time she would feel a light tickle of wind on her neck, she would jerk around, looking for the wasp that was about to sting her. Her concentration was so divided that when the exam question was "What was the effect of growing European fractionism?" she could only answer that European fractionism made her nervous and anxious, and reminded her of wasps. Her professor was less than understanding.

So why handicap yourself? If you were running in a race, you wouldn't want to have to weave through a crowd of people to get to the finish line. Any one of them could knock you down and out of the race. If you have the opportunity, give yourself the best chance of success.

Let's Get Physical

Look at a group of perfect students in the moments before taking an essay test. You should see alert, focused people who, the minute the exam begins, open their test booklets and scan the pages deftly for the important information. They are rapidly and efficiently trying to derive the primary questions from their test books.

Look at how these perfect students physically engage themselves in the test: they are slightly hunched over the reading, completely engrossed. Bombers could be flying overhead—they wouldn't notice. They have a pen in one hand, the other on the desk in front of them. They become physically involved with their reading—and you should, too.

We're not asking you to recreate testing situations—no one needs (or deserves) that much stress in her life. But you should become physically involved with your reading. If your posture is poor, and your back begins to hurt after ten minutes of reading, your speed, comprehension, and stamina will all suffer. If you sit back and wait for the book to grab you, you've already lost. No matter how engrossing or difficult any reading is, the most effective reading comes from involving yourself in the subject.

Be aggressive with your approach to reading, both mentally and physically. If you are intimidated by a book, you're going to have a struggle on your hands, and in the end the book always wins. If you go away, leave the book on a table, join the French Foreign Legion, travel to the four corners of the world, win a Nobel Peace Prize, and conquer a nation, when you come back to the book, it will be exactly the same, and you will feel the same way about it. It's not going to change. That means *you* have to.

READING RACETRACK #2

Read the following passage and answer the questions after it to find your speed and comprehension levels. Time yourself on a watch with a second hand. Time only the reading portion of the exercise, not the question portion. Then calculate your reading speed and comprehension level, using the formulas at the end of the questions.

On Tuesday, May 22, 1980, a man named Henry Hill did what seemed to him the only sensible thing to do: he decided to cease to exist. He was in the Nassau County jail, facing a life sentence in a massive narcotics conspiracy. The federal prosecutors were asking him about his role in the $6 million Lufthansa German Airlines robbery, the largest successful cash robbery in American history. The New York City police were in line behind the feds to ask him about the ten murders that followed the Lufthansa heist. The Justice Department wanted to talk to him about his connection with a murder that also involved Michele Sindona, the convicted Italian financier. The Organized Crime Strike Force wanted to know about the Boston College basketball players he had bribed in a point-shaving scheme. Treasury agents were looking for the crates of automatic weapons and Claymore mines he had stolen from a Connecticut armory. The Brooklyn district attorney's office wanted information about a body they had found in a refrigeration truck, which was frozen so stiff it needed two days to thaw before the medical examiner could perform an autopsy.

When Henry Hill had been arrested only three weeks earlier, it hadn't been big news. There were no front-page stories in the newspapers and no segments on the evening news. His arrest was just another of dozens of the slightly exaggerated multimillion-dollar drug busts that police make annually in their search for paragraphs of praise. But the arrest of Henry Hill was a prize beyond measure. Hill had grown up in the mob. He was only a mechanic, but he knew everything. He knew how it worked. He knew who oiled the machinery. He knew, literally, where the bodies were buried. If he talked, the police knew that Henry Hill could give them the key to dozens of indictments and convictions. And even if he didn't talk, Henry Hill knew that his own friends would kill him just as they had killed nearly everyone who had been involved in the Lufthansa robbery. In jail Henry heard the news: his own protector, Paul Vario, the seventy-year-old mob chief in whose house Henry had been raised from childhood, was through with him; and James "Jimmy the Gent" Burke, Henry's closest friend, his confidant and partner, the man he had been scheming and hustling with since he was thirteen years old, was planning to murder him.

Under the circumstances, Henry made his decision: he became part of the Justice Department's Federal Witness Protection Program. His wife, Karen, and their children, Judy, fifteen, and Ruth, twelve, ceased to exist along with him. They were given new identities. It should be said that it was slightly easier for Henry Hill to cease to exist than it might have been for the average citizen, since the actual evidence of Hill's existence was extraordinarily slim. His home was apparently owned by his mother-in-law. His car was registered in his wife's name. His Social Security cards and driver's licenses—he had several of each—were forged and made out to fictitious names. He had never voted and never paid taxes. He had never even flown on an airplane using a ticket made out in his own name. In fact one of the only pieces of documentary evidence that proved without doubt that Henry Hill had lived—besides his birth certificate—was his yellow sheet, the police record of arrests he had begun as a teenage apprentice to the mob.

Now try some questions. If you saw *Goodfellas,* keep in mind that the movie doesn't follow this book exactly, because we kept it in mind as we wrote the questions.

1. According to the passage, Henry Hill's arrest was described by police as

   (A) slightly exaggerated
   (B) big news
   (C) just another drug bust
   (D) a "prize beyond measure"
   (E) the beginning of the end for the Mafia in the United States

2. Why was Hill's arrest so important?

   (A) Hill's friends and colleagues were scheming to kill him.
   (B) He had deep-frozen a body.
   (C) It allowed him to join the Witness Protection Program.
   (D) He had information on many unsolved crimes.
   (E) He was the head of a major organized crime empire.

3. Why was it so easy for Hill to "disappear?"

   (A) His mother-in-law bought his house.
   (B) There was little legal evidence of his existence.
   (C) His family came with him.
   (D) He had a long "yellow sheet."
   (E) He had many underworld contacts.

4. According to the passage, Henry Hill was accused of:

   (A) the murder of Michele Sindona
   (B) the hijacking of a Lufthansa flight
   (C) shaving points in a Boston College basketball game
   (D) All of the above
   (E) None of the above

5. Which of the following, if any, were interested in Henry Hill?

   (A) The Drug Enforcement Agency
   (B) The Anti-terrorism arm of the United Nations
   (C) The Department of the Treasury
   (D) All of the above
   (E) None of the above

6. The Lufthansa crime

    (A) was the only sucessful hijacking in American
         history
    (B) was the crime for which Hill was first arrested
    (C) was the biggest successful robbery in the U.S.
    (D) made Hill kill ten people
    (E) was masterminded by James "Jimmy the Gent"
         Burke

7. Which best describes Hill's position in the mob?

    (A) Powerful and knowledgeable
    (B) Low but powerful
    (C) Low but knowledgeable
    (D) High and knowledgeable
    (E) Relative of Paul Vario

8. What's the implied message of the passage?

    (A) Crime does not pay.
    (B) Crime pays until you get busted.
    (C) Hill played both sides for his own benefit.
    (D) Hill is a unique and interesting figure.
    (E) The Mafia is a family that protects its members.

9. According to the passage, Paul Vario

    (A) was murdered by Henry Hill
    (B) had ten people murdered following the Lufthansa
         crime
    (C) raised Henry Hill
    (D) knew Henry from the age of thirteen
    (E) headed an international crime family

10. Hill's three relatives mentioned in the passage were named

    (A) Karen, Jimmy and Paul
    (B) Paul, Henry and James
    (C) Karen, Jennifer and Ruth
    (D) Ruth, Judy and Karen
    (E) Ruth, Karen and Jimmy

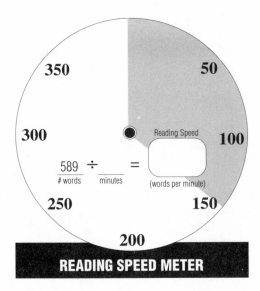

Calculate your reading speed using the following formula. First, mark down how long it took you, in minutes, to read the passage (if it took you 2 minutes, 15 seconds, then it took you 2.25 minutes). Divide the number of words in the passage by that number. This is your reading speed in words per minute. For example, there are 589 words in this passage. If it took you 3.5 minutes to read the entire selection, then divide 589 by 3.5. This would result in a reading speed of 168 w.p.m.

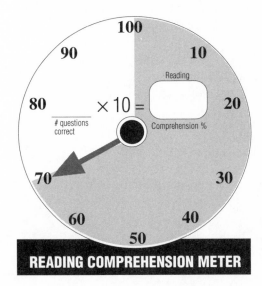

Calculate your comprehension rate using the following formula. Multiply the number of questions you answered correctly by 10. That is your comprehension percentage. You want to keep your percentage above 70 percent for any type of reading. Below that, you start losing important information presented in the passages.

CHAPTER 3

Mechanics

"Reading is to the mind what exercise is to the body."

—Richard Steele

Y ou've found your comfortable, well-lighted spot. You have your new-age music going in the background. You have a pen in hand, a back pillow and the phone unplugged. You're ready to read and you open the book; then, suddenly, you start to read and nothing changes. It still takes you a long time to get through a few pages; you don't recall many of the ideas or details; and you start thumbing through the phone book looking for the number of the store that sold you this stupid book. You want to give the clerk who talked you into it a piece of your mind.

Don't do that just yet. After all, a journey of a thousand miles begins with a single step, and you've just learned to tie your shoes. Let's talk about the mechanics of reading: how anyone, from the slowest to the fastest of readers, actually reads. Much of the technical stuff is not necessary for you to be a smarter reader, but it helps you understand why you are not reading as effectively as you could.

THE EYES HAVE IT

How does a person read? There is the physical side of reading (what your body does) and the mental side (what your brain does). Physically, reading begins with the eyes. Although you think your eyes travel smoothly across the page, they don't. They jerk across the page, grabbing clumps of information and sending them to your brain. Your eyes don't do any actual reading (understanding)—that takes place in your brain. But they do determine one side of how fast and how efficiently you can read.

The other side is what goes on in your head while you read. Your brain takes these clusters of information and sorts through them looking for patterns that it recognizes. These patterns are words or groups of words. It assembles these groups into coherent thoughts and sentences, and that's reading. Of course, all this stuff happens simultaneously—your eyes are grabbing clusters and sending them to your brain while one part of your brain is sorting and another is assembling.

Two things immediately come to mind: one, the faster you can train your eye to take in these clusters, the faster you can read. The second is that the more efficiently you can train your brain to recognize these patterns, the more rapidly and the more effectively you can read. (A corollary of this is that the larger your vocabulary, the more patterns you can recognize.)

Everyone Has Healthy Fixations

Most time spent reading is due to the way you use your eyes. Reading is not a fluid process—your eye stops a number of times on each line and focuses on various words or clusters of words. Every time your eyes stop at a position on a line of text, that stop is called a **fixation**. It's like driving—when you're on the highway, you can travel a great distance in a short time because there are no traffic lights. If you tried to travel the same distance through city streets, you would stop a number of times at traffic lights, and it would take a much longer time. So any time we talk about "reducing your fixations" we're just reducing the number of times your eye stops on a line.

> **The movement of your eyes across a line of text is called a *saccade*. You can improve your saccade speed, but there is only one way to do that—by practicing your fixations and making them more precise.**

By using your peripheral vision, you can reduce the number of fixations you have per line of text. Peripheral vision is the ability to look directly at one thing, but take in things on either side of it. Most professional athletes have great peripheral vision. Does this mean they are the fastest readers? No, you have to know how to use that skill.

The slowest readers have fixations at almost every word. The best readers have two to three fixations per line. We'll show you how to reduce the number of fixations per line and increase your speed, but remember—if you start losing comprehension because you're trying to minimize your fixations, it's not worth it. Speed at the cost of comprehension is worthless.

The following drill is designed to improve your eye fixations. Remember: a lifetime of use is difficult to change. The way you read has been dictated by the way you *originally learned* to read. In other words, don't expect to find this reading natural, easy, or effective as you first try it. It will seem stilted and awkward, and will slow you down initially. As it becomes more natural and you integrate it into your reading patterns, you'll jump a level in terms of speed and comprehension. If you are going to start reading smart, you have to start with the basics.

KEEP YOUR EYES ON THE PRIZE

See this black dot? • This dot indicates that you should focus your eyes on this point. This will be your fixation point. Try focusing on the black dot and using your peripheral vision to read the words on either side of it. Use the first exercise to get used to the feel of reading without moving your eyes so often. Read across the page, traveling from dot to dot, taking in the words on either side of the dot without moving your eyes. Then jump to the next dot. This gets your eyes used to traveling in jumps rather than words. Give it a try.

EXERCISE #3

All day • I work	for lousy • pay	I hate • my job
When • Brian was	a • little	fat • baby
his hands • were small	his eyes • were blue	he had • gas a lot
He asked • me for	a toy • soldier	and a • pop gun
How I • wish you	were • here	darling • of mine
Spock • didn't see	why • humans were	so utterly • emotional
Someone • is always	lying • to you	about how • they feel
People • get ready	there's a • train to	Georgia at • noon
Golf is • a sport	for biddies • and for	salty sailors • on leave
Waltzing • Mathilda	is all • I want	to do • today
Don't hit • anyone	unless you • can	get away • with it
Larry is • as ugly	as a • buffalo in	a pond • of mud
If you • go out	with my • sister	I will • smack you
Don't go • out with	my nice • sister	for any • reason
You went • out with	my sister • last	night • to dance
Prepare • yourself	to meet • your	maker • now

Can you feel your eyes quickly moving from black dot to black dot? Just make sure you don't move from word to word. You don't need to look directly at a word to have your brain register what word it is.

Try reading the next two passages focusing on the black dots. Their frequency will decrease as the passage continues. Train your eyes to make fewer and fewer jumps, and you'll increase your speed in no time.

EXERCISE #4

Max • leafed through • the help-wanted
• section, • looking for • jobs • which suited • his
talents. He • was smart, • strong, reliable • and
handsome. • Modest, too, • he thought. His • father
had • called him • "King Max" and • his mother had
referred • to him as • "the emperor." • He had been
• to the best • schools, the brightest • tutors, and
now • was ready • to unleash • his abilities • on the
world. The • question he posed was, • "Is the
world • ready for me?" • He chuckled to • himself when
the • perfect ad caught • his eye. It was • as if they
were advertising • for him. It would • take daring, risk
and • creativity. He would be • tested twenty-
four • hours per day by • its intricate and • varied
demands. The salary • wasn't what he had hoped, • but
what was • salary compared with • the chance of a lifetime? He • closed the paper with a • flourish. He had
found his dream. • Max Hoober was going to • become a
chicken plucker • and no one in this world, or any • other,
was going to • stop him.

When • greeting Aunt • Sally, make • certain
that • your cheeks • are out of • her reach, for • she
will pinch • them if she • has the chance. • Smearing
them • with Crisco • or any • other lubricant • will
increase • your chances • of emerging unscathed. • Also,
it will be • helpful for • removing the • industrial
lipstick • Aunt Sally is • known to apply. • If you are
greeting • her at her apartment, • the smell of mothballs
and • aged lace may be • enough to overwhelm • you.
Do not be surprised if • one of your cousins • succumbs to
the scents and • passes out. This • is normal. • Do not
panic. Just make • sure it is not you. Keep • a capsule
of smelling salts • available at all times. • If Aunt Sally

offers • you a piece of • candy, do • not ingest! I
repeat, do • not ingest! Most likely it • is a relic from the
Pleistocene • era, at most recent, • from the crusades of
the • fifteenth century. The butterscotch • candies are the
worst • (common wisdom holds • that the
peppermint • should be the worst, • but only three
peppermint • striped candies are known • to still be in
existence). Scientists • have been unable to • date them
using carbon-14 methods. • In fact, speculation
continues • on whether they are • artifacts of this world,
or • another.

That may have seemed a little artificial, but anything new does
at first. Now try the same thing on the following passage, but *you*
determine where the fixation points should be. Work on putting more
and more space between them as you get further into the piece. It
might help to go through the passage a few times, so you know
what's coming and can concentrate on where you're putting your
eyes rather than what's in the passage.

EXERCISE #5

When Warren moved into the tree, no one was really too
concerned. "He'll be down as soon as *My Three Sons* is on, you
bet," said his mom. "He probably just owes Mr. Katz for all
those anchovies," said Slats, eyeing the ever-growing pile of
empty cans beneath the spreading oak. "Warren is just trying to
work out a post-arboreal trauma through confrontation," said Dr.
Pease, who just happened to be walking by. But Mr. Katz didn't
complain, and Dr. Pease admitted he had just made it up, so we
all began to wonder just what was up (besides Warren) as the
leaves yellowed and then fell. No one is really sure, but the
Rotary has the fundraiser every year and Warren seems happy,
so we just put up a sign saying "please don't shake the tree"
and let him alone.

Learning to train your eyes to stop fewer times per line is *so*
important, we've included an extra five eye fixation exercises in the
"A Day at the Races" section at the end of the book. Don't try all
five at once. Read a chapter, do a fixation exercise. If you don't
cut down your fixations, your reading speed will stay way below
its potential.

CLUSTER COMBINATIONS

In addition to eye fixations, it's important to learn a mechanical trick called clustering. **Clustering** is the learned ability to see words in groups rather than as individual words. How does clustering work? Certain words will slow you down if read individually. You can read the sentence "Mary goes to the store" word by word: "Mary—goes—to—the—store." However, the phrase "to—the—store" is (logically, grammatically, and otherwise) a unit. A smart reader takes in most prepositional phrases (phrases that start with words like "to," "against," and "in") as self-contained units. It is also useful with appositive phrases: units of information that are secondary to the immediate information. (If you are saying "What on earth is he talking about?" bear with us. Just remember that you want to slow down for important stuff. Background stuff you can take in larger chunks because it is not as important.) In the sentence, "Mr. Johnson, who owned the clothing store, was drunk," the information that he owned the clothing store is secondary to the main information, and should be read in its own fixation.

EXERCISE #6

Try the following exercise, letting your mind read the prepositional phrases as one unit. Put slashes between each of the clusters you would make when reading. We did the first two sentences to help you start seeing words in logical clusters. Clustering is a cousin to the previous eye fixation drill. By decreasing your fixations, you improve your speed. By increasing your clustering, you make the transition between fixations smoother and more rapid. One without the other is like paddling with one oar. The more you paddle, the faster you will go, but you won't get anywhere. That's because fewer fixations without larger clusters means you'll be missing words.

1. The ball was/on the stairs.

2. My fingers,/stained with nicotine, pointed/to the west.

3. Vincent called for his sister after the storm.

4. Albert Einstein married his cousin on the sly.

5. Uncle Walvis plays bagpipe music in the house too loudly.

6. I like to read *Catcher in the Rye* over and over and over and think about the president.

7. Marva wrapped tape around her finger until the digit turned a delicate vermillion.

8. Vlad is quite the man about town.

9. In a town like this, you should go to your house and stay there after dark.

10. Vampires feast upon the blood of the living.

11. Fogerty was down on the corner, then out in the street.

12. Uncle Walvis likes to shout Gaelic curses at the cars as they pass.

13. No one believed me about the alien pods until it was too late.

14. They come to your house while you sleep.

15. The fiends take over your mind and teach you about reading.

16. I liked the Stones in the sixties, but their new stuff is for the birds.

17. Dogs in the morning, cats in the night—I like pets if they don't bite.

18. A sunrise from space is beautiful above all things.

19. They bowl in the summer and skate in the winter.

20. You light up my life with halogen lamps.

21. Christine fell down the stairs but landed on her feet.

Exercise #7

Circle the phrases that should be read as clusters in the following sentences. Don't simply try to identify them—try to read the sentences in clusters.

Kathy left her address book on the top of the coffee maker.

After she noticed it was missing, she retraced her steps.

Her path took her, a vice president, to the mailroom.

In a fit of anger, she fired everyone.

She called the police and reported they were all stealing.

Holding her phone, she gripped the receiver with claw-like hands.

The police told her she couldn't prove anything.

They refused her request, and then she wrote the president.

After her anger subsided, she rehired everyone and gave them raises.

It was a bad day at the office for Kathy to switch to decaf.

Efficiency Rules

Fixations and clustering are the two major techniques for improving your reading speed. Being able to read rapidly means you can take in more text, finish assignments faster, and generally lead a better life. Now what additional techniques can you use to stop inefficient behavior?

SUBVOCALIZING

When you are reading through some difficult or choppy texts, do you ever find yourself mouthing the words or speaking them out loud? If you do, you are doing something called **subvocalization**. Don't feel bad about it. That's the way most people are taught— sound out the words, listen to the information. But mouthing or speaking the words slows you down, so it's best to get over it.

Getting over subvocalizing can be rough. Many times, if you are used to mouthing the words every time you read, the minute you stop subvocalizing, the words stop making any sense. It's as if the page were suddenly translated into a foreign language. Imagine a person whose job is to type written notes into a computer. That person can type at, let's say, 120 words per minute. Now imagine they had to speak each word before they had to type it. Their typing rate drops to 60 words per minute. You might as well ask them to juggle oranges between words.

The best way to get over a subvocalizing tendency is to place a couple of fingers in your mouth as you read. If you begin to mouth the words, you'll find yourself chewing your own fingers. That is not pleasant. Your eyes can move much faster if they don't have to wait for your mind to translate the words to your lips, and your lips to mouth the words. And if you are concentrating on the pain in your fingers, you can't concentrate on what you are reading. The minute you feel your mouth start to move, stop reading. Close the book. Think of the same words you just read, picturing them in your mind without saying them. Open the book again. Put your finger in your mouth. After you have closed the book six or seven times, and have two or three bandages on your fingers, you'll find that you can't stand this stopping and starting.

That's when your brain makes you stop subvocalizing.

READING WITH YOUR HANDS

Now, let's talk about another reading approach that can slow you down. Are you a pointer? Be honest. Confess it. Sometimes, when you really concentrate on reading difficult material, do you move your hand or finger across the page to keep your place?

If you don't, then congratulations. You're not supposed to. Your eyes can move much faster than your hand, and your brain considerably faster than your hand. If you are really concentrating on the piece, you know where you are on the page, and you do not need your hand to keep your place. If you find yourself unable to stop, sit on your hands. You've got to stop this habit right away. Marking with your finger slows you down.

REGRESSION

Do you check your facts as you read by returning to earlier sentences and earlier paragraphs? Don't. You only need to reread earlier text if you weren't concentrating in the first place. You can double the amount of time it takes you to read a given passage by jumping backwards and searching to verify things you've already read. Think about it—when you do anything, do you want to do it twice or three times? In a recipe, if it says put in a teaspoon of salt, do you want to do it three times? If you are going to the store in your car, and you are not sure if the last light you passed was yellow or red, are you going to go back and check? Regressive reading only happens when you stop concentrating. If you find yourself regressing, read one of the passages at the end of any chapter in this book and practice not regressing. Force yourself to plow through the passage without rereading any sentence. You'll find you remember more than you think.

OVERALL APPROACH

Overall, you want to approach your reading with intensity—nothing else will do. You can master all the other steps and improve your comprehension or your speed slightly, but nothing will substitute for a stubborn refusal to allow a piece of writing to defeat you. Be aggressive with your body and your mind. Attack the reading. The next few chapters will tell you how.

THINGS TO TAKE WITH YOU

Learning these skills is the physical part of learning to read faster. If you don't reduce your fixations, start to cluster, and eliminate your poor reading habits, the help in the subsequent chapters will still greatly improve your comprehension, and even your enjoyment of your reading. But the goal is to do both—that is when your quality of life improves considerably. You can double the number of books you read and, at the same time, double what you get out of each book.

READING RACETRACK #3

Read the following passage and answer the questions that follow to find your speed and comprehension levels. Time yourself on a watch with a second hand. Time only the reading portion of the exercise, not the question portion. Then calculate your reading speed and comprehension level, using the formulas at the end of the questions.

Based on its record since the 1950s, one might suppose that the Court has had a splendid history of protecting the fundamental rights of otherwise defenseless minorities against encroachment by the president and Congress. In this view of the Court's role we would expect to find a considerable number of important cases in which the justices have declared unconstitutional laws passed by Congress, or orders by the president, on the ground that they impaired the rights of citizens granted by the first ten amendments (the Bill of Rights).

Looking over the annals of the Court, however, two conclusions are strikingly evident. First, most of the cases in which the Court has defended the rights of unpopular minorities against majorities are quite recent. They mainly occurred between 1954 and 1968, during a period of "judicial activism," as it has been called, when the Court was presided over by Chief Justice Earl Warren. Second, even then, most of these cases involved state or local laws, not acts of Congress. An inspection of the historical records shows:

1. There have been only a handful of cases, all since 1964, in which the Court has held a provision of *federal* law to be unconstitutional—as contrary to the fundamental liberties of religion, speech, press and assembly guaranteed by the First Amendment. Two cases involved federal legislation

directed toward alleged Communists. In two others, parts of certain federal acts were held to violate rights of anti-war protesters.

2. In about ten cases prior to 1964, the Court has held congressional acts unconstitutional because they violated other provisions of the Bill of Rights. An inspection of the issues in all the earlier cases indicates that the lawmakers and the Court were not very far apart. Moreover, the issues were mainly of such a minor sort that it is doubtful whether the fundamental conditions of liberty were altered by more than a hair's breadth as a result.

3. Over against these decisions we must put the substantial number of cases in which the Court used the protections of the Bill of Rights, or the constitutional amendments enacted after the Civil War to protect the rights of the newly freed blacks, not to uphold the weak against the strong but quite the reverse: to preserve the rights and liberties of a relatively privileged group at the expense of the rights and liberties of a submerged group. The victors in these cases were chiefly slave holders at the expense of slaves, whites at the expense of nonwhites, and property holders at the expense of wage earners and other groups....

These cases, unlike some of the relatively unimportant ones previously discussed, all involved liberties of genuinely fundamental importance, where an opposite policy would have meant basic shifts in the distribution of rights, liberties, and opportunities in the United States. Moreover, the policies sustained by the Court's action have since been repudiated in every civilized nation of the Western world, including our own.

In a dozen or more cases since 1964, however, the Court *has* struck down provisions of federal laws directed against unpopular minorities. Beginning in 1964 the Court all but single-handedly dismantled the Subversive Activities Control Act of 1950, which was explicitly directed against Communists. The court also struck down laws denying certain of the constitutional rights of other unpopular groups, such as welfare clients, gamblers, and drug dealers. In 1977, for the first time, the Court also held laws unconstitutional because they discriminated against women.

1. Which of the following statements would the author most likely agree with?

   (A) The Court consistently protects minority rights.
   (B) The Court consists mostly of minorities.
   (C) In the past, the Court protected minority rights.
   (D) Only in the 1950s did the court begin to protect minority rights.
   (E) Communists should not have minority rights.

2. It can be inferred from the passage that "judicial activism" means

   (A) the Court assuming an active role
   (B) people supporting the Court
   (C) the Court before Chief Justice Earl Warren
   (D) a conscious violation of the Bill of Rights
   (E) the court from 1954 to 1977

3. Which of the following <u>supports</u> the idea that the Court has not been an aggressive protector of minority rights?

   (A) Only a handful of cases has held a provision of federal law to be unconstitutional.
   (B) In 1977, the Court held laws unconstitutional because they discriminated against women.
   (C) Both
   (D) Neither

4. In which of the following years was the Supreme Court most likely to uphold minority rights?

   (A) 1883
   (B) 1930
   (C) 1941
   (D) 1953
   (E) 1957

5. Which characterizes best the relationship of the Court to Congress on the issue of minority rights <u>prior</u> to 1964?

   (A) In perfect harmony
   (B) Extremely close, but differing slightly
   (C) Often disputing, but engaging in discussion
   (D) Often at odds, rarely agreeing
   (E) Opposites who fought regularly

6. The Subversive Activities Control Act was aimed at

   (A) judicial activists
   (B) the court
   (C) Congress
   (D) communists
   (E) women

7. In the second-to-last paragraph, the term "repudiated" is used to mean

   (A) disavowed
   (B) copied
   (C) embraced
   (D) imported
   (E) despised

8. According to the passage, prior to 1964 the Court

   (A) provided a forum for state, local, and federal grievances
   (B) maintained the *status quo* in terms of distribution of rights and liberties
   (C) reversed the *status quo* in terms of distribution of rights and liberties
   (D) provided a battleground for state, local, and federal grievances
   (E) broke with a tradition of social upheaval

9. Cited in the passage as examples of First Amendment rights are

   (A) freedom of religion
   (B) freedom of speech
   (C) freedom of press
   (D) freedom of assembly
   (E) all of the above

10. "Unpopular groups," as mentioned in the passage, can best be described as

   (A) groups not supported by political parties
   (B) groups with no power
   (C) groups against the public morality
   (D) small minorities groups
   (E) groups who are grudgingly afforded rights

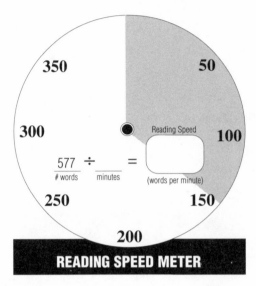

*Calculate your reading speed
using the following formula.
First, mark down how long it took
you, in minutes, to read the
passage (if it took you 2 minutes,
15 seconds, then it took you 2.25
minutes). Divide the number of
words in the passage by that
number. This is your reading
speed in words per minute. For
example, there are 577 words in
this passage. If it took you 4
minutes to read the entire
selection, then divide 577 by 4.
This would result in a reading
speed of 144 w.p.m.*

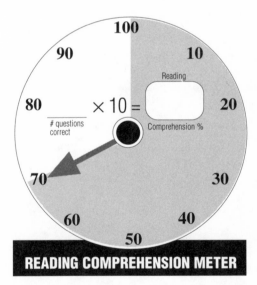

*Calculate your comprehension
rate using the following formula.
Multiply the number of questions
you answered correctly by 10.
That is your comprehension
percentage. You want to keep
your percentage above 70 percent
for any type of reading. Below
that, you start losing important
information presented in the
passages.*

CHAPTER 4

Know What You're Reading

"Literature is the art of writing something that will be read twice; journalism what will be grasped once."

—Cyril Connolly

So you're ready to be aggressive, to attack your reading, to approach it smartly, smoothly and with no reservations. Great. What next? Are you just going to dive into any different type of reading with one blasting approach? Would you read a physics manual and a Stephen King novel in the same way, or a book of poetry and a newspaper? Such an approach would lead you back to reading the way you did before.

IDENTIFY WHY

You must identify the type of reading you are about to undertake. In the first chapter, we talked about three different types of reading you may encounter. These are large, inclusive groups which are meant as guidelines (and will be repeated here—don't turn back). The most important questions about your reading will be addressed here. And before you pick up a single piece of paper to read, you should have these questions answered somewhere in your mind. The first question you must ask yourself before you sit down to read something is *why am I reading this?* ("Because I have to" is not a valid response.) Unless you know what you need to get out of your reading, you are not ready to begin reading yet. Remember: *Identify Why.*

> **Why you read something is as important as what you are reading. If you won a ten-minute shopping spree in a supermarket, you wouldn't just take one of everything, or only get forty bags of dog food. You'd tailor your shopping to the things you needed. You'd get the biggest cart. You'd make a plan to use those ten minutes to your greatest advantage. *Identifying Why* tells you how you need to approach the reading, and how to tailor your approach.**

As a student, business person, casual reader, or professional, you cannot afford to begin reading without first knowing what you need to get out of it. Ask yourself the following questions before you begin reading:

1. What degree of knowledge do I need to take from this: Intimate, Casual or Passing? Or to put it another way: Final, Test, or Quiz?

2. What type of reading is it: Fast, Medium, or Slow?

3. How long will I need this knowledge: Tomorrow, Long Time, Life?

After you have answered these questions, you will be in a better position to read smart. How do you answer these questions? Let's look at the questions one by one.

1. WHAT DEGREE OF KNOWLEDGE DO I NEED TO TAKE FROM THIS INFORMATION?

Ask yourself why you are reading the material. Is it an assignment? Will you be tested on the contents? Do you need it for work, and will you use it every day? Or is it just a secondary piece of information you will need every now and then? Or is it a newspaper, or magazine, where you enjoy the articles but are not sure you will ever need to know the details? The speed at which you want to read these pieces depends mainly on your answers to these questions.

2. WHAT TYPE OF READING IS IT?

Is it casual, chatty reading with lots of dialogue and action that you can just whip through? Or is it a series of symbols and graphs, explaining a very esoteric concept? Is this an argument or a presentation (a trick question—nearly all good writing is an argument of some kind). This is a sub-category of questions which should be answered by your first question. You want to keep in your mind the speed and the way you should read each piece.

3. HOW LONG WILL I NEED THIS KNOWLEDGE?

If you are reading a book on how to hypnotize people into doing your absolute bidding, you'll want to remember that for the rest of your life. If you are reading the menu in a restaurant you never intend to eat in again, you are not going to want to remember a single thing two minutes after you order. The way you remember very important things is by rewriting them in your own words. Once you remember it in your own way, it is yours forever. If you need something in the short term, you should mark the text. You don't want to rewrite everything in your own words. That would be ineffective, because nothing would stand out.

EXERCISE #8

In the following exercise, identify how you would classify the types of reading according to these three questions: 1) What degree of knowledge do I need to take from this information—intimate, casual, or passing? 2) What type of reading is it? 3) How long will I need this knowledge? We've done the first one for you.

1. You are reading a chapter in a physics textbook which will be on the final.
   (1) intimate   (2) slow   (3) long time

2. You pick up a magazine at the haircutter's while waiting for a chair to be free.

3. You are reading the business section of a newspaper before you go to your job as a stockbroker.

4. You are lying in bed, reading a novel about an English spy in World War II Germany.

5. You are reading a report on the environment you requested for work.

6. You are reading a speed-reading book.

7. You are reading a police report on your cousin Willie.

8. You are reading a math textbook to review some concepts for your physics final.

9. You are reading your spouse's old love letters you found at the top of the closet.

10. You are reading the recommendations of a prospective employee.

11. You are reading a "Far Side" cartoon.

12. You are reading *War and Peace* the night before the final exam.

READING RACETRACK #4

Read the following passage and answer the questions after it. To find your speed and comprehension levels, time yourself on a watch with a second hand. Time only the reading portion of the exercise, not the question portion. Then calculate your reading speed and comprehension level, using the formulas at the end of the questions.

Sherwood Anderson in his *Memoirs* testifies to the nearly miraculous sense of ease and liberation with which the stories of *Winesburg, Ohio* were written—poured out in a Chicago room in a concentrated fury of creations, sometimes two or three stories in a week. If his account of their composition is literally true, it is a symbolic parallel to the creative exuberance of the Twenties. The *Winesburg* stories speak with the voice of the Twenties, too, in their rebellion against lingering Victorianisms, middle-class repressions, Midwestern pieties, Puritan hypocrisies, village narrownesses—all the things which hampered and limited the "life of realization" upon which Anderson and his whole generation were bent.

Individually the stories of *Winesburg, Ohio* do not represent Anderson's best and richest work, and we have acknowledged that fact by selecting a story from another book, *The Triumph of the Egg*. But collectively they are both impressive and of absolutely first importance. They were revolutionary in more than their disregard of conventional morals. The outraged protest that they inspired may even have been obscurely aesthetic in part, for these were no stories by conventional standards; even Anderson's friend Floyd Dell said so; Mencken said so; the reviewers said so. They were little vignettes of buried lives, throbs of muffled desire, sketches of characters foundering among the village tribalisms, glimpses of torment behind drawn (and sometimes undrawn) blinds. They were not only plotless, but they did not even make use of the sensuous impressionism by which Crane and Steele could impress by mere vividness. These stories moved obscurely, like night-things. To this day the warmest admirers of Anderson cannot quite say how they get their effects. The style is flat, the method more narrative than dramatic; and yet Winesburg's people have the terrible shamefaced look of people caught in something unspeakably personal. The suppressed emotions of their lives burst out of them like moans or cries, and they compel attention and exact sympathy as more cunningly made and steered characters could not. The influence of Chekhov, obviously, is strong here: Chekhov was one of the new and exciting writers of whom Anderson's mind was full, and it was not entirely unjust that a reviewer should later call him

the "phallic Chekhov." It may be precisely the strong
Chekhovian sympathy that makes *Winesburg, Ohio* a great
book—William Faulkner says it is the only great book that
Anderson ever wrote. "Unlighted Lamps" is our choice because
it contains, along with the themes of frustration and loss and
yearning and human waste that were the soul of *Winesburg*,
the rich and warmly felt background of the county fairgrounds
and race tracks where many of his best non-*Winesburg* stories
are laid. If a single story is to represent Anderson, this will
serve as well as any, and better than most.

And after Anderson, the deluge. Two of the major novelists
of the Twenties, Dreiser and Sinclair Lewis, were never
successful with the short story, but consider those who were:
Fitzgerald, Hemingway, Faulkner, Katherine Anne Porter,
Steele, Lardner, and, in addition, Edith Wharton and Willa
Cather and Ellen Glasgow, in the twilight of their powers
but still producing. On its short stories alone the Twenties
would have been notable. And supporting the great figures,
packed around them like excelsior in a tight box, was an
astonishingly large and astonishingly good body of lesser
writers upon whose work and against whose competition the
best ones grew. You do not sharpen an axe against a wheel
of cheese; neither do you produce great writers without the
pressure of a solid body of competing talent. It is from its
secondary figures as well as from its great ones that a period
gets its quality.

Yet the great ones make themselves known unmistakably.
From his earliest stories—dismissed as mere *contes* by some
of the editors to whom he sent them—Hemingway impressed
those who knew him as somebody inevitably special. His
first books, *Three Stories and Ten Poems* and *In Our Time*
were hardly more than a sample of what was to come, and
yet there was a widespread feeling that a giant was on his
way up, as witness Edmund Wilson's early review in *The
Dial* for October, 1924.

It may be, as William Faulkner has said, that Hemingway
found out early what he could do, and has continued to do
it, and that this constitutes a deficiency in him, a lack of
daring. On the other hand, most readers will find plentiful
signs of progress and growth from "Up in Michigan" and
the early vignette of *In Our Time* to "The Snows of
Kilimanjaro," or "The Old Man and the Sea." Incorporated
in this change is evidence that Hemingway, like Chekhov
and James, has increasingly chafed against the artificial con-
strictions of the short story, and has moved more and more
toward James's "blessed nouvelle." His first stories were
vignettes less than a page long; his last one, just as true
a short story, is long enough to make a small book. It is

a long way from the things he was producing when as a
young correspondent in Paris he was learning to write,
"beginning with the simplest things."

1. The primary subject of the passage can best be
    summarized as

    (A) short story writers of the Twenties
    (B) a book called *Winesburg, Ohio*
    (C) Sherwood Anderson and Anton Chekov
    (D) Sherwood Anderson and Ernest Hemingway
    (E) Ernest Hemingway and Anton Chekov

2. What Sherwood Anderson story is mentioned by name in
    the passage?

    (A) Unlighted Lamps
    (B) Winesburg, Ohio
    (C) The Triumph of the Egg
    (D) Up in Michigan
    (E) The Snows Of Kilimanjaro

3. Anderson's stories could best be described as

    (A) conventional
    (B) similar to Hemingway's
    (C) revolutionary
    (D) supportive of Victorianism
    (E) intricately structured and plotted

4. What makes secondary writers important?

    (A) They have an axe to grind.
    (B) They make bad writers feel better.
    (C) They make primary writers look better.
    (D) The competition improves all writers.
    (E) They make good packing material.

5. How do most readers feel about Hemingway's artistic progress?

    (A) His lack of daring made him just keep doing what
        he was good at.
    (B) "In Our Time" is better than "The Old Man and
        the Sea."
    (C) He eventually advocated "beginning with the
        simplest things."
    (D) His success was inevitable.
    (E) Over time, he began to flourish within the
        boundaries of the short story.

6. On whom did Chekov have great influence?

   (A) Faulkner
   (B) Hemingway
   (C) Anderson
   (D) Hemingway *and* Anderson
   (E) None of the above

7. Anderson's style can be most appropriately described as

   (A) ornate
   (B) impressionistic
   (C) phallic
   (D) frustrated
   (E) flat

8. Initially, Hemingway was seen as

   (A) innovative and important
   (B) redundant and unimportant
   (C) promising by some, unimportant by others
   (D) the primary voice of his age
   (E) a boy from Michigan with usurptuous ideas

9. Crane and Steele are cited as

   (A) examples of the preeminent twenties' voices
   (B) counterexamples to the flat style
   (C) Anderson's closest contemporaries
   (D) Anderson's inspirations
   (E) reviewers for *The Dial*

10. The "deluge" referred to in the passage means

    (A) the uncontrolled downpouring
    (B) the unstoppable flooding
    (C) the unanticipated promulgation
    (D) the rapid decrease
    (E) the overwhelming emergence

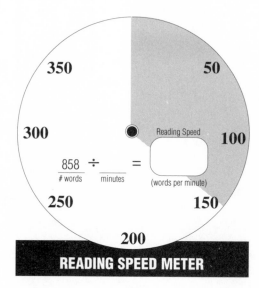

*Calculate your reading speed
using the following formula.
First, mark down how long it took
you, in minutes, to read the
passage (if it took you 2 minutes,
15 seconds, then it took you 2.25
minutes). Divide the number of
words in the passage by that
number. This is your reading
speed in words per minute. For
example, there are 858 words in
this passage. If it took you 6
minutes to read the entire
selection, then divide 858 by 6.
This would result in a reading
speed of 143 w.p.m.*

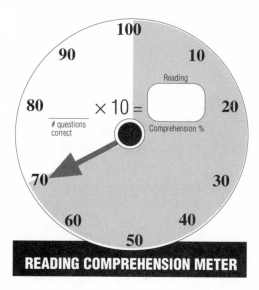

*Calculate your comprehension
rate using the following formula.
Multiply the number of questions
you answered correctly by 10.
That is your comprehension
percentage. You want to keep
your percentage above 70 percent
for any type of reading. Below
that, you start losing important
information presented in the
passages.*

CHAPTER 5

Let's Talk About Reqs

"There are no dull subjects. There are only dull writers."

—H.L. Mencken

R equired reading is the most demanding of all types of reading. Unfortunately, it's usually the most necessary (you can't get around it) and the most boring (you can't stand it). Often the texts are dense with important information, poorly written, and so dull they will put you into a sleep deeper than NyQuil. You ask the most from it—details—and it asks the most from you— memorization. It is the easiest type of reading to view as a chore, and it is the easiest type of reading to let whiz by you, letting your retention levels fall into the sub-cellar.

Who can wade through all this information and make any sense of it? Facts—dates, equations, and names—seem impossible to remember and all you can do is wish for a merciful end to the subject, and pray that your boss doesn't ask you any questions, or your teacher doesn't cover it on the exam. When the final or presentation comes, and you need them most, all the ideas jump out of your mind like rats leaving a sinking ship.

One basic principle can help you through this kind of molasses. Remember that *reading without understanding ensures you will not remember the facts you need, or that if you do, you will not be able to use them wisely.* No teacher will give you credit if you remember only that the Treaty of Versailles was signed in 1919. What was it? Who was there? What were the effects? Every textbook has a larger agenda—whether it is teaching the principles of physics or the history of the United States—that it uses its facts to support. Slow yourself down during the first or second reading of any textbook and put the information you are reading into its context. What larger ideas are being presented? What part of physics is being examined? Then the facts have something to grab on to. When you can put facts into context, you are much much more likely to remember them.

GET A CLUE: SEEING THE BIG PICTURE

> **Clue yourself into the main idea and context of what you are reading. Don't just learn facts—learn about how they fit into the bigger picture.**

Let's take the Watergate/Nixon events. Sure, Nixon resigned in disgrace, but the effects on the presidency, and how people changed their view of government officials, is more important than the details of the Watergate break-in (believe it or not, people used to have *faith* in elected officials). Ask yourself: what are the lasting effects of any action or event? Why is an equation important to memorize? That's when these things stay in your head.

READ WITH YOUR PEN

A good way to make sure you are not just blindly reading facts is to **read every textbook with your pen in hand**. In the margin, jot down the main idea of the section, and when you get to the part of that paragraph that relates to the main idea, <u>underline it</u>. Then ⟨circle⟩ the facts you'll need to memorize later. Distinguish quickly between reading and studying. Reading should give you the overall picture presented by the facts: studying is the way to memorize the facts themselves.

WHEN IN DOUBT, DRAW IT OUT

Another way to remember facts from a textbook is to make a picture that relates facts to each other. This picture could be a **timeline,** a **tree chart,** or a **circular chart**.

A **timeline** is useful for the study of history, political science, and any events which progress over a period of time. It is a straight line which places all the facts in chronological order. A timeline of the American Revolution (a sparse one at that) might look like this:

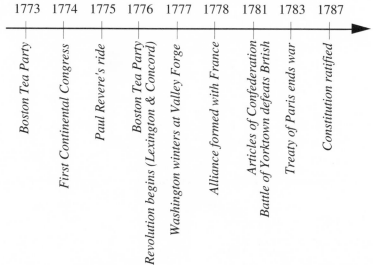

1773 1774 1775 1776 1777 1778 1781 1783 1787

Boston Tea Party
First Continental Congress
Paul Revere's ride
Boston Tea Party
Revolution begins (Lexington & Concord)
Washington winters at Valley Forge
Alliance formed with France
Articles of Confederation
Battle of Yorktown defeats Brtish
Treaty of Paris ends war
Constitution ratified

A **tree chart** is useful for political movements, for the study of fiction, and for understanding some hard-science reactions. It begins at the top with a main idea or an initial state, and then progresses through the various options. We've given you two examples, one for fiction and one for hard science.

SCIENTIFIC TREE CHART

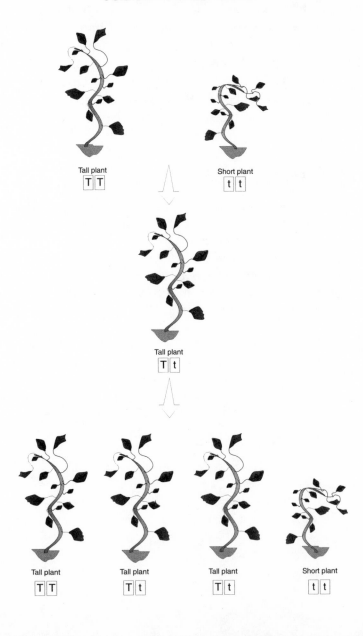

Tall plant
T T

Short plant
t t

Tall plant
T t

Tall plant
T T

Tall plant
T t

Tall plant
T t

Short plant
t t

FICTION TREE CHART

"The Cask of Amontillado"

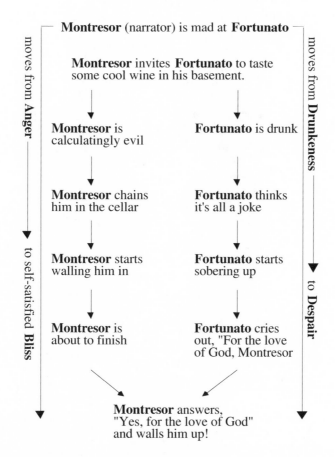

Montresor (narrator) is mad at **Fortunato**

moves from **Anger** — *to self-satisfied* **Bliss**

Montresor invites **Fortunato** to taste some cool wine in his basement.

moves from **Drunkeness** — *to* **Despair**

Montresor is calculatingly evil

Fortunato is drunk

Montresor chains him in the cellar

Fortunato thinks it's all a joke

Montresor starts walling him in

Fortunato starts sobering up

Montresor is about to finish

Fortunato cries out, "For the love of God, Montresor

Montresor answers, "Yes, for the love of God" and walls him up!

Circular charts are used for the hard sciences. They indicate relationships that can go in either direction. The most common circular chart is an equation: 2 + 2 = 4 means both "when you add two and two you get four" and "four is the same as adding two and two." Once you have your picture, the relationship between facts becomes apparent. Then, you don't have to remember a string of unconnected facts; the relationship is apparent from the picture. Sounds weird? It works like a charm. Let's look at an example. Here's a textbook selection which can be simplified by a diagram.

> Water consists of two hydrogen molecules and one oxygen
> molecule. The combination of the molecules requires energy,
> otherwise the combination will not take place. Conversely,
> the liberation of the molecules requires energy as well if
> you are to release the gaseous elements from their recom-
> binant state.

Wouldn't this be oh-so-much-fun to memorize? Why not just draw a picture. A picture is worth more than a thousand words—it can be worth a full grade on a test. Here is one way you could draw this (and, no, you don't have to be an artist—all you have to do is draw it in a way that makes sense to you).

You can't be a vegetable when you read. If you understand what's going on, your retention is going to zoom. After you see a movie, it's pretty easy to describe the sets, costumes, actors, and so on, but if you were just handed a list of these items, it would be hopeless to try to memorize them in a reasonable amount of time. That's because the movie integrates it all into a larger whole, so each item has a meaning beyond "T-shirt" or "Chevy." Instead, they are "Patrick Swayze's T-shirt that becomes so nastily sweaty after he throws those drunk guys out of the bar" and "the van that Arnold drives through the police station wall." Understanding a reading passage provides a framework you can hang each individual fact on, and it will still be hanging there when you come looking for it on exam day.

For any discipline, the facts are useful, but they are not the most important part of any course of study. An overwhelming number of people try to memorize facts as they read them. Every fact. Every date. Every name. That is what we have textbooks for—to keep track of all that stuff. Work to distinguish reading from sheer memorization, comprehension from studying. On a first read of any textbook, your primary goal should be understanding the relationship between parts, the main point, and the direction of the text.

READING RACETRACK #5

Read the following passage, marking in the side your understanding of the larger issues, the important parts of each passage, and the facts that you think will be useful. There will be questions following the passage. DO NOT TIME YOURSELF. The point in textbook reading is to do it smarter. When you start worrying about whipping through textbook material, you're missing the point.

CONSERVATION OF ENERGY

The concept of energy appears throughout every area of physics, and yet it is difficult to define in a general way just what energy *is*. Energy plays a central role in one of the fundamental natural laws called *conservation laws*, and looking at this role is as good a way as any to approach the question of what energy is.

A conservation law always concerns a transformation or an interaction that occurs within some physical system or in a system and its surroundings. Some quantities that describe the state or condition of the system and surroundings may change during the transformation or interaction, but there may be one or more quantities that remain constant or are *conserved*. A familiar example is conservation of *mass* in chemical reactions. It has been established by a very large amount of experimental evidence that the total mass of the reactants in a chemical reaction is always equal to the total mass of all the products of the reaction. That is, the total mass is always the same after the reaction occurs as before. This generalization is called the principle of *conservation of mass,* and it is obeyed in all chemical reactions.

Something similar happens in collisions between bodies. For a body of mass m moving with speed v we can define a quantity $\frac{1}{2mv^2}$, which we call the *kinetic energy* of the body. When two highly elastic or "springy" bodies (such as two hard steel ball bearings) collide, we find that the individual speeds change but that the total kinetic energy (the sum of the $\frac{1}{2mv^2}$ quantities for all the colliding bodies) is the same after the collision as before. We say that kinetic energy is *conserved* in such collisions. This result doesn't tell us what kinetic energy *is,* but only that it is useful in representing a conservation principle in certain kinds of interactions.

When two soft, deformable bodies, such as two balls of putty or chewing gum, collide, experiment shows that kinetic energy is *not* conserved. However, something else happens; the bodies become *warmer.* Furthermore, it turns out to be possible to work out a definite relationship between the temperature rise of the material and the loss of kinetic energy. We can define a new quantity, which we may call *internal energy,* that increases with temperature in a definite way, so that the *sum* of kinetic energy and internal energy *is* conserved in these collisions.

The significant discovery here is that it is *possible* to extend the principle of conservation of energy to a broader class of phenomena by defining a new form of energy. This is precisely how the principle has developed. Whenever an interaction has been studied in which it seems that the total energy in all known forms is *not* conserved, it has been found possible to define a new form of energy so that the *total* energy, including the new form, *is* conserved. These new forms have included energy associated with heat, with elastic deformations, with electric and magnetic fields, and, in relativity theory, even with mass itself. Conservation of energy has the status, along with a small number of partners, of a *universal* conservation principle; no exception to its validity has ever been found.

1. The main question addressed by the passage is

    (A) What is conservation of energy?
    (B) What is an elastic deformation?
    (C) What is internal energy?
    (D) What happens in collisions between bodies?
    (E) What is energy?

2. Conservation of energy, as described in the passage, is exhibited in

    (A) Two ball bearings colliding
    (B) Reducing the speed of your car
    (C) Turning off lights when not in use
    (D) Resting after exercise
    (E) The conservation of mass in chemical reactions

3. The formula for kinetic energy is

   (A) $\dfrac{1}{2}MV$

   (B) $\dfrac{1}{2}{}^2MV$

   (C) $\dfrac{1}{2}M^2V$

   (D) $\dfrac{1}{2}M^2$

   (E) $\dfrac{1}{2}MV^2$

4. Conservation of mass is mentioned in the passage because

   (A) chemistry and physics are related disciplines
   (B) chemistry is a sub-category of physics
   (C) it is the same as conservation of energy
   (D) it is a concept in chemistry which is similar to
       the conservation of energy in physics
   (E) it is necessary for an understanding of work and
       energy in physics

5. Internal energy is measurable through changes in

   (A) mass
   (B) temperature
   (C) size
   (D) velocity
   (E) kinetic energy

6. The conservation of energy

   (A) occurs in most chemical reactions
   (B) occurs in most collisions
   (C) is, as a rule, almost never violated
   (D) is, as a rule, almost always violated
   (E) is never violated

7. If a car were to slam into a large mound of wet clay, a
   probable result would be

   (A) a loss of energy
   (B) a loss of mass
   (C) a preservation of kinetic energy
   (D) a deformation of mass energy
   (E) a rise in clay temperature

8. By defining new forms of energy, a greater understanding of which of the following has been developed?

   (A) Magnetic fields
   (B) Nuclear energy
   (C) Momentum energy
   (D) All of the above
   (E) None of the above

9. Conservation of energy is defined by

   (A) an analogy
   (B) a series of examples
   (C) defined scientific terms
   (D) None of the above
   (E) All of the above

10. In the passage, the term "elastic" means

   (A) steep
   (B) pliable
   (C) able to be stretched
   (D) hard and springy
   (E) heavy

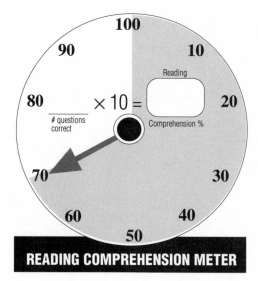

Calculate your comprehension rate using the following formula. Multiply the number of questions you answered correctly by 10. That is your comprehension percentage. You want to keep your percentage above 70 percent for any type of reading. Below that, you start losing important information presented in the passages.

No Suprises, No Failures

In mysteries, love, and sporting events, not knowing the eventual outcome is exciting, and most of the time, desirable. Surprises and unexpected turns are par for the course. How much fun would a Sherlock Holmes book be if you knew exactly who killed the victim and how and when and why? You wouldn't need a detective at all. You also wouldn't keep reading.

In required reading, unpredictable events are a mortal sin. Who wants to be suprised by a textbook or a proposal? Imagine reading a book that seems to argue, in every chapter, that Burt Reynolds was the greatest actor ever. And the final three pages turn everything on its head, and argue that, in fact, he was the worst actor ever (this is a hypothetical, Burt, so don't have your lawyers send us any nasty letters—we love your work). All the facts you've read and noted and marked are useless! If you had known that the book was heading toward smashing Burt, you could have picked out different bits of information that would support trashing Burt (*Cannonball Run*, for example). For every chapter you read, before you get to the actual text, you should have an understanding of what you are about to be reading.

Pre-Read for Profit

The most effective way of checking out where the book is heading before you read it is to pre-read the chapter. **Pre-reading** is looking ahead at all the clues the text provides to describe what kind of material you are about to read. First, look at the title of the chapter. Does it spell out the larger concept that will be covered in the chapter? A physics textbook offers some of the following chapter headings: "Newton's Second Law: Gravitation," "Work and Energy," and "Heat Transfer." When you study these chapters, you should understand that the information contained within will pertain to these topics and, in your mind, associate them easily with the equations or subheadings. Say to yourself, "Oh, gravitation. The idea of orbiting bodies, and why things fall are both just parts of gravitation. One is *between* planets, the other is *on* planets." In each chapter, there may be subheadings for sections or paragraphs. You should quickly read all the subheadings, centered or bolded as they may be, to get a quick idea of how the ideas are going to progress. You've seen examples here in this book. Go back through the first few chapters, looking at the subheadings. They should give you a good idea of what comes right after each one. Try pre-reading for the rest of this book. You'll be glad you did.

If your textbook contains questions at the end of each chapter, read them before you begin the chapter. It's like your teacher telling you what's going to be on the final exam before the class begins. Take the hint—make sure you look for that stuff aggressively before you read the chapter. One of the most difficult things to do in textbooks is to figure out on your first read what is important and what you can whiz by. These questions are your road map through the passage.

READING RACETRACK #6

Read the next passage, pre-reading subheads and the questions. Your speed should improve as you disregard the information which you already know you won't need. Still, don't time yourself—you shouldn't be concerned with speed through textbooks yet. This is a long passage, so pre-reading is very important.

The Dutch in Indonesia

The saga of the Dutch in Indonesia began in 1596, when four small Dutch vessels led by the incompetent and arrogant Cornelius de Hoetman anchored in the roads of Banten, then the largest pepper port in the archipelago. Repeatedly blown off course and racked by disease and dissension, the Houtman expedition had been a disaster from the start. In Banten, the sea-weary Dutch crew went on a drinking binge and had to be chased back to their ships by order of an angry prince, who then refused to do business with such unruly *farang*. Hopping from port to port down the north coast of Java, de Houtman wisely confined his sailors to their ships and managed to purchase some spices. But on arriving in Bali, the entire crew jumped ship and it was some months before de Houtman could muster a quorum for returning to voyage.

Arriving back in Holland in 1597 after an absence of two years, with only three lightly laden ships and a third of their crew, the de Houtman voyage was nonetheless hailed as a success. So dear were spices in Europe at this time, that the sale of the meager cargoes sufficed to cover all expenses and even produced a modest profit for the investors! This touched off a veritable fever of speculation in Dutch commercial circles, and in the following year five consortiums dispatched a total of 22 ships to the Indies.

The Dutch East India Company

The Netherlands was at this time rapidly becoming the commercial centre of Northern Europe. Since the 15th century, ports of the two Dutch coastal provinces, Holland and Zeeland, had served as entrepots for goods shipped to Germany and the Baltic states. Many Dutch merchants grew wealthy on this carrying trade, and following the outbreak of war with Spain in 1568, they began to expand their shipping fleets rapidly, so that by the 1590s they were trading directly with Levant and Brazil.

Thus when a Dutchman published his itinerary to the East Indies in 1595-6, it occasioned the immediate dispatch of the de Houtman and later expeditions. Indeed, so keen was the interest in direct trade with the Indies, that all Dutch traders soon came to recognize the need for cooperation—to minimize competition and maximize profits. In 1602, therefore, they formed the United Dutch East India Company (known by its Dutch initials VOC), one of the first joint-stock corporations in history, It was capitalized at more than 6 million guilders and empowered by the states-general to negotiate treaties, raise armies, build fortresses, and wage war on behalf of the Netherlands in Asia.

The VOC's whole purpose and philosophy can be summed up in a single word—monopoly. Like the Portuguese before them, the Dutch dreamed of securing absolute control of the East Indies spice trade, which traditionally had passed through many Muslim and Mediterranean hands. The profits from such a trade were potentially enormous, in the order of several thousand percent.

In its early years, the VOC met with only limited success. Several trading posts were opened, and Ambon was taken from the Portuguese (in 1605), but Spanish and English, not to mention Muslim, competition kept spice prices high in Indonesia and low in Europe. Then in 1614, a young accountant by the name of Jan Pietieszoon Coen convinced the directors that only a more forceful policy would make the company profitable. Coen was given command of VOC operations, and promptly embarked on a series of military adventures that were to set the pattern for Dutch behavior in the region.

The Founding of Batavia

Coen's first step was to establish a permanent headquarters at Jayakarta on the northwestern coast of Java, close to the pepper-producing parts of Sumatra and the strategic Sundra Straits. In 1618, he sought and received permission from Prince Wijayakrama of Jayakarta to expand the existing Dutch post, and proceeded to throw up a stone barricade mounted with cannon. The prince protested that fortifications were

not provided for in their agreement and Coen responded by
bombarding the palace, thereby reducing it to rubble. A
siege of the fledgling Dutch fortress ensued, in which the
powerful Bantenese and a recently arrived English fleet joined
the Jayakartans. Coen was not so easily beaten, however
(his motto: "Never Despair!"), and escaped to Amboton leaving
a handful of his men in defense of the fort and its valuable
contents.

Five months later, Coen returned to discover his men
still in possession of their post. Though outnumbered 30-
to-1 they had rather unwittingly played one foe against another
by acceding to any and all demands, but were never actually
required to surrender their position due to the mutual suspicion
and timidity of the three attacking parties. Coen set his
adversaries to flight in a series of dramatic attacks, undertaken
with a small force of 1,000 men that included several score
of fearsome Japanese mercenaries. The town of Jayakarta
was razed to the ground and construction of a new Dutch
town begun, eventually to include canals, drawbridges, docks,
warehouses, barracks, a central square, a city hall and a
church—all protected by a high stone wall and a moat—
a copy, in short, of Amsterdam itself.

The only sour note in the proceedings was struck by
the revelation that during the darkest days of the siege, many
of the Dutch defenders had behaved themselves in a most
unseemly manner—drinking, singing, and fornicating for
several nights in succession. Worst of all, they had broken
open the company storehouse and divided the contents up
amongst themselves. Coen, a strict disciplinarian, ordered
the immediate execution of those involved, and memories
of the infamous siege soon faded—save one. The defenders
had dubbed their fortress "Batavia," and the new name stuck.

Coen's next step was to secure control of the five tiny
nutmeg- and mace-producing Banda Islands. In 1621, he
led an expeditionary force there and within a few weeks
rounded up and killed most of the 15,00 inhabitants on the
islands. Three of the islands were then transformed into
spice plantations managed by Dutch colonists and worked
by slaves.

In the years that followed, the Dutch gradually tightened
their grip on the spice trade. From their base at Ambon,
they attempted to "negotiate" a monopoly in cloves with the
rulers of Ternaate and Tidore. But "leakages" continued to
occur. Finally, in 1649, the Dutch began a series of yearly
sweeps of the entire area. The infamous *hongi* (war-fleet)
expeditions defended islands other than Ambon and Ceram,
where the Dutch were firmly established. So successful were
these expeditions, that half of the islanders starved for lack
of trade, and the remaining half were reduced to abject poverty.

Still the smuggling of cloves and clove trees continued. Traders obtained these and other goods at the new Islamic port of Makassar, in southern Sulawesi. The Dutch repeatedly blockaded Makassar and imposed treaties theoretically barring the Makassarese from trading with other nations, but were unable for many years to enforce them. Finally, in 1669, following three years of bitter and bloody fighting, the Makassarese surrendered to superior Dutch and Buginese forces. The Dutch now placed their Bugis ally, Arung Palakka, in charge of Makassar. The bloodletting did not stop here, however, for Arung Palakka embarked on a reign of terror to extend his control over all of southern Sulawesi.

The Dutch in Java
By such nefarious means the Dutch had achieved effective control of the eastern archipelago and its lucrative spice trade by the end of the 17th century. In the western half of the archipelago, however, they became increasingly embroiled in fruitless intrigues and wars, particularly on Java. This came about largely because the Dutch presence at Batavia disturbed a delicate balance of power on Java.

1. Cornelius de Hoetman could be described as

   (A) a daring adventurer
   (B) the father of the spice trade
   (C) the first casualty of the Dutch in Indonesia
   (D) an ineffective commandant
   (E) an inspirational leader

2. The Dutch East India Company at first encountered

   (A) enormous success
   (B) limited success
   (C) limited failure
   (D) enormous failure
   (E) horrendous weather

3. Coen's motto was

   (A) "Never Despair"
   (B) "Never Forget"
   (C) "Never Give Up"
   (D) "Never Again"
   (E) "VOC Forever"

4. The Dutch control of the spice trade in Java was achieved through

   (A) diplomatic negotiation
   (B) military conquest
   (C) sordid alliances
   (D) commerce and trade
   (E) correspondence and requisition

5. During the siege of Coen's position, his soldiers behaved

   (A) with military decorum
   (B) with vengeance and anger
   (C) with honor and discipline
   (D) with dipsomaniac fervor
   (E) until the fourth month of the siege

6. The rush to Indonesia was initiated by the promise of

   (A) power
   (B) land
   (C) religious fervor
   (D) profit
   (E) vengeance

7. It can be inferred from the passage that the word *farang* means

   (A) friends
   (B) foreigners
   (C) Dutchmen
   (D) drunkards
   (E) sailors

8. In their conquest of the Banda islands, the Dutch

   (A) assimilated the natives
   (B) enslaved the natives
   (C) befriended the natives
   (D) exterminated the natives
   (E) ignored the natives

9. The Dutch East India company's philosophy can be summed up in the word:

   (A) exploration
   (B) expansion
   (C) monotony
   (D) profit
   (E) monopoly

10. It is implied that the historical relationship between the Indonesian people and the Dutch is

(A) filled with animosity
(B) filled with brotherly love
(C) distant trading partners
(D) occasional allies
(E) None of the above

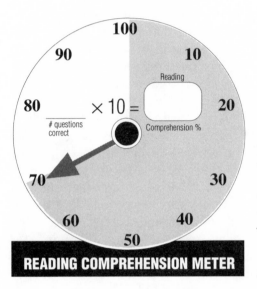

Calculate your comprehension rate using the following formula. Multiply the number of questions you answered correctly by 10. That is your comprehension percentage. You want to keep your percentage above 70 percent for any type of reading. Below that, you start losing important information presented in the passages.

THE SCIENTIFIC METHOD

In scientific texts, don't worry about the questions that merely serve to reinforce your ability to manipulate a set of equations when pre-reading. Look for questions that ask about larger themes and overarching principles, not just plug-ins or word problems. Those are useful, but not as pre-reading. Pre-reading is designed to help you anticipate a line of thought—not to resolve its every intricacy.

By now, you're beginning to see a split in how you should approach scientific texts and social-scientific texts, like math versus history. Each type has some problems and idiosyncrasies unique to it, and a closer look at each will clear some of them up.

STRAIGHTFORWARD SCIENCE

In scientific texts, the authors will begin with the fundamentals of the discipline and build from there. The first few chapters should provide you with most of the background that you will need for all later chapters, so if you are going to spend more time on any one part, make it the beginning. Unfortunately, the beginning chapters are usually dull because background information is usually dull. It becomes a lot more exciting when the background you decided to skip shows up on a test, though, so don't leap ahead to the good stuff. Jumping into a difficult textbook midstream is like deciding you're going to become a doctor by practicing surgery on yourself. There are certain things you really need to know, and you're going to get hurt if you don't.

Some people view texts as bibles, to remain pristine and untouched. Certainly your library does. If you are going to use a text often, get your own copy, because useful reading in scientific texts is done not only with the eyes, but also with a pen. **Mark up the book, underline, take notes.** We cannot emphasize enough that this will improve your reading. By doing this, you will not only know what is important to study when finals come around, but also where the good examples are that explain abstract principles. Gravity, for example, is such a nebulous concept that when explained in abstract terms, it is easily misconstrued. But if you can think of gravity as a giant vacuum, sucking everything toward its center, then all of a sudden you have a concrete image of the effects of gravity, and it becomes easier to remember.

MAKE A MESS

> **Mark up your books and take notes in them. Even if you doodle, do it around important ideas or concepts. Then you have something to identify the concept with. Unmarked books are useless during review time. Each page looks like every other page, with nothing to identify it for you. By circling facts, by noting important ideas in the margin, you increase the chance that they will stay in your head and you can picture the things you circled on the page or wrote in the margin.**

In scientific texts, ideas are usually broken into one idea per paragraph. Identifying that idea and summarizing it in the margin next to the paragraph is a good idea. In that way, you construct an outline of the chapter while reading it. When you need to memorize the important information from the chapter, you have an outline at your fingertips, and needn't waste valuable phone and/or TV time constructing one. If this sounds overwhelming, think of the work and torn hair it will save at the end of the semester.

WORDS IN CONTEXT

Most dense texts have their own language, their own specific vocabulary. Do you need to know the precise meaning of every term? Hardly. It doesn't hurt to look up words you don't know, especially words that appear over and over again in a text. Technical jargon has the effect of droning you to sleep, making you feel lost and confused, and deflating your aggressive attitude in approaching the material. Do not let this stop you from being a more effective reader.

DON'T STOP

The key to getting around technical jargon is twofold. First, stopping at every word and looking it up is counterproductive. By letting the word reveal itself in context, you can keep your reading rhythm without stopping and starting. This first technique is important for keeping the fluidity (and therefore the pace) of your reading as continuous as possible.

Read the following passage and see if you can figure out the meaning of the word without knowing exactly what is being described.

> *Criatus Micanscropus* uses all eight legs to support its weight. Though too small to be seen by the human eye, its sting can raise small welts and can be thought of as a mosquito by the uninitiated. *Criatus Micanscropus* lives in colonies of 7–12, and thrives on scalp decay, skin detritus, and spins minute webs which, if embedded in the dermic layer, can cause infection.

Can you picture a tiny, spiderlike bug? It is tough to train yourself to keep reading when you don't recognize a word, but it is important that you don't get bogged (or bugged, in this case) down by unfamiliar terms. By letting words reveal themselves in context, you avoid getting thrown by what you don't immediately recognize.

Exercise #9

Try to figure out what's being described in bold, and put your answer in the blank underneath the question. We've done the first one for you.

1. **To engage the selective-access unit, insert one of the provided selective-access unit actuators into the selective-access unit actuator slot and rotate until the access-denial bolt has audibly engaged. To disengage the access-denial bolt, reverse procedure.**

   A Lock and Key

2. The adventurous traveler crossed **any half of the Earth's surface**.

   _____

3. Polar Bears and penguins are apt to be found in the **region in the northernmost area of the Earth.**

   _____

4. Charles looked for his eventual destination, the heart of Africa, in his **bound collection of maps.**

   _____

5. While strolling through the department store, Jennifer casually picked up a fifteen-dollar bracelet and slipped it into her purse without paying. Jennifer suffered from **a compulsion to steal, usually without economic need.**

   _____

6. The days of the specialized craftsman for popularly accessible goods is gone; once Henry Ford made his presence known, nothing has worked more effectively than **a linear grouping of factory workers and equipment along which a product being assembled passes consecutively from operation to operation until complete.**

   _____

7. The difficulty with the physics of the waterslide rests on one basic principle: **the resistance of an object to the medium through which or on which it is traveling.**

---

8. As an editor, Laurice worked daily with **an often sextagonal, long stem of graphite surrounded by wood, occasionally tipped on one end by vulcanized rubber.**

---

9. Any operation on the trachea must take into accout the proximity of the **two folds of tissue located in the larynx that vibrate when air passes over them.** If these folds of tissue are damaged, speech patterns could become impaired.

---

10. Aside from his mutton-chopped later incarnation, initially this **American rock-and-roll singer of the twentieth century known for his distinctive throaty tone in such songs as "Hound Dog"** was viewed as both the primary American clean-cut rebellious sex symbol, and as a patriotic member of our armed forces.

People don't always write as simply or as clearly as they should. It's up to you to make sense of their long-winded gibberish. By figuring out words in context, you save yourself a trip to the dictionary and keep your concentration in the book. Whenever you stop reading and do something else, you lose something from the book. If during a dinner you tasted a spice you couldn't identify, would you get up in the middle of the meal and go through the spice rack to find out what spice it was? No, because when you came back, your dinner would be cold. So will your concentration for the book be cold. Use the context to tell you the word, and later you can look up a textbook definition.

TRANSLATION

The second technique, which is important for comprehension, is called translation. **Translation** involves taking a piece of technical jargon and identifying it with a common-sense phrase or definition in your mind. Then, every time you see this phrase, you link it with a definition which makes sense. Most technical books are written by people who have an expertise in a particular discipline. These people have no sympathy for our lack of knowledge. They are so far removed from common vocabulary problems that they don't even realize there could possibly be a problem. It's up to you to turn their technical stuff into meaningful words.

Let's look at an example. Read the following passage and look at how we would translate it.

> A property of matter that is closely related to mass is *mass density*. **Mass density** refers to the amount of matter in a given amount of space and is defined as the *mass per unit volume of a substance*.

This definition is functionally useless. It's like saying "Shpleg" is defined as "Grheg" (which means nothing, in case you were wondering). It might be more helpful if it were translated into the following:

> Density is matter per amount of space. Hmm. Well, density is just the amount of stuff in a space. If I have a lot of stuff, something is very dense. If I have a little bit of stuff in the same space, it's not very dense. It's like my room. If I have a bunch of my clothes and stuff all over, it is tough to navigate through my room. If there is just a little bit of stuff, it is easy to get through my room. Density, then, is just clutter.

Now for some of you, this definition will be equally useless. The key is to find the definition which makes sense for you. Then every time you see "density," you can say, "Oh, that's just clutter," and all that the definition means for *you*.

Now you wouldn't write this entire paragraph in the margin. What you would do is figure this out in your head, and write in the margin "Density = Clutter." Then, the next time you see the word "density," think "clutter."

The more you translate, the less mystical complex subjects will appear to you. What does this have to do with reading? A lot. Reading is making sense of symbols. The harder your brain has to work to translate symbols, the slower you will read. Translation is a way of speeding up that process. That's why a large vocabulary is such a big help—you've pre-translated a lot of stuff already. More about that in chapter nine.

EXERCISE #10

Try the following exercises, translating the terminology from its scientific doublespeak into something which makes sense.

1. Heating a mixture of substances usually provides activation energy and increases the rate of chemical reaction. A high temperature would not be a good way for a cell to obtain activation energy. Too much heat would harm a cell. It might produce reactions that would would cause cells to disintegrate. There is one way to increase the rate of reactions, however, that is not harmful. When certain chemicals, called **catalysts** (CAT-uh-lists), are present, molecules can interact without the need for extra heat. This means that catalysts act to lower the amount of activation energy needed.

2. **The Nichiren Sect**
   This is a Japanese sect, founded in the 13th century by Nichiren, a fiery patriot who thought he had discovered original Buddhism in the *Lotus of the Good Law*. He thought the other Buddhist sects had missed the true way. The implicit patriotism of this sect is seen in its three vows: "I will be a pillar of Japan; I will be eyes to Japan; I will be a great ship for Japan." The contemporary militant *Soka Gakkai* movement is a revival of the Nichiren sect, even to the constant repitition of the *daimoku* formula: *Namu Myoho Renge Kyo*, "Hail to the Lotus of the Good Law."

3. On a superficial view, direct or indirect or circumstancial evidence would appear to be distinct species of evidence; whereas these words denote only the different modes in which those classes of evidentiary facts are adduced to produce conviction. Circumstantial evidence is of a nature identically the same with direct evidence; the distinction is that by direct evidence is intended evidence that applied directly to the fact which forms the subject of inquiry, the *factum probandum;* circumstantial evidence is equally direct in its nature, but, as the name imports, is a direct evidence of minor fact or facts of such a nature that the mind is led into intuitively, or by a conscious process of reasoning, towards or to the conviction that from it or them some other fact may be inferred. A witness disposes that he saw A inflict on B a wound of which he instantly dies; this is a case of direct evidence. B dies of poisoning; A is proved to have had malice and other threats against him, and to have clandestinely purchased poison, wrapped in a particular paper, and of the same kind as that which has caused death. The paper is found in his secret drawer, and the poison gone. The evidence of these facts is direct; the facts themselves constitute indirect and circumstantial evidence as applicable to the inquiry whether a murder has been committed, and whether it was committed by A.

4. Mathematically, a worm is difficult to distinguish from a virus, and a communications network cannot be distinguished from the "network" formed by the busses inside a computer (unless the network includes workstations with independent processing capability, such as microcomputers). Colloquially, a virus alters other "programs" and a worm does not; however, mathematically the environment (sequence of bits in the address space) in which a worm moves is a "program." A virus does not propagate by itself, and it modifies other programs; the lack of independence may offer a mathematically definable difference between virus and worm. The physical implementation of a network implies very different countermeasures for a worm than for a virus.

5. For income tax reporting, firms generally use the Accelerated Cost Recovery System (ACRS), which specifies depreciation charges accelerated in three distinct ways. First, the depreciable lives themselves are generally shorter than economic lives. (Straight-line depreciation for a shorter period will produce depreciation charge accelerated when compared to straight-line over a longer period.) Second, for assets other than buildings, ACRS provides for depreciation over the specified life based on the 150-percent and 200-percent declining-balance depreciation method, which is more rapid than straight-line. ACRS assumes, however, that each asset is acquired at mid-year of the year of acquisition, so the first-year percentage represents only a half-year of depreciation. Third, ACRS allows the entire depreciable basis to be written off over the depreciation period; salvage value is ignored.

These approaches to scientific texts should save you time, decrease your frustration, and improve your retention. If there were some magic way of putting a math book underneath your pillow at night, going to sleep and waking up with a full knowledge of the text, believe me, we'd be the first to show you. But there isn't. You just have to tough through these texts, using the techniques above. You should see a dramatic improvement in your understanding of these materials, and at the same time, an increase in speed.

THE NON-SCIENTIFIC METHOD

But not all required reading is scientific texts (thank heavens). Project reports, psychology, history, philosophy, and other social sciences all contain information you need to understand a discipline, but they usually aren't so terminology- or number-heavy. You need a different approach for this kind of reading, because it's just as important to keep your comprehension rates up here. "He who does not learn from history is doomed to repeat it," said George Santayana, and by the same token, he who does not learn from history textbooks is doomed to repeat history class.

In the social sciences, history, sociology, literature, psychology, and others, many of the textbooks will argue points of view. The first thing you should do is look at the title. Does it argue a point, or state a fact? If a book is called *Capitalist Patriarchy and the Case for Socialist Feminism,* you can have a pretty clear idea that the book will involve those issues. It is less helpful if the title is *The American Revolution.*

EXERCISE #11

Look at the following titles and mark down if the title is helpful or not helpful in identifying what the author's argument or point of view might be.

Financial Accounting for Beginners

Vietnam: The Untold Story of Government Corruption

From Fish to Man: Evolution's Progress

Russia's Quiet Threat

America the Beautiful

Society and Social Structures

Myths of Gender

Why I Kill: A Psychological Study

Parents and Children: The Communication Gap

The Evolution of Nuclear Strategy

Zen and the Art of Motorcycle Maintenance

Advanced Pascal

On Becoming a Novelist

Reading Smart

Information, Incentives, and Bargaining in the Japanese Economy

The point is to use all the clues any book has to offer. In particular, any text that argues a point of view offers you a great advantage: there will be a linear discussion which will lead you to a conclusion, often stated in the opening chapter. **Reading with your pen is essential in cases like this.** Mark up the first and last chapters ruthlessly; if an author makes an argument the focus of an entire book, you must keep that argument in mind the whole time you read the book. It would be like playing baseball without knowing the goal of the game. You would know all of these facts, but have no idea how they relate to each other. You are more likely to remember them if you know that the goal of the game is to score the most runs by the end of the ninth inning.

TRACE THE THEME

Each paragraph will further the argument and back it up, or refute other arguments. Using your pen you can quickly identify the main theme of the book and then trace that theme in the margin of your text. If the first paragraph says "Revolution is a good thing," then you should look for how the next paragraphs support or illuminate that statement by taking notes and underlining text. When you are done, you will have a complete outline of the book.

SEPARATE THE FACTS

After understanding what the larger endeavor is, then the reader should distinguish primary facts from secondary facts. **Primary facts** are dates, names, and equations without which you couldn't begin to discuss the subject. **Secondary facts** are all interesting, but non-necessary information about the event. If the subject were the American Revolution, then 1776, George Washington, and The Boston Tea Party would be primary facts, critical to any discussion of the American Revolution. The precise number of troops in Boston Harbor, the amount of the tea tax, and the age of King George III of England are all interesting and related to the discussion, but the American Revolution can be discussed without knowing any of them. They should be treated as secondary facts. If this seems arbitrary, just ask yourself the question: "Can I talk about this subject completely without using these facts?" Don't confuse little stuff with more important larger issues—see how the facts relate to the main idea of the book. Once you've caught that magic thread of the main idea, then the important facts seem to leap out at you.

Primary vs. Secondary Fact

The best way to tell if a fact is primary or secondary is to pare an event down to its simplest scenario, and then keep adding until you get to the level of information which describes the subject in sufficient detail.

Let's take the American Revolution (again). Start with the basics:

1. There was a conflict.

This doesn't fully capture the subject. So expand.

2. There was a conflict between the colonies (America) and the empire (Britain).

Still, more is needed.

3. There was an eighteenth-century conflict between the colonies (America) and the empire (Britain) which came to a head over the "taxation without representation" issue. America's army was led by General George Washington, who later became the first president of the United States. Great Britain was led (though not militarily) by King George III. America won.

This is enough to get a fair idea of the subject, and to go much further gets into secondary facts. Tailor your expansion to the subject. You may want to have a larger group of primary facts to describe World War I than you would use to describe your local dogcatcher elections.

EXERCISE #12

Read the following passage and list the important facts on the left. Be careful to exclude secondary facts that may be interesting, but are not related or important to the main idea.

About 30,000 years ago Neanderthal man disappeared, displaced by Homo sapiens, a taller, slimmer, altogether agile and more handsome—at least to our eyes—race of people who arose in Africa 10,000 years ago, spread to the Near East, and then were drawn to Europe by the retreating ice sheets of the last great ice age. These were the Cro-Magnon people, who were responsible for the famous cave paintings at Lascaux in France and Altamira in Spain—the earliest signs of civilization in Europe, the work of the world's first artists. Although this was an immensely long time ago—some 20,000 years before the domestication of animals and the rise of farming—these Cro-Magnon people were identical to us: they had the same physique, the same brain, the same looks. And, unlike all previous homonids that roamed the earth, they could choke on food. That may seem a trifling point, but the slight evolutionary change that pushed man's larynx deeper into his throat, and thus made choking a possibility, also brought with it the possibility of sophisticated, well-articulated speech.

Other mammals have no contact between their airways and their esophagi. They can breathe and swallow at the same time, and there is no possibility of food going down the wrong way. But with Homo sapiens food and drink must pass over the larynx on the way to the gullet and thus there is a constant risk that some will be inadvertently inhaled. In modern humans, the lowered larynx isn't in position from birth. It descends sometime between the ages of three and five months—curiously, the precise period when babies are likely to suffer from Sudden Infant Death Syndrome. At all events, the descended larynx explains why you can speak and your dog cannot.

According to studies conducted by Philip Lieberman at Brown University, Neanderthal man was physiologically precluded from uttering certain basic sounds such as the /e/ sound of *bee* or the /oo/ sound of *boot*. His speech, if it existed at all, would have been nasal-sounding and fairly imprecise—and that would have no doubt have greatly impeded his development.

It was long supposed that Neanderthal man was absorbed by the more advanced Homo sapiens. But recent evidence indicates that Homo sapiens and Neanderthals coexisted in the Near East for 30,000 years without interbreeding—strong evidence that the Neanderthals must have been a different species. It is interesting to speculate what would have become of these people had they survived. Would we have used them for slaves? For sport? Who can say?

At all events, Neanderthal man was hopelessly outclassed. Not only did Homo sapiens engage in art of astonishingly high quality, but they evinced other cultural achievements of a comparatively high order. They devised more specialized tools for a wider variety of tasks and they hunted in a far more systematic and cooperative way. Whereas the food debris of the Neanderthals shows a wide variety of animal bones, suggesting that they took whatever they could find, archaelogical remnants from Homo sapiens show that they sought out particular kinds of game and tracked animals seasonally. All of this strongly suggests that they possessed a linguistic system sufficiently sophisticated to deal with concepts such as "Today let's kill some red deer. You take some big sticks and drive the deer out of the woods and we'll stand by the riverbank with our spears and kill them as they come towards us." By comparison Neanderthal speech may have been something more like "I'm hungry. Let's hunt."

It may be no more than intriguing coincidence, but the area of Cro-Magnon's cave paintings is also the area containing Europe's oldest and most mysterious ethnic group, the Basques. Their language, called Euskara by its speakers, may be the last surviving remnant of the Neolithic languages spoken in Stone Age Europe and later displaced by Indo-European tongues. No one can say. What is certain is that Basque was already old by the time the Celts came to the region. Today it is the native tongue of about 600,000 people in Spain and 100,000 in France in an area around the Bay of Biscay stretching roughly from Bilbao to Bayonne and inland over the Pyrenees to Pamplona. Its remoteness from Indo-European is indicated by its words for the numbers one to five: *bat, bi, hirur, laur, bortz.* Many authorities believe there is simply no connection between Basque and any other known language.

Don't Forget the Pretty Pictures

Often overlooked are graphs, charts and photographs. Examine them carefully. Usually, they are intended to be a snapshot of something important in the chapter. Read the captions and the keys. Nothing can give you a quicker overview of a way of life, a problem, or a representation, than a chart, graph, or photograph. Don't rely on these, though: a student of ours did that once, and ended up having to draw pretty little pictures in her exam book.

THINGS TO TAKE WITH YOU

Textbook reading depends on concentration and using techniques to keep you focused on the text. We all know that most of this information is dense, difficult to get through, and confusing. But the best readers give themselves a fighting chance by reading with their pens, by tracing main ideas and picking out important details. They use pictures, subheadings, translation, and derive the meaning of words in context. They don't try to memorize everything—they try to understand everything, and give themselves the best chance of remembering the important stuff.

READING RACETRACK #7

Read the next passage, using pre-reading and the questions as guidelines for reading the passage. You'll find your speed improves as you can disregard the information which you already know you won't need. Still, don't time yourself—you shouldn't be concerned with speed through textbooks yet. This is a long passage, so pre-reading is very important.

> Gauguin left France on 3 July 1895, never to return. He had presided over a failed sale of his earlier work and had left the majority of his paintings in the hands of at least two obscure men, Auguste Bauchy and Georges Chaudet. Together with his literary agent Charles Morice, his faithful friend Daniel de Manfried, and later, Ambroise Vollard, his dealer, these men kept Gauguin informed about his business affairs in France and made it possible for him to enjoy periods of prosperity amid bouts of depression, illness, and poverty. Because they oversaw Gauguin's financial well-being from afar, the many letters he wrote to them are full of information about financial matters and the state of his health. When these letters are read as an ensemble, his life sounds more miserable than it was, and almost masks the brillint paintings, drawings, and prints that survive him.
>
> During the eight years that elapsed between Gauguin's final departure from France and his death on the distant island of Hivaoa in the Marquesas, he was in the hospital at least four times, often for prolonged periods; claimed to have

attempted suicide once and perhaps succumbed to its temptations in 1903; built three houses; fathered at least three children; edited one newspaper and wrote, designed, and printed another; completed three book-length texts; sent paintings and drawings to many European exhibitions; finished nearly 100 paintings; made over 400 woodcuts; carved scores of pieces of wood; wrote nearly 150 letters, and fought both civil and ecclesiastical authorities with all the gusto of a youth. He was only fifty-four years old when he died, but he had lived his life with such fervor and worked so hard when he was healthy that we must remember the achievements even as we read the litany of the failures and miseries in the chronology.

Unfortunately, none of the great monographic exhibitions devoted to Gauguin since his death has done justice to this extraordinary phase in his working life. By the time the French organizers of the 1906 exhibition had begun their work, a good many of the most important paintings had already left France for private collections in Russia and Germany. Indeed, without the paintings bought by Karl Ernst Osthaus, Sergei Shchukin, and Ivan Morosov, it is difficult to understand the late Gauguin fully, and many of these paintings were not in France to be loaned to the 1906 Gauguin exhibition. Only the 1903 exhibition held in Vollard's gallery a few month after Gauguin's death had a generous enough selection of major paintings and transfer drawings to give full measure to the achievement of the artist in his last years. Yet even this large exhibition was insufficient for a full understanding of his oeuvre from 1896 to 1903 because it contained almost exclusively works made in the last three years of his life.

There are several important ways in which Gauguin's oeuvre from the last Polynesian period can be differentiated from that of the first. During the first trip, Gauguin's work took two different directions, both of which were recognized by critics of the 1893 exhibition. First, he represented scenes of daily life just as his hero, Delacroix, had done in Morocco; second, he created idealized illustrations of Polynesian tales of religious and mythical events about which he read. Both these enterprises were characterized by a sort of ethnographic focus on Tahiti before its colonialization. Indeed, hints of the colonial presence are so rare in the paintings that, even when they do exist, one must be sensitized to recognize them.

Neither of these ethnographic concerns was so evident in Gauguin's work of the last Polynesian period. Indeed, Gauguin returned to Tahiti with his mind full of new ideas about comparative religion, politics, and social philosophy. He also took with him an even larger stock of photographs and reproductions of other works of art than he had in the years 1891 to 1893, and, as many scholars have pointed out, he made considerable use of this material. Two of the photographs often referred to were of the Javanese temple of Borobudur. The Tahiti to which Gauguin returned in 1895 had become even more colonial in the two years since he had left, and there is little doubt that Gauguin disliked most of the "progress" that he saw. Yet we must also remember that Tahiti had changed in those years perhaps less than Gauguin himself had, and that given his earlier experience, the painter could have predicted what he was going to find on his return.

His late paintings, traced and transferred drawings, and sculpture lack the vivid directness of the work from his earlier, ethnographic phase. In these years, he was more interested in the creation of works of art that transcended the particular place in which they were made. His late work is more obviously meditated than the earlier, and he created works of art as if to decorate a new mythic universe. His overt wordliness, his conflation of religious traditions of East, West, and Oceania, of ancient and modern, must have seemed strange to the majority of Eurocentric Parisians for whom his art was made. Today, in an age of rampant international capitalism, his world view is easier to find relevant and even important.

1. From 1895 to 1903, Gauguin's artistic activity can best be described as

    (A) impoverished
    (B) alien
    (C) ethnographic
    (D) frenzied
    (E) transcendental

2. Paintings important to understanding the late Gauguin were purchased by

    (A) Charles Morice
    (B) Daniel de Manfried
    (C) the temple of Borobudur
    (D) Ivan Morosov
    (E) Georges Chaudet

3. It can be inferred from the passage that the word "oeuvre" means

   (A) style
   (B) area of obsession
   (C) overtness
   (D) work
   (E) openess

4. Which of the following statements is best supported by the passage?

   (A) Paul Gauguin was impressed by the physical beauty of Tahiti.
   (B) Paul Gauguin believed in civil reform.
   (C) Paul Gauguin committed suicide.
   (D) Paul Gauguin was not confined to one area of expression.
   (E) Paul Gauguin, in his later years, abandoned Europe due to religious pressure.

5. Paul Gauguin's later work was

   (A) obsessively involved in ethnography
   (B) casually informed by ethnography
   (C) revered in Europe
   (D) informed by philosophical issues
   (E) imitative of Javanese life

6. Gauguin's exhibition of 1893 was marked by

   (A) scenes from daily life
   (B) ideas of comparative religion, politics, and social philosophy
   (C) the lack of the vivid directness of earlier work
   (D) photographs of the Javanese temple of Borobudur
   (E) an abandonment of the island of Hivaoa as subject

7. Gauguin's financial situation for his final eight years can best be described as

   (A) impoverished
   (B) vacillatory
   (C) profitable
   (D) mismanaged
   (E) well diversified

8. Gauguin's later work was inspired by

   (A) native life
   (B) mythic representation
   (C) Sergei Shchukin
   (D) the 1903 exhibition in Vollard's gallery
   (E) rampant international capitalism

9. According to the passage, Gauguin's later work has

   (A) been comprehensively chronicled at a number of
       exhibitions
   (B) all been destroyed by Gauguin's fourth wife
   (C) gone down in value
   (D) received short-shrift compared to his earlier work
   (E) influenced many young artists

10. The last eight years of Gauguin's life can best be
    described as

   (A) languid
   (B) goofy
   (C) serene
   (D) very productive
   (E) inexplicable

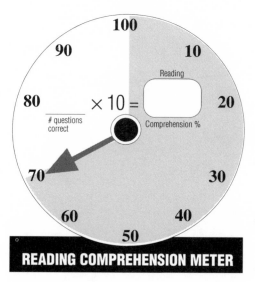

Calculate your comprehension rate using the following formula. Multiply the number of questions you answered correctly by 10. That is your comprehension percentage. You want to keep your percentage above 70 percent for any type of reading. Below that, you start losing important information presented in the passages.

CHAPTER 6

In
The
News

"Journalism is the ability to meet the challenge of filling space."

—Rebecca West

[Before you start this chapter, grab a newspaper or a magazine—try to find one without a lot a perfume ads—those things will give you a headache and make you think of many, many things that are not related to reading at all.]

When you get a chance, go to the newsstand, or your local magazine store. Look at the ridiculous number of magazines and newspapers that each cater to a specific audience: *Glamour, Vogue, The New York Times, Wall Street Journal, Mad Magazine, Bride's Magazine, U.S. News and World Report.* It seems that if you are interested in anything, there is a magazine for you (or there will be one shortly). And most of the time, when you pick up a magazine to read, you're not exactly sure what you're going to need it for. An article may seem interesting for the first few paragraphs, but often people just put down the magazine or newspaper, bored, confused, or angry, because the article didn't turn out to be about what they expected to read.

"What could I do? It jumped off the newsstand."

Drawing by C. Barsotti: © 1993 The New Yorker Magazine, Inc.

Journalism is one of the most diverse fields of literature, in both style and content. You have to be prepared for anything, from a dull, sleep-inducing recitation of events (snore journalism) to a vibrant, argumentative piece on a volatile issue based mainly on opinion (catch-your-breath journalism). Once you learn quickly to identify what kind of piece you're looking at, you're in good shape with this type of reading.

The first thing you must keep in mind is that for any piece of journalism, the author is arguing a point. Oh, sure, the *Wall Street Journal* sounds a lot less opinionated than *Revolution Today*, but if you look closely, it is arguing its point just as fiercely—only it's more subtle.

The second thing you have to look for is the difference between opinion and fact. Often, it's the journalist's job to use certain facts to get you to feel a certain way (this is the cynical point of view, but anyone who's read the *Weekly World News* knows what we're talking about). By distinguishing fact from opinion, you can tell what the true situation is and what the author wants you to feel. Sometimes the author is wrong—and by figuring out what the facts are, you can start to argue with the article's conclusions. Let's look at an example of a journalistic piece which appears just to be stating the facts, but in reality argues a point. Make an effort to distinguish fact from opinion.

For example, read the following article:

> Legend has it that Thomas Edison was a champion napper. A couple of times every day, he would sit peacefully in a chair with a solid iron ball in each hand. As he moved from light sleeping to deep slumber, the balls would drop and wake him up, thus preventing him from falling into a deep sleep.
>
> Edison knew what he was doing. Says Dr. Claudio Stampi, a sleeping disorders expert at the Institute for Circadian Physiology in Cambridge, Mass.: "The most restful nap with the least amount of sleep-hangover is between 15 and 30 minutes."
>
> Many historical figures have enhanced their productive powers, and probably increased their life spans, by napping. Among them: Leonardo da Vinci, Winston Churchill, Albert Einstein, John F. Kennedy, Ronald Reagan, and basketball's Wilt Chamberlain. Yet when asked, nearly half of all adult Americans stoutly deny that they ever nap. Stampi, who is one of the few scientists to focus on the subject of napping, thinks most people equate the practice with indolence or old age.
>
> Stampi is bent on making napping respectable. Some intriguing new research supports his cause. Historically, American society had been geared to what biologists call a "monophasic" sleep/awake pattern, in which the day is rigidly divided into one period of wakefulness, followed by one period of sleep. Under the monophasic model, napping has been considered culturally inappropriate and, according to some experts in the field of sleep research, even unhealthy, in that is cuts into night-time sleeping.

But new data suggest that human beings may in fact be "biphasic" creatures whose days are broken up into two periods of sleep, nocturnal and midafternoon. Lunch is commonly blamed as the cause of midafternoon drowsiness, but it turns out that food intake has little or nothing to do with the urge to nod off. Much more important, according to recent research at the Circadian Institute and the University of Pennsylvania, is simply the time of day.

Circadian's Claudio Stampi is convinced that Americans will be better rested, healthier, and more productive if they give in to that urge to take a siesta. Like many sleep disorder researchers, he believes that Americans' "sleep deficit" has steadily grown as people experience more stress in managing the competing needs of careers and families. Far from being a sign of laziness, napping, he says, is really a biological imperative that allows people to whittle away at the deficit.

After you read this article, did you start thinking, "Maybe I should start napping?" Be honest. We did. But once you look closely at the article, you can see how the author manipulates us into reaching that conclusion. Let's take a look at how the article does this.

Now, what is the author arguing? You can breeze quickly through the facts of the opening paragraphs. It's interesting that Edison, Kennedy, and da Vinci all napped, but did napping make them geniuses? Many people we know nap, and they have yet to discover a basic scientific principle, give moral guidance to a nation, or paint a single chapel ceiling (this principle is an example of the difference between primary and secondary facts, which we've explained earlier). The author is presenting a little snapshot of Claudio Stampi and, in so doing, arguing his point that people should nap. How does the author do this without saying straight out she believes Stampi? In a few ways. First, she cites historical figures meant to inspire us who support Stampi's point of view. This is meant to ally us with Stampi's opinion (implied: Do you want to be like Albert Einstein? Then nap!). Second, when she describes Stampi's research she uses the adjective "intriguing." Intriguing means "thought-provoking," which she tries to do, to change the way we think about sleep. She cites only Stampi's new research, and doesn't present any opposing point of view. And finally, she ends up agreeing with Stampi's conclusion. If *her* conclusion is Stampi's conclusion, then *our* conclusion should be Stampi's conclusion. This piece masterfully manipulates the reader by choosing selective facts and presenting them in a certain way. Should we be mad at Kate Bohner for doing this to us in her piece? Absolutely not. It's her job to get us to feel a certain way about facts. Heck, if we feel anything, she's done a good job. Bohner has here argued successfully for us to change our thoughts. We should be impressed by her good work.

THE POINT BEING . . .

Be careful. Don't take opinion or selective fact as the final truth. If someone tells you that seventy-five percent of Americans are in favor of burning witches, would you believe him? How about twenty-five percent? How about five percent? Big manipulations of fact (lies, that is) are easy to spot. To spot the small manipulations of numbers or facts which subtly support the author's point, you have to be vigilant. By uncovering the author's argument, you can start to look at the facts and see how objective they are.

But the above example about burning witches can't be manipulated, can it? What if the question was asked in the following way:

> "If we could prove that certain people, without any doubt, were witches, and had ceased to be human hundreds of years ago, that they were planning an overthrow of the world which would succeed and lead to pain and misery for all humankind, and the only way to stop them (regrettably) would be to immolate them, in that case, would you object to our saving your way of life?"

You would expect a large response of "No, I don't mind. Immolate 'em." Also, people might not realize that "immolate" means "setting on fire." The following question might get a different response:

> "If I think someone's a witch, I should burn them, right?"

People would be less likely to agree with the second question. But both percentages could be used as facts in an article to support a point of view. You must be suspicious of articles that claim to present only the truth, particularly ones which appear to have no point of view. Those are the most dangerous of all—they are working behind the scenes to get you to feel one way or another. The best defense against being manipulated by an article is to quickly identify the author's argument.

How do you figure out an author's argument? Ask yourself some questions about the article. First of all, where is it from? Usually, a magazine or a newspaper will have a tradition of a certain point of view. For example, the *Utne Reader* contains alternative, non-traditional approaches to contemporary issues. So if an article in the *Utne Reader* is titled "Cars and America" you can probably expect something which challenges your traditional notion of the relationship between cars and America. The same article in *Car and Driver* will have completely different content and a completely different point of view. Where you are reading is important—don't forget about it.

BEGIN AT THE BEGINNING

The second thing that you want to know is the title of the article. Many articles will have a heading and then a subheading. You can use these things to identify what the article is going to be about. For example, several articles can be titled "The Year 2000" but have different subheadings which quickly identify which one is more important to you.

> The Year 2000: Global Crisis or World Peace?
>
> The Year 2000: The Stocks to Buy for the Future
>
> The Year 2000: An Adventure in Cooking
>
> The Year 2000: Numerology for You
>
> The Year 2000: Your Horoscope for the Future
>
> The Year 2000: Helpful Dating Tips
>
> The Year 2000: Will My Acne Be Gone By Then?

All of these are written for different groups, and one is not necessarily more important than another. It depends on what is most important in your life and what you are interested in. Use all the available information to tell you what is the right article for you. Headlines, kickers, and headers are useful ways to scan quickly which articles will be of interest to you.

FIND OUT WHEN

When was it written? You might think this isn't important, but it helps you figure out some of the author's direction. The title of an article from the *Bethlehem Gazette* reads "How Smoking Matures You" and the article goes on to support smoking as a healthy, pleasant endeavor. This article was written in 1911. An article from 1986 on the stock market might read "Why The Market Will Never Fall." In 1987, the stock market lost 22.8% of its value in one day, falling over 508 points. With the knowledge you have now, you judge these articles differently. The date of publication affects how current, useful, and trustworthy the information is.

These ideas aren't new. You've known about identifying what you read from chapter one. We're just asking you to take it to a different level now. The more you know about what you're reading, the more you'll retain.

Of course, as we've stressed before, *why* you're reading is as important as *what* you're reading, and should affect your approach to the material. If you're reading for pleasure, take what you like from the material (as long as you take enough to follow the author's argument). If you're reading for retention or to bolster your knowledge on a certain topic, sort out irrelevant facts from what you really need, and keep only the good stuff.

ARE YOU HORTENSE OR EUNICE?

For example, Hortense and Eunice are both at the zoo. Hortense has to write a paper for school on the Stinky Crested Wallabee, but Eunice is there for fun.

It would be silly for Hortense to wander through every exhibit, memorizing the feeding periods of the Flaming Pit Viper or the number of eggs laid by the Flemish Hooting Walloon, until she gets to the Wallabee cage, just as it would be silly to pay great attention to the Thomas Edison bit in the previous article when you really need to research REM sleep. Conversely, Eunice is at the zoo for fun, and doesn't have to see any pit vipers at all if she doesn't want to. If you're reading for fun and only like stories about Thomas Edison, then that's the only part you have to read.

READING RACETRACK #8

Read the following passage and answer the questions after it to find
your speed and comprehension levels. Time yourself on a watch with
a second hand. Time only the reading portion of the exercise, not
the question portion. Then calculate your reading speed and comprehension level, using the formulas at the end of the questions.

The demise of the Soviet Union has, paradoxically, given
Vietnam a strategic usefulness to the United States that it
never had during a war in which fifty-eight thousand Americans
perished. The Soviet collapse has created a power vacuum
in East Asia. The American withdrawal from the Philippines
and the shrinking of the United States military because of
the end of the Cold War and economic troubles at home
are contributing to the sense of a power vacuum. This may
be more perception than reality, since the United States retains
the air and naval capability to assert itself in East Asia, but
perception has a reality of its own. The Chinese perceive
it, and they are intent on filling the vacuum.

Southern China is an economic astonishment. Guangdong
Province's economy, for example, grew at an average annual
rate of fifteen per cent from 1981 to 1991. The Chinese are
using their new wealth to make themselves the big military
power in the region. They are creating a sophisticated Air
Force, purchasing long-range Sukhoi-27 fighter-bombers, MIG-
31 interceptors, and airborne surveillance-and-control planes
from Russia. They are bringing their Army up to date with
Russia's latest T-72 main-battle tanks. Beijing is also building
a "blue water" Navy to project force beyond China's shores,
negotiating with Russia and Ukraine for an aircraft carrier
that was under construction at a Soviet shipyard.

Like it or not, the United States is going to have to
play the role of regional balancer—the guarantor of stability
in the last resort—to keep China from unsettling East Asia
in the post-Cold War era. There is too much to lose for us
to refuse the role. Americans tend to view their current
relationship with Asia as a one-way drain of cash to Japan.
The street has lanes that go in both directions. American
two-way trade with Asia and the Pacific exceeded $360 billion
in 1992, and roughly 2.6 million jobs in the United States
are dependent on it. United States exports more to Singapore
than it does to Spain or Italy, and American firms have about
$66 billion invested in that part of the world.

Lifting the economic embargo, opening diplomatic relations, and backing the cause of economic reform in Vietnam
to strengthen the country by quickening its development would

serve the American need to counter Chinese regional ambitions. The relationship suits the Vietnamese, because big nations that do not threaten their independence, as the United States no longer does, are the kinds of friends the Vietnamese want. The Vietnamese assume, rightly or wrongly, that the more involved American business is in Vietnam, the more China will hesitate to move against them. Tom Vallely, a Harvard Vietnam specialist, who first went to the country as a nineteen-year-old Marine infantryman and is now trying to help the Vietnamese shift to a market economy, quipped "One Mobil oil rig in the South China Sea is worth the whole Seventh Fleet."

The looming threat of China propels the Vietnamese attempt to make peace with the United States. When Deng Xiaoping invaded Vietnam in 1979, after the Vietnamese drove China's Cambodian protégé, the homicidal Khmer Rouge, out of Phnom Penh, Vietnamese troops were able to halt the Chinese rapidly and bloody them badly, because they were in excellent fighting trim. Yet the ultimate checkrein on Chinese behavior that has since vanished was the threat of Soviet retaliation. The Vietnamese also relied on the Soviet Union for their weaponry. With their benefactors now history, Vietnamese armament has become outmoded.

While Vietnam has made peace with China and full trade and diplomatic relations have resumed, the Chinese seem to want more: they seem to want submission. The visit to Vietnam last December of Li Peng, the Chinese premier, went badly. Peng behaved as if he were visiting a tributary. China has so far been the winner in Cambodia, because its cat's-paw, the Khmer Rouge, has succeeded in sabotaging the United Nations peace plan and once again constitutes a menace to the Vietnamese.

1. Which of the following excerpts is not an opinion?

   (A) "[A] checkrein on Chinese behavior that has since vanished was the threat of the Soviet Union."

   (B) "Like it or not, the United States is going to have to play the role of regional balancer...to keep China from unsettling East Asia in the post-Cold War era. There is too much to lose for us to refuse the role."

   (C) "Lifting the economic embargo, opening diplomatic relations, and backing the cause of economic reform in Vietnam to strengthen the country by quickening its development would serve the American need to counter Chinese regional ambitions."

   (D) "One Mobil oil rig in the South China Sea is worth the whole Seventh Fleet."

   (E) "The looming threat of China propels the Vietnamese attempt to make peace with the United States."

2. Which of the following quotations is a primary fact?

   (A) "Guangdong Province's economy...grew at an average annual rate of fifteen percent from 1981 to 1991."

   (B) "American two-way trade with Asia and the Pacific exceeded $360 billion in 1992, and roughly 2.6 million jobs in the United States are dependent on it."

   (C) "When Deng Xiaoping invaded Vietnam in 1979...Vietnamese troops were able to halt the Chinese rapidly and bloody them badly."

   (D) "The Chinese are using their new wealth to make themselves a big military power in the region."

   (E) "[The Chinese] are purchasing long-range Sukhoi-27 fighter-bombers, MIG-31 interceptors, and airborne surveillance-and-control planes from Russia."

3. Which sentence best summarizes the author's argument?

(A) The Chinese may attack Vietnam again.
(B) The United States views Vietnam as a bulwark against Chinese aggression.
(C) Both Vietnam and the United States would benefit from a normalization of relations.
(D) Vietnam fears Chinese domination.
(E) The dissolution of the Soviet Union has fundamentally changed the United States— Vietnam relationship.

4. According to the passages, all of the following contributes to the perceived power vacuum in East Asia EXCEPT

(A) the American withdrawal from the Philippines
(B) the shrinking U.S. military budget
(C) the Vietnamese disarmament along Cambodian borders
(D) the collapse of the Soviet Union
(E) American domestic economic struggles

5. According to the author, which of the following is the primary reason behind Vietnam's attempt to make peace with the United States?

(A) Investment opportunities in U.S. oil companies
(B) The looming threat of China
(C) Li Peng's ill-fated visit
(D) The threat of the Khmer Rouge
(E) China's annual economic growth rate

6. America's financial relationship with the East is

(A) often misconstrued
(B) dependent in both directions
(C) valued at approximately 66 billion dollars
(D) All of the above
(E) None of the above

7. According to the passage, in the face of global demilitarization, China is

(A) seeking most-favored nation trading status
(B) ignoring human rights violations
(C) aggressively pushing into Cambodia
(D) rearming with modern weaponry
(E) pursuing economic growth aggressively

8. The author's main reason why the United States must "play the role of regional balancer" is inherently

(A) economic
(B) moral
(C) political
(D) military
(E) social

9. We can infer from the passage that since 1979 Vietnam's relationship with China has been

(A) improving
(B) degenerating
(C) satisfactory to China
(D) satisfactory to Vietnam
(E) satisfactory to both

10. What, according to the passage, would the United States gain from an open relationship with Vietnam?

(A) A downsizing of the United States military presence
(B) The capability to assert itself financially in eastern Europe
(C) A Vietnamese shift to market economy
(D) A military presence in the Far East
(E) Oil resources

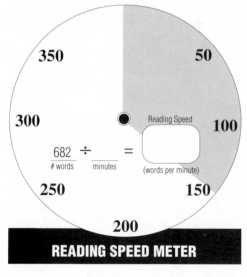

Calculate your reading speed using the following formula. First, mark down how long it took you, in minutes, to read the passage (if it took you 2 minutes, 15 seconds, then it took you 2.25 minutes). Divide the number of words in the passage by that number. This is your reading speed in words per minute. For example, there are 682 words in this passage. If it took you 5.25 minutes to read the entire selection, then divide 682 by 5.25. This would result in a reading speed of 130 w.p.m.

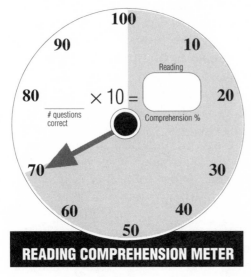

Calculate your comprehension rate using the following formula. Multiply the number of questions you answered correctly by 10. That is your comprehension percentage. You want to keep your percentage above 70 percent for any type of reading. Below that, you start losing important information presented in the passages.

SIGNS, SIGNS, EVERYWHERE SIGNS

Much in the way that highway signs tell you where a road leads, what towns are accessible from each exit, and what other roads are available, headers and quotations pulled out from an article ("kickers," they are called) tell you what to expect from different parts of an article. Remember pre-reading? Scan the article quickly for headers and kickers which tell you about the way the facts are broken up. Use them to guide your reading through any article. Do you need certain information about the history of a neighborhood? Do you need the facts in a murder case? Are you just looking for the scores in a sporting event? The headers and kickers will tell you where to look.

For example, in a *Business Week* cover story article on President Bill Clinton's second year, the following headers subdivided the article into parts

- Policy Grafts
- Shooting Sprees
- Health Security
- Pension Security
- Education and Training
- Competitiveness Policy
- Personal Safety
- "No Testosterone"

Each of these can point you to a section of the article which would provide details and opinions on that facet of Clinton's second year. By using the headers, you can quickly jump to the portion of the article you need to read without having to read all the other stuff. Each section contains one discrete subject (except for the "No Testosterone" heading which is, by definition, indiscreet).

This brings us to an important point. Do you want to read everything in every article in every paper and every magazine? Never. You want to choose the articles which are important to you, so scan the headlines, headers, photographs, and quotes that go with each article. If it is even tangentially related to a topic that is important to you, pre-read the whole thing. If it isn't, move on to the next article. In this way, you've made sure you've covered all your bases. What if you don't know? Read it anyway. It's better to err on the side of being overinformed than underinformed. That's not to suggest that you should read every part of every article: overinformed and out of time is no improvement at all. You've got to read smart— use your judgment on what's important in any given article.

READ LESS, KNOW MORE — RIDICULOUS

Even when you want to read an article, do you want to read every word and phrase? Again, absolutely not. If you do that, why not just handwrite them out on a sheet of paper twice, and then translate them into Rumanian? In other words, why waste time? Use the techniques of fixation and clustering to increase your speed. But when you read an article or opinionated piece, only read as far into any paragraph until you get the main idea of that paragraph. Do not read any further. This sounds strange, but it really works. For a dramatic example, let's look at the first sentence—and only the first sentence— of each paragraph of a newspaper article on the President's proposed budget:

> *Senate Minority Leader Bob Dole said yesterday that he anticipated there would be some Republican support for the budget President Bill Clinton unveiled today.*

> *Clinton will need all the support he can get for this budget.*

Rep. Kwesi Mfume (D-Md.) said yesterday he "was not satisfied."

Clinton will propose cutting mass transit operating subsidies, low-income heating assistance, and new construction money for low-income public housing.

White House budget director Leon Panetta defended the budget.

Panetta said the Federal Government will continue to fund mass transit capital spending.

Panetta said the budget will include healthy increases for technology, training, and education.

Dole, meanwhile, noted the President's budget was in some ways incomplete.

Purists and news junkies are probably tearing their hair after reading the above "news," but face it, our condensed version is about as informative as most TV news programs, and reading it took far less time than either watching TV news or reading the entire article would have taken. Sure, you're poorly read and ill-informed, but think of the time you've saved! Now you have the time to get in loud blustering arguments about issues of unimaginable complexity, like the budget, based on just a few sentences you lifted out of context from your local paper.

EXERCISE #13

Here's an exercise that you'll have to grade yourself on. Grab that newspaper you've had sitting by you since you started this chapter, and find a dull article about something important. The business section is a good place to start, and any article about local school boards or zoning will probably work. Now read only the first sentence of each paragraph (if you can't help peeking, use an index card to block the rest of the paragraph, but only this once). Using your newfound powers of retention, write down every important fact you can remember: names, dates, amounts, and, of course, the subject of the article. Now go back and read the whole article, and make a similar list. If you compare the two, you'll find that your lists are similar in length, meaning that you absorbed about the same amount of information from each reading. Your second list may be a little longer, but look at the items which appear only on the second list. Are they primary or secondary facts? Do they really add to your basic understanding of the topic? No, because if they did, they'd have their own paragraph with their own intro sentence.

Repeat this exercise with a couple of different articles. Try a sports article. Try a fashion article. Try topics you wouldn't normally read about. Not only will you be learning about reading more efficiently, you'll also become a more well-rounded human being.

You'll find that the first sentence technique allows you to stay informed while leaving you enough time to lead a real life (assuming you had one to begin with) and to get the newsprint off your fingers (hot water and a little lemon juice).

MAPPING THE ARGUMENT

Argument mapping means laying out all the points an author makes in the order she makes them. This process exposes the structure of the argument, and therefore, its weaknesses. You'd want your surgeon to know anatomy, wouldn't you? Maybe a little chemistry? Knowledge of structure tells you the author's position, point of view, the facts of the argument, and the flaws. Without seeing the structure, some of these flaws can slip on by you, and on your final that could very well mean disaster.

SEE THE STRUCTURE

You'll notice that when you look at the beginning of each paragraph, the first sentences form an outline of the story. That's intentional. Given their strict space requirements, reporters have to get their information across in as direct a manner as possible. They have to connect logically one point to the next. This isn't always easy. It's difficult for a reporter to piece everything together and still get across the impact of the event. Many good writers are bad reporters, because they can't conform to this way of writing. Even many good reporters find this artificial restriction a problem.

What's a problem for the reporter is good for us, though, because it provides us with a way to examine the author's argument. Every paragraph is a building block in the author's argument. Identify the main point of each paragraph, which most often is in the first sentence. Write that idea in the margin next to the paragraph. When you move to the next paragraph, identify its main idea. See how that relates to the main idea of the previous paragraph. Write that in the margin. Stringing together all your marginal comments should provide a map of the author's argument. For example, "illustrates author's point about small yapping dogs," "provides counterexample from dog lovers," "possible solution to the plague of small yapping dogs," and so on are possible margin-notes from an article on "Schnauzer Love."

At first, you can expect your summaries to be too long. Don't panic. One hint is that your summaries shouldn't be longer than the paragraph you're summarizing. With more practice, you'll get more concise. The best way to get really good at margin-noting and argument mapping is to do it. A lot. A real lot. As much as you can, really. Not only will this help you get more out of your journalistic reading, it gets your brain to condense information. This skill translates into faster reading rates and higher retention rates for all types of reading.

EXERCISE #14

Practice mapping and summarizing on the following passage. Pay close attention to primary facts (as opposed to secondary facts). Use the margins for noting, and answer the questions after the passage using your marginal notes—try not to return to the passage once noted.

The 1996 Conventions/Defying History

Not since the Democrats held their riotous meeting there in 1968 has Chicago offered its hospitality to a big-party convention. That convention was supposed to draw the world's attention to the proud city of Mayor Richard M. Daley, then the Democratic party's kingmaker. It turned into a well-televised brawl between the police and anti-Vietnam-war protesters, with fights along South Michigan Avenue in front of the convention headquarters. Now the Vietnam war is history, the Black Power movement has subsided, and Chicago's boosters think the city is overdue for a return to the political limelight.

Chicago's current Democratic mayor, Richard J. Daley, son of the late Richard M., is making bids for both the conventions at which the big parties will name their presidential candidates in 1996. He and Illinois' Republican governor, Jim Edgar, have set aside their quarrels to make a bipartisan pitch for the two events. The last city to win both nominating conventions was Miami, in 1972. The Chicago meetings would be held in the city's new United Center, a 21,500-seat, $175m arena due to open this August. It expects to do well with basketball and ice hockey during the winter, but would welcome the late-summer boost the parties' delegates would bring in 1996.

If the city got both conventions, it could pull in more than $200m from spending by delegates. New York recouped from convention-related tax revenues the $28m it is reckoned to have spent on organising the Democrats' 1992 meeting, and then earned $104m from convention visitors. Houston estimates it got $100m in direct spending from the Republican convention that year.

Chicago thinks it should get the Democrats in 1996, anyway. David Wilhelm, chairman of the Democratic party's national committee (DNC), which has the final say on the convention site, has lived in Chicago for years and is a former campaign adviser to Mayor Daley. The mayor's lawyer-brother, William Daley, was President Clinton's back-room ally in the fight to get the North American Free Trade Agreement through Congress. Another Chicago lawyer, John Schmidt, helped Mr. Clinton bring the GATT deal to its successful conclusion. He has yet to call in his political chips.

The DNC, which is also considering Los Angeles, San Antonio, Kansas City, and New Orleans, is expected to announce its choice by June. The Republicans' schedule is more sedate: they may not choose their site until the summer of 1995. The Republicans, however, have fixed the time of their convention: August 1996. The Democrats have yet to name their day. Since they hold the presidency, and the ruling party generally likes to meet after its rival, that could push 1996's political season into the last steamy days of summer.

Some Republicans are not keen on sharing a convention city with their rivals, saying that each party needs its own style and therefore its own site. But Chicago has a historical tilt toward the Republicans (it has been the site of 14 Republican conventions, as opposed to ten Democratic ones). And Governor Edgar's people point out that Illinois will be a key state in the 1996 presidential race, so holding the party's convention there might be a shrewd idea. They add that television and the press, which present the conventions to the nation, prefer to have both in the same city because it costs them less.

Answer the following questions based only on your marginal notes.

1. Is the mayor of Chicago a Democrat or a Republican?

2. Which party is most likely to hold *their* convention first in 1996?

3. Give two reasons the Democrats might hold their convention in Chicago?

4. Give two reasons the Republicans might hold their convention in Chicago?

5. What is the current relationship between the mayor of Chicago and the governor of Illinois?

6. Why would Chicago want to host either convention?

7. What factors work against Chicago holding either convention?

Journalistic reading is the type of reading you should try to do every day of your life. You'll find that after a time, it becomes addictive. It's like a huge soap opera, except that people in real life (especially politicians) do things that aren't allowed on daytime TV. If you like guns, crime, car chases, violence, sex, and generally low behavior, just grab today's paper. You won't be disappointed.

CHAPTER 7

The Pleasure Principle

"To have great poets, there must be great audiences, too."

—Walt Whitman

The way we first learn to read is through stories, and the way we first learn about people, about anyone outside ourselves and our friends and our family, is through fiction. If you're reading books for pleasure, for school, to impress the boss—it doesn't matter. You're trying to learn something and be entertained at the same time. In a Sherlock Holmes novel, you're trying to figure out "whodunit," and how. In an Isaac Asimov novel, you're trying to imagine his created universe, and how it resembles your own. Sometimes the struggle is less visible. Sometimes all the author offers you is a little slice of life—a view into someone else's world that may be as clouded as your own.

The reason we're talking about what fiction does is that the first question you have to ask yourself about a work of fiction is what do I need it for? It will be rare that you will read a textbook only for fun. A journalistic piece will inform you and entertain you, but it is not a commitment like a novel or a collection of short stories. Reading fiction for pleasure and reading it for school are separate disciplines. I'll go into why, and how you should read each, in a second, but be very, very aware of why you are reading each book. A book gets discussed in a class in a very different way than at a cocktail party. If you and a co-worker are grabbing handfuls of cocktail weenies at a company gathering, and you start spouting off about the "post-modernist anagrammatical games in Lolita, and the ubiquitous self-referencing aspect visible once one knots symbolism and linguistic play," either your co-worker will leave, bored to tears, or your co-worker will slug you (and well she should) for your turning what used to be a fun book to read into a dull literary exercise. When you read books for pleasure, lighten up. It's good to notice the scholarly stuff—but that isn't the point when reading for pleasure.

HAVE A PLAN

A little general strategy never hurts. Have a plan before you pick up a book. Don't intend to sit down and read the whole thing in one sitting. If you love the book, and your reading is going fine, then go beyond what you've planned. But when you pick up a book, you should read it every day until you are done, even if you can only devote fifteen minutes a day to it. Set a goal of ten days for every book. If you can't reach that goal, finish as fast as you can. Why? The more you set stuff aside, the less you remember about earlier stuff. The book loses all its momentum. The characters, which once seemed real, now seem flat, like soda with the cap left off. Think of it as a commitment (if commitment is a problem for you, buy yourself a copy of *Relationship Smart*). If a book is fifteen chapters, break it up into three-chapter segments. Tell yourself you're going to read a segment today, two tomorrow, and one segment each day until you finish it. If you fall behind, you stand a much greater chance of not finishing the book or losing track of the events, characters and language. Plan your reading before you pick up the book—then you can tell how you're doing.

READING FICTION FOR SCHOOL

Oh boy, another assignment. You figure, hey, it's a fiction book. No problem. You struggle through it, slowly, searching word by word, and it's a chore. More than a chore. It's the worst thing in the world. But if you sat down by the pool, and had nothing else to read, this book would fly by. What is this event called "assigned reading" that drives people up a tree? A student of ours says that if eating Nestle's Crunch bars were required, everyone would all of a sudden hate them. While we disagree with that specific example, the idea that an assignment must be a back breaking chore is worth looking at.

How do you keep your head in the book? Most assigned fiction is going to be given to you in paperback. Look at the back. There should be a blurb about the book or a blurb about the author. Read that stuff. If it's not there, look at the first few pages. The more you know about an author, the more interested you become in their work. Sometimes their lives are even more fascinating than their books (don't let a teacher hear you say that, though). But the best information helps make the author's work more lively for you. Virginia Woolf, a famous British author (*To the Lighthouse, A Room of One's Own, Orlando,* etc.), suffered from bouts out depression so deep it would take her months to recover. She heard voices, had delirious visions, and in spite of all this, she produced some of the most complicated, inventive work in the English language. Raymond Carver, a twentieth-century short-story writer (*Cathedral, Where I'm Calling From,* etc.) was an alcoholic and a chain smoker for most of his life. Ernest Hemingway was dressed by his mother as a girl up to the age of six. Most writers, come to think of it, are all slightly screwed up in some way. All of these things make their fiction more real, more lively, because they write about these things. If you make an effort to learn about an author, it pays you back come exam time, and besides, there's nothing more interesting than other people's vices.

How Does It Start?

Next, look at the title and any quotes the author has chosen to introduce their book—keeping in mind you are doing all this before you hit page one of the book. For example, Ernest Hemingway wrote a book called *The Sun Also Rises*. He introduces it with two quotations. First, one from Gertrude Stein, a writer who was seen as an oracle for the writers of the twenties in Paris. "You are a lost generation," she says. You want to keep that in mind when you read this book. The people who are involved in the book are all coming right after World War I, and they have lost their belief in anything. The second quotation is one from a book of the Bible, from Ecclesiastes, which explains the title of the book (if you are interested, look it up yourself—this isn't *Literature Smart*). The point is use all the clues provided for you. These are things to keep in your mind as you read the book—often they'll explain the weird things going on. The characters in *The Sun Also Rises* are all wounded in some way, all drunkards and all behave very badly. If you know that he's writing about a generation decimated by WWI, you might also sympathize a little more.

Big Picture, Small Picture

How is reading for school different than reading any other way? At first glance, it seems to be the exact same thing. Your eyes take in the information—your brain decodes it. But when you have to read for school, you have to remember what you've read (the details) and you have to see larger things the author is doing (symbols, plot, metaphor, etc). Now, in a textbook, you would mark significant ideas in the margin. Would you do the same thing in a work of fiction? You bet. But you have to mark the things that are important to fiction, the symbols, plot, metaphor, etc.

"And what's the story behind the story?"

Drawing by Levin, © 1993 The New Yorker Magazine, Inc.

In your own mind, you have to get the action clear. That's the primary thing. If you don't know what's going on, you're going to have trouble seeing larger, hidden themes. Authors don't like to make everything as simple as they could (although the best authors do that and more). You have to keep track of what's going on. And where better than the margin of the book itself? At the end of each chapter summarize the events of the chapter. If there are section breaks, you can do it there. We're just talking plot here. By plot, we mean what happens. That's it. For now, nothing else.

So you know what's going on. So what? Your teachers will expect you to know more. Like what images, what themes come back, what hidden stuff there is underneath what happens. You can do something called theme-marking. **Theme-marking** means keeping track of all instances of a single image or single character. Look for things which keep appearing. You don't have to know what it means. Just mark where it occurs. Let's look at an example: If a dove keeps appearing, make a mark where it appears. Then, after you're done reading the book, you can start to make connections about where that bird appears. It doesn't have to be the exact same thing—it can be a type of thing, like death images, or birth images, or a color. Maybe that bird appears just before the same type of scene happens. Maybe just after. But theme-marking makes it clear that something's going on. And as you read your book and you start to mark it up, the connection between those themes will become clearer.

EXERCISE #15

Read the next passage, summarizing at the end, and marking on the side of the text the types of images that keep coming back. Read quickly, keeping in mind the kind of images that appear. Try to see what kind of tone is set by the images. Is the meeting this guy is going to a good meeting or a bad one? Is he scared? Is he tough? Try to see what the images tell you.

> The car was a dark blue seven-passenger sedan, a Packard of the latest model, custom-built. It was the kind of car you wear your rope pearls in. It was parked by a fire-hydrant and a dark foreign-looking chauffeur with a face of carved wood was behind the wheel. The interior was upholstered in quilted grey chenille. The Indian put me in the back. Sitting there alone I felt like a high-class corpse, laid out by an undertaker with a lot of good taste.
>
> The Indian got in beside the chauffeur and the car turned in the middle of the block and a cop across the street said: 'Hey,' weakly, as if he didn't mean it, and then bent down quickly to tie his shoe.
>
> We went west, dropped over to Sunset and slid fast and noiseless along that. The Indian sat motionless beside the chauffeur. An occasional whiff of his personality drifted back to me. The driver looked as if he was half asleep but he passed the fast boys in the convertible sedans as though they were being towed. They turned on all the green lights for him. Some drivers are like that. He never missed one.
>
> We curved through the bright mile or two of the Strip, past the antique shops with famous screen names on them, past the windows full of point lace and ancient pewter, past the gleaming new night clubs with famous chefs and equally famous gambling rooms, run by polished graduates of the

Purple Gang, past the Georgian-Colonial vogue, now old hat, past the handsome modernistic buildings in which the Hollywood flesh-peddlers never stop talking money, past a drive-in lunch which somehow didn't belong, even though the girls wore white silk blouses and drum majorettes' shakos and nothing below the hips but glazed kid Hessian boots. Past all this and down a wide smooth curve to the bridle path of Beverly Hills and lights to the south. All colours of the spectrum and crystal clear in an evening without fog, past the shadowed mansions up on the hills to the north, past Beverly Hills altogether and up into the twisting foothill boulevard and the sudden cool dusk and the drift of wind from the sea.

It had been a warm afternoon, but the heat was gone. We whipped past a distant cluster of lighted buildings and an endless series of lighted mansions, not too close to the road. We dipped down to skirt a huge green polo field with another equally huge practice field beside it, soared again to the top of a hill and swing mountainward up a steel hill road of clean concrete that passed orange groves, some rich man's pet because this is not orange country, and then little by little the lighted windows of the millionaires' homes were gone and the road narrowed and this was Stillwood Heights.

The smell of sage drifted up from a canyon and made me think of a dead man and a moonless sky. Straggly stucco houses were moulded flat to the side of the hill, like bas-reliefs. Then there were no more houses, just the still dark foothills with an early star or two above them, and the concrete ribbon of road and a sheer drop on one side into a tangle of scrub oak and manzanita where sometimes you can hear the call of the quails if you stop and keep still and wait. On the other side of the road was a raw clay bank at the edge of which a few unbeatable wild flowers hung on like naughty children that won't go to bed.

Then the road twisted into a hairpin turn and the big tyres scratched over loose stones, and the car tore less soundlessly up a long driveway lined with the wild geraniums. At the top of this, faintly lighted, lonely as a lighthouse stood an eyrie, an eagle's nest, an angular building of stucco and glass brick, raw and modernistic and yet not ugly and altogether a swell place for a psychic consultant to hang out his shingle. Nobody would be able to hear any screams.

PIECE TOGETHER THE PUZZLE

A summary of the passage could read:

> *I got in a car with a chauffeur and an Indian, and drove*
> *through L.A. to a deserted spot in the hills.*

If this were all there were to it, Chandler could have saved an awful lot of time and paper by just summarizing. Unlike journalism, the writing itself contains the point. Images and emotions are evoked while the plot develops—two for the price of one. There has to be a reason for these images. Chandler is no dummy. But it's not his job to explain them; it's your job to figure out why he chose what he did. This process doesn't have to be a chore. View it as a puzzle, as a mystery you have to solve. All the pieces are in front of you, and the author's even given you hints how to assemble them.

Look back at the story. Repeated images are of light and color. The street he travels on is called "sunset" and he travels from "light," to his destination which is "moonless." His journey from light to dark should give you the creeps. Something ominous is happening here—circling all the words about light and color will show you the progression.

Some other images should leap out at you from the passage. He lies in the backseat "like a corpse." He is reminded of a "dead man." There is "raw" clay and the car "twisted" and "tore." His final observation is that "[n]obody would be able to hear any screams." He feels like he's becoming part of death, that somehow, this meeting scares him to death. Look for the meaning in images, but start with identifying the images themselves. You'll find these images stay in your mind long after finishing the book.

THE MIND'S EYE

Why do we remember so much from fiction? I mean, we can read a two-hundred page textbook and only remember bolded headings and a few chapter titles, while we can read a two-hundred page novel and remember nearly every scene in the book. What is unique to fiction?

It's not really about fiction—it's about the way humans are built. We all come with active imaginations. It's not just the ability to visualize things not present—research shows that most animals have that capability. First, it is the ability to piece together a whole out of incomplete information. For example, if you were on vacation in the Adirondack mountains, and returned to your cabin to find large paw tracks covering the floor, claw marks on the walls, your bed torn to ribbons, and all your honey gone, you could reasonably imagine the bear that went through your stuff. Second, it is the ability to place yourself sensually (hearing, seeing, smelling) and emotionally in other places and other peoples' minds. For example, to imagine the joy felt at defeating a dragon and saving the kingdom, or the frustration of being the dragon, defeated by a tiny mortal. Fiction releases those abilities, encourages us to use them. And so we remember. Because it makes us use a part of ourselves that we normally try to control. Face it—day-to-day existence is dull. We use our imaginations to escape that boredom, but we have to use it in small doses. If you're too caught up in your imagination while driving your car, the repair bills will be enormous. Fiction invites you to imagine all day long and get something out of it.

As a reader, you must exploit the power to imagine. When dialogue is spoken, you have to make an effort to hear it. When a landscape is described, you have to make an effort to see it. The best authors make it easy for you. Look at a John Steinbeck landscape, or listen to a Toni Morrison character speak. Once you make the leap from fiction being merely words on a page to concrete images and experiences, your retention will jump a level.

Think of a movie. Why the heck can we remember even more from a movie (specific lines, images) than we can from a book (except for the *Cannonball Run* movies, of course)? Because first, most of the way we deal with the world is visual. A movie is primarily a visual experience. Second, a movie has sound reinforcing the visual, providing another reason to remember. A movie plays to the way our mind works. If you can make a book do the same, you'll find your enjoyment of the book increases too. Try and imagine it as a movie—examine the difference between Burt's real hair and his toupee, see the lasagna stain on Dom DeLuise's ambulance driver's outfit. Get specific, visual images which bring the story to life.

This is a good moment to bring back one important idea. Remember how we said you had to be involved in your reading? Well, fiction is the real test. If you get involved, and start using your own abilities when you read fiction, you'll rarely find yourself wondering where you are and what you are reading. Keep focused on the book—a high concentration level here reaps even higher rewards.

Exercise #16

Look for the visual clues in the next passage which allow you to picture it. Try and get a feel for how the author describes the situation. Keep in mind the physical action, and the underlying important stuff should come through.

At noon of Sunday, the 6th of July, the fiesta exploded. There is no other way to describe it. People had been coming in all day from the country, but they were assimilated in the town and you did not notice them. The square was as quiet in the hot sun as on any other day. The peasants were in the outlying wine-shops. There they were drinking, getting ready for the fiesta. They had come in so recently from the plains and the hills that it was necessary that they make their shifting in values gradually. They could not start in paying cafe prices. They got their money's worth in the wine-shops. Money still had a definite value in hours worked and bushels of grain sold. Late in the fiesta it would not matter what they paid, nor where they bought.

Now on the day of the starting of the fiesta of San Fermin they had been in the wine-shops of the narrow streets of the town since early morning. Going down the streets in the morning on the way to mass in the cathedral, I heard them singing through the open doors of the shops. They were warming up. There were many people at the eleven o'clock mass. San Fermin is also a religious festival.

I walked down the hill from the cathedral and up the street to the cafe on the square. It was a little before noon. Robert Cohn and Bill were sitting at one of the tables. The marble-topped tables and the white wicker chairs were gone. They were replaced by cast-iron tables and severe folding chairs. The cafe was like a battleship stripped for action. Today the waiters did not leave you alone all morning to read without asking if you wanted to order something. A waiter came up as soon as I sat down.

"What are you drinking?" I asked Bill and Robert.

"Sherry," Cohn said.

"Jerez," I said to the waiter.

Before the waiter brought the sherry the rocket that announced the fiesta went up in the square. It burst and there was a gray ball of smoke high up above the Theatre Gayarre, across on the other side of the plaza. The ball of smoke hung in the sky like a shrapnel burst, and as I watched, another rocket came up to it, trickling smoke in the bright sunlight. I saw the bright flash as it burst and another little cloud of smoke appeared. By the time the second rocket had burst there were so many people in the arcade, that had been empty a minute before, that the waiter, holding the bottle high up over his head, could hardly get through the crowd to our table. People were coming into the square from all sides, and down the street we heard the pipes and the fifes and the shrill and the drums pounding, and behind them came the men and boys dancing. When the fifers stopped they all crouched down in the street, and when the reed-pipes and the fifes shrilled, and the flat, dry, hollow drums tapped it out again, they all went up in the air dancing. In the crowd you saw only the heads and shoulders of the dancers going up and down.

Did you begin to actually see the crowd in your mind? Did you get the feel for the dancers, and the music and the rockets? Those are the things that can stay with you long after your class is over. More than one person has taken a trip to Pamplona, Spain, to see the festival Hemingway described above.

ANOTHER WAY IN

Sometimes, it's not the action that makes writing interesting. When a story seems to have not much happening, you're going to need to look elsewhere to find the involving part of the book. In cases like these, you're going to need to look at the writing itself. What kind of language does the author use? Are the words ten-syllable monsters you have to look up all the time? Or does it sound like Uncle Otto, sipping his soda while he tells you about driving his pickup off the Talahache bridge? The way the writing sounds is the author's tone, and tone can give you an understanding of the author's attitude and relationship to his characters and their situation.

EXERCISE #17

Read the following passage from Raymond Carver, looking at the tone of the piece. What kind of voice is this? Be aware of how everything sounds.

He was here at Frank Martin's to dry out and to figure how to get his life back on track. But he wasn't here against his will, any more than I was. We weren't locked up. We could leave any time we wanted. But a minimum stay of a week was recommended, and two weeks or a month was, as they put it, "strongly advised."

As I said, this is my second time at Frank Martin's. When I was trying to sign a check to pay in advance for a week's stay, Frank Martin said, "The holidays are always bad. Maybe you should think of sticking around a little longer this time? Think in terms of a couple of weeks. Can you do a couple of weeks? Think about it, anyway. You don't have to decide anything right now," he said. He held his thumb on the check and I signed my name. Then I walked my girlfriend to the front door and said goodbye. "Goodbye," she said, and she lurched into the doorjamb and then onto the porch. It's late afternoon. It's raining. I go from the door to the window. I move the curtain and watch her drive away. She's in my car. She's drunk. But I'm drunk, too, and there's nothing I can do. I make it to a big chair that's close to the radiator, and I sit down. Some guys look up from their TV. Then they shift back to what they were watching. I just sit there. Now and then I look up at something that's happening on the screen.

Later that afternoon the front door banged open and J.P. was brought in between these two big guys—his father-in-law and brother-in-law, I find out afterward. They steered J.P. across the room. The old guy signed him in and gave Frank Martin a check. Then these two guys helped J.P. upstairs. I guess they put him to bed. Pretty soon the old guy and the other guy came downstairs and headed for the front door. They couldn't seem to get out of this place fast enough. It was like they couldn't wait to wash their hands of all this. I didn't blame them. Hell, no. I don't know how I'd act if I was in their shoes.

A day and a half later J.P. and I meet up on the front porch. We shake hands and comment on the weather. J.P. has a case of the shakes. We sit down and prop our feet up on the railing. We lean back in our chairs like we're just out there taking our ease, like we might be getting ready to talk about our bird dogs. That's when J.P. gets going with his story.

These are the type of guys for whom "a couple of weeks" is an unusually long time. They speak in short sentences. They can't even trust long words. These are people living word to word. Do

you think these guys will succeed? Is it fact that leads you to this
conclusion, or is it the overall tone and attitude of the piece? Is
this guy likable? Does he seem like the type to lie? Does this matter?
These guys, the narrator and J.P., are struggling against alcoholism
at Frank Martin's, a drying-out place. How people speak and how
the author describes things can provide another way for you to get
interested in the book and in the characters.

You might remember that I said a few chapters back that it's
not worth looking up every word you don't know. Well, that's dou-
bly—no *triply*—true in fiction. Often authors will use a foreign or
specific word to say exactly what they mean. They know when they're
doing this and will try to make it clear in context why they are
using it and just what they mean by it. If they're not using a word
in this way, don't worry about it, because it's probably not that
important. If they are, don't let that word you don't know slow you
down. Put a mark next to it, and plow through to the end of the
chapter. If you still haven't figured out the word, then (and only
then) look it up. Usually, looking stuff up is counterproductive because
it's distracting and time-consuming.

READING RACETRACK #9

Read the following passage and answer the questions after it to find
your speed and comprehension levels. Time yourself on a watch with
a second hand. Time only the reading portion of the exercise, not
the question portion. Then calculate your reading speed and comprehension level, using the formulas at the end of the questions.

> The village of Holcomb stands on the high wheat plains of
> western Kansas, a lonesome area that other Kansans call "out
> there." Some seventy miles east of the Colorado border, the
> countryside, with its hard blue skies and desert-clear air, has
> an atmosphere that is rather more Far Western than Middle
> West. The local accent is barbed with a prairie twang, a
> ranch-hand nasalness, and the men, many of them, wear
> narrow frontier trousers, Stetsons, and high-heeled boots with
> pointed toes. The land is flat, and the views are awesomely
> extensive; horses, herds of cattle, a white cluster of grain
> elevators rising as gracefully as Greek temples are visible
> long before a traveler reaches them.
>
> Holcomb, too, can be seen from great distances. Not
> that there is much to see—simply an aimless congregation

of buildings divided in the center by the main-line tracks of the Santa Fe Railroad, a haphazard hamlet bounded on the south by a brown stretch of the Arkansas (pronounced "Ar-kan-sas") River, on the north by a highway, Route 50, and on the east and west by prairie lands and wheat fields. After rain, or when snowfalls thaw, the streets, unnamed, unshaded, unpaved, turn from the thickets dust into the direst mud. At one end of the town stands a stark old stucco structure, the roof of which supports an electric sign— DANCE—but the dancing has ceased and the advertisement has been dark for several years. Nearby is another building with an irrelevant sign, this one in flaking gold on a dirty window—HOLCOMB BANK. The bank closed in 1933, and its former counting rooms have been converted into apartments. It is one of the town's two "apartment houses," the second being a ramshackle mansion known, because a good part of the local school's faculty lives there, as the Teacherage. But the majority of Holcomb's homes are one-story frame affairs, with front porches.

Down by the depot, the postmistress, a gaunt woman who wears a rawhide jacket and denims and cowboy boots, presides over a falling-apart post office. The depot itself, with its peeling sulphur-colored paint, is equally melancholy; the Chief, the Super Chief, the El Capitan go by every day, but these celebrated expresses never pause there. No passenger trains do—only an occasional freight. Up on the highway, there are two filling stations, one of which doubles as a meagerly supplied grocery store, while the other does extra duty as a cafe—Hartman's Cafe, where Mrs. Hartman, the proprietress, dispenses sandwiches, coffee, soft drinks, and 3.2 beer. (Holcomb, like all the rest of Kansas, is "dry.")

And that, really, is all. Unless you include, as one must, the Holcomb School, a good-looking establishment, which reveals a circumstance that the appearance of the community otherwise camouflages: that the parent who sent their children to this modern and ably staffed "consolidated" school—the grades go from kindergarten through senior high, and a fleet of buses transport the students, of which there are usually around three hundred and sixty, from as far as sixteen miles away—are, in general, a prosperous people. Farm ranchers, most of them, they are outdoor folk of very varied stock— German, Irish, Norwegian, Mexican, Japanese. They raise cattle and sheep, grow wheat, milo grass seed, and sugar beets. Farming is always a chancey business, but in western Kansas its practitioners consider themselves "born gamblers," for they must contend with an extremely shallow precipitation (the annual average is eighteen inches) and anguishing irrigation problems. However, the last seven years have been years of droughtless beneficence. The farm ranchers in Finney County, of which Holcomb is a part, have done well; money has been made not from farming alone but also from the exploitation of plentiful natural-gas resources, and its acquisition is reflected in the new school, the comfortable interiors of the farmhouses, the steep and swollen grain elevators.

Until one morning in mid-November of 1959, few Americans—in fact, few Kansans—had ever heard of Holcomb. Like the waters of the river, like the motorists on the highway, and like the yellow trains streaking down the Santa Fe track, drama, in the shape of exceptional happenings, had never stopped there. The inhabitants of the village, numbering two hundred and seventy, were satisfied that this should be so, quite content to exist inside ordinary life—to work, to hunt, to watch television, to attend school socials, choir practice, meetings of the 4-H Club. But then, in the earliest hours of that morning in November, a certain Sunday morning, certain foreign sounds impinged on the normal nightly Holcomb noises—on the keening hysteria of coyotes, the dry scrape of scuttling tumbleweed, the racing, receding wail of locomotive whistles. At the time not a soul in sleeping Holcomb heard them—four shotgun blasts that, all told, ended six human lives. But afterward the townspeople, theretofore sufficiently unfearful of each other to seldom trouble to lock their doors, found fantasy re-creating them over and again— those somber explosions that stimulated fires of mistrust in the glare of which many old neighbors viewed each other strangely, and as strangers.

1. According to the passage, the word "hamlet" could best be defined as:

    (A) an urban center
    (B) a Prince of Denmark
    (C) a train station
    (D) a small town
    (E) a river-bounded island

2. The tone of the passage can best be described as primarily

    (A) journalistic
    (B) explosive
    (C) technical
    (D) tragic
    (E) personal

3. Farming in Holcomb is viewed as

    (A) popular
    (B) easy
    (C) dangerous
    (D) risky
    (E) unpleasant

4. How many lives were ended by the "shotgun blasts?"

    (A) 3
    (B) 3.2
    (C) 4
    (D) 4-H
    (E) 6

5. The best description of Holcomb before the shotgun blasts would be

    (A) homogeneous and peaceful
    (B) volatile and isolationist
    (C) frightened and unfriendly
    (D) placid and picturesque
    (E) impoverished and picaresque

6. The best description of Holcomb after the shotgun blasts would be

    (A) fearful and unfriendly
    (B) violent and aggressive
    (C) armed and dangerous
    (D) somber and dissatisfied
    (E) hysterical and panicked

7. The village of Holcomb has inhabitants numbering

    (A) between 50 and 100
    (B) between 100 and 200
    (C) between 200 and 300
    (D) between 300 and 350
    (E) between 350 and 400

8. The violence of the shotgun blasts seemed, to the author, to be

    (A) an expected occurrence, predictable in this violent town
    (B) a rare occurrence in an otherwise regularly violent town
    (C) a shocking occurrence, forever changing this otherwise peaceful town
    (D) a welcome occurrence, breaking the monotony of the otherwise boring town
    (E) a painful occurrence, embraced and forgiven by this otherwise picturesque town

9. A train which runs through the town is called the

    (A) Express Chief
    (B) Rapid Chief
    (C) Super Train
    (D) Rapid Train
    (E) Super Chief

10. It can be inferred from the passage that the people killed by the shotgun blasts were

    (A) strangers visiting the town
    (B) relatives of a member of the town
    (C) criminals who lived near the town
    (D) residents of the town
    (E) the founders of Holcomb, Kansas

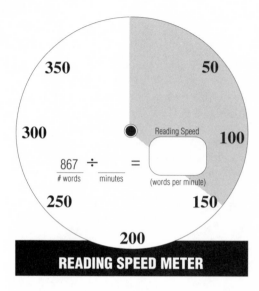

READING SPEED METER

Reading Speed

$$\frac{867}{\text{\# words}} \div \frac{}{\text{minutes}} = \frac{}{\text{(words per minute)}}$$

Calculate your reading speed using the following formula. First, mark down how long it took you, in minutes, to read the passage (if it took you 2 minutes, 15 seconds, then it took you 2.25 minutes). Divide the number of words in the passage by that number. This is your reading speed in words per minute. For example, there are 867 words in this passage. If it took you 5 minutes to read the entire selection, then divide 867 by 5. This would result in a reading speed of 173 w.p.m.

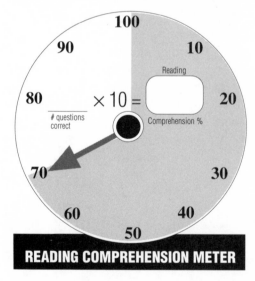

READING COMPREHENSION METER

Reading

$$\frac{}{\substack{\text{\# questions} \\ \text{correct}}} \times 10 = \frac{}{\text{Comprehension \%}}$$

Calculate your comprehension rate using the following formula. Multiply the number of questions you answered correctly by 10. That is your comprehension percentage. You want to keep your percentage above 70 percent for any type of reading. Below that, you start losing important information presented in the passages.

Fiction on Your Own

Now that you don't have to theme-mark, and you don't have to keep track of every single fact, you are somewhat liberated. Doesn't it feel good? It's like the difference between playing an organized game of basketball and just shooting some baskets. Enjoy the process—you don't need to remember everything, and no one is going to yell at you if you don't do everything perfectly.

Don't use this as an excuse to read without a plan, or to keep the television on in the background. If you do that, you're just going to read the same way as before, too slowly and without enough involvement. Use this chance to throw yourself only into the parts that really interest you. Pay attention to the things you like. If you are going to read things passively, and pay no attention at all, you might as well take up squash—at least you'll get in shape while doing something pointless.

How do you know that you're going to want to put some effort into a book? Well, read the first chapter. Many bookstores are allowing readers to sit in the aisle, grab a copy, and check it out. Take advantage of their good nature.

The author uses the first chapter to set up the plot, the characters, and the ideas that should be followed throughout the novel. If the first chapter doesn't grab you, then it is unlikely the rest of the novel will. Some books do take a while to get going—but usually they don't have terrible first chapters; only mildly unpleasant ones. Many novels don't live up to the promise of their first chapters, but you can certainly eliminate the novels which you immediately hate, don't understand or are in a language you don't know.

Divide and Conquer

Most modern popular fiction divides itself into sections within chapters. Often, each section will take care of some requirement of the author, whether it's plot development, character development or description. You can quickly tell by reading the first few sentences of a section what the focus of the section is going to be. If only one of these three interests you, you can skip the other two types of sections. Of course, you're going to miss a whole bunch of the book, but if you can still piece together the story, who cares? It's not like a dinner where you have to eat your vegetables to get your dessert. If you want to skip to the last chapter of a murder mystery, go ahead. The literature police won't come after you. There are no rules—you get out of a book what you put in.

EXERCISE #18

See if you can quickly tell what each of these sections is going to be: plot, character, or setting. Mark next to each one what type of section you think it is.

1. Paul set the timer on the explosive for two minutes. Barely enough time to get out of the warehouse. If the guards were asleep, and if the silent alarms had not been tripped, he would have a chance. A slim chance.

2. Carl's hair was like liquid fire. His nails, manicured crescent moons of delight. As his fingers danced along the piano keys, one was reminded of dolphins jumping from the water in the sparkling Aegean.

3. In the past, his brother had helped him out of jams like this. Before that, it was his father. And as a little kid, it had been his mother. People were always taking care of Johnny. But here, alone in a strange town, with no one who knew his face, his name, he started helping others, and, one morning, as he was jump-starting a car stuck in a snowbank, he realized that he had become his own person.

4. Mathilda thought that kissing John had been fun, but pointless. He was always making these silly noises, and she was always afraid her older sister would see her smeared lipstick. She would rather ride the carnival rides, feel the whooping feel of the up-and-down roller coaster, the arms of the octopus, the drop of the free-fall machine.

5. Uncle Walvis stumbled through the streets of Newark, raising the sleeping residents with his bagpipe music. He lurched from side to side, warbling out his unsteady tunes, as a strange thing, almost like a vision, began to take place. Walvis noticed people watching from the windows, staring in disbelief and pointing at him as he played. Uncertain, confused, he turned around:

he was followed by an army of wombats, wombats of all sizes, entranced by the uneven grating of Walvis' pipes.

6. Charles browsed through the library looking for a book on Mary Queen of Scots, or, if they didn't have one, a book on the lottery. He didn't care. He liked the feel of shelves, filled with books, of dusty, unused leather, and of enforced silence. Often, in his room, late at night, he would imagine he was in the library and force himself to be silent, and if he was bad, he would fine himself fifty cents.

7. Brenda slapped Dillon with a paternity suit. He was shocked. Sure, he had a gambling problem. And contract negotiations for next year weren't going well. But everyone knew that being slapped with a paternity suit would mean the end of his career. He wished, prayed, that he was related to the producer of his show, and that he could be talentless but be guaranteed a job.

8. Satan was thrown out of the bar by Rocco, a steroid-created throwback to Pleistocene Man.

    "Whassa matta," Satan slurred, "never seen the Prince of Darkness have a little drinky too many?" He tripped over a garbage can and sprawled in the street between a green Audi and a garbage truck.

    Rocco was not amused. He grabbed Satan by his cape and belt and slung him into the back of the garbage truck. No one hit on his girlfriend, especially in his bar. Even if he was evil incarnate.

    "Wait," Satan said, "Les' make a deal."

    Rocco pressed the button on the side of the truck, starting the jaws downward, and by the time Satan realized what was happening, it was too late. Rocco, unlikely hero, had eliminated the king of the underworld.

9. Vicki didn't just hate Carol—she despised her. Everything Carol did was great, and universally loved, even that stupid ear pull she closed every show with. And everything Vicki did was a copy, a rip-off, a no-talent solution. She would show them all. She planned in her sleep all the secrets she would tell to the tabloids. When she was done, Carol would wish she had never trifled with a redhead like Vicki!

10. The sun fell like light rain on the copper roof, sparkling with golden glares and sharp points. It was difficult to look at—it hurt the eyes. But everything else looked dull, unwashed next to that roof. The porch looked cracked and rotting, the railing looked worm-eaten and dying. The brown patch of dirt which was called the lawn lifted small dust-devils of turf smoke across the base of the stairs and up to the crack underneath the flapping screen door.

THE SHORT STORY

If you think that reading a short story will take you less time than a novel, you're right. It's shorter. But you should put just as much thought into it. A short story can be as complicated, as dense, and as powerful as any novel. Because it is a distilled form of fiction, every image and symbol becomes correspondingly more important and significant. If you don't believe me, try reading any Flannery O'Connor or Charlotte Perkins Gilman story. By the time you're done theme marking and summarizing and figuring it all out, we'll be nothing but dust and worm meal. And hopefully, the story will be exciting and interesting to you because the hidden elements all add to the dynamic, creative storytelling.

Some people really dislike short stories; they see them as unsatisfying, incomplete and confusing. Some people also hate chocolate—there's no accounting for taste. Be open-minded about the short story. Take each story on its own merits. You're going to like some more than others. When you're done, then make a decision on the book containing them. But if you start one story, and you think it stinks, don't condemn them all. Give it a chance. O.K. Enough preaching. Sermon over.

READING RACETRACK #10

Read the following passage as if you were reading it merely for pleasure. Do not time yourself. See how, even when you don't have a pen near you, you remember a whole bunch about the passage. Answer the questions. You know the drill.

Sheppard sat on a stool at the bar that divided the kitchen in half, eating his cereal out of the individual pasteboard box it came in. He ate mechanically, his eyes on the child, who was wandering from cabinet to cabinet in the paneled kitchen, collecting the ingredients for his breakfast. He was a stocky blond boy of ten. Sheppard kept his intense blue eyes fixed on him. The boy's future was written in his face. He would be a banker. No, worse. He would operate a small loan company. All he wanted for the child was that he be good and unselfish and neither seemed likely. Sheppard was a young man whose hair was already white. It stood up like a narrow brush halo over his pink sensitive face.

The boy approached the bar with a jar of peanut butter under his arm, a plate with a quarter of a small chocolate cake on it in one hand and the ketchup bottle in the other. He did not appear to notice his father. He climbed up on the stool and began to spread peanut butter on the cake. He had very round large ears that leaned away from his head and seemed to pull his eyes slightly too far apart. His shirt was green but so faded that the cowboy across the front of it was only a shadow.

"Norton," Sheppard said," I saw Rufus Johnson yesterday. Do you know what he was doing?"

The child looked at him with a kind of half attention, his eyes half forward but not yet engaged. They were a paler blue than his father's as if they might have faded like the shirt; one of them listed, almost imperceptibly, toward the outer rim.

"He was in an alley," Sheppard said, "and he had his hand in a garbage can. He was trying to get something to eat out of it." He paused to let this soak in. "He was hungry," he finished, and tried to pierce the child's conscience with his gaze.

The boy picked up the piece of chocolate cake and began to gnaw it from one corner.

"Norton," Sheppard said, "do you have any idea of what it means to share?"

A flicker of attention. "Some of it's yours," Norton said.

"Some of it's *his*," Sheppard said heavily. It was hopeless.

Almost any fault would have been preferable to selfishness—
a violent temper, even a tendency to lie.

The child turned the bottle of ketchup upside-down and
began thumping ketchup onto the cake.

Sheppard's look of pain increased. "You are ten and
Rufus Johnson is fourteen," he said. "Yet I'm sure your shirts
would fit Rufus." Rufus Johnson was a boy he had been
trying to help at the reformatory for the past year. He had
been released two months ago. "When he was in the reformatory, he looked pretty good, but when I saw him yesterday, he was skin and bones. He hadn't been eating cake
with peanut butter on it for breakfast."

"It's stale," he said. "That's why I have to put stuff
on it."

Sheppard turned his face to the window at the end of
the bar. The side lawn, green and even, sloped fifty feet
or so down to a small suburban wood. When his wife was
living, they had often eaten outside, even breakfast, on the
grass. He had never noticed then that the child was selfish.
"Listen to me," he said, turning back to him, "look at me
and listen."

The boy looked at him. At least his eyes were forward.

"I gave Rufus a key to this house when he left the
reformatory—to show my confidence in him and so he would
have a place he could come to and feel welcome any time.
He didn't use it, but I think he'll use it now because he's
seen me and he's hungry. And if he doesn't use it I'm going
out and find him and bring him here. I can't see a child
eating out of garbage cans."

The boy frowned. It was dawning on him that something
of his was threatened.

Sheppard's mouth stretched in disgust. "Rufus's father
died before he was born," he said. "His mother is in the
state penitentiary. He was raised by his grandfather in a shack
without water or electricity and the old man beat him every
day. How would you like to belong to a family like that?"

"I don't know," the child said lamely.

"Well, you might think about it sometime," Sheppard
said.

Sheppard was City Recreational Director. On Saturdays
he worked at the reformatory as a counselor, receiving nothing
for it but the satisfaction of knowing he was helping boys
no one else cared about. Johnson was the most intelligent
boy he had worked with and the most deprived.

Norton turned the rest of the cake over as if he no longer
wanted it.

"You started that, now finish it," Sheppard said.

"Maybe he won't come," the child said and his eyes brightened slightly.

"Think of everything you have that he doesn't!" Sheppard said. "Suppose you had to root in garbage cans for food? Suppose you had a huge swollen foot and one side of you dropped lower than the other when you walked?"

The boy looked blank, obviously unable to imagine such a thing.

"You have a healthy body," Sheppard said, "a good home. You've never been taught anything but the truth. Your daddy gives you anything you need or want. You don't have a grandfather who beats you. And your mother is not in the state penitentiary. "

The child pushed his plate away. Sheppard groaned aloud.

A knot of flesh appeared below the boy's suddenly distorted mouth. His face became a mass of lumps with slits for eyes. "If she was in the penitentiary," he began in a kind of racking bellow, "I could go to seeeeee her." Tears rolled down his face and the ketchup dribbled on his chin. He looked as if he had been hit in the mouth. He abandoned himself and howled.

Sheppard sat helpless and miserable, like a man lashed by some elemental force of nature. This was not a normal grief. It was all part of his selfishness. She had been dead for over a year and a child's grief should not last so long.

"You're going on eleven years old," he said reproachfully.

The child began an agonizing high-pitched heaving noise.

"If you stop thinking about yourself and think what you can do for somebody else," Sheppard said, "then you'll stop missing your mother."

The boy was silent but his shoulders continued to shake. Then his face collapsed and he began to howl again.

"Don't you think I'm lonely without her too?" Sheppard said. "Don't you think I miss her at all? I do, but I'm not sitting around moping. I'm busy helping other people. When do you see me just sitting around thinking about my troubles?"

The boy slumped as if he were exhausted but fresh tears streaked his face.

"What are you going to do today?" Sheppard asked, to get his mind on something else.

The child ran his arm across his eyes. "Sell seeds," he mumbled.

Always selling something. He had four quart jars full of nickels and dimes he had saved and he took them out of his closet every few days and counted them. "What are you selling seeds for?"

"To win a prize."

"What's the prize?"

"A thousand dollars."

"And what would you do if you had a thousand dollars?"

"Keep it," the child said and wiped his nose on his shoulder.

"I feel sure you would," Sheppard said. "Listen," he said and lowered his voice to an almost pleading tone, "suppose by some chance you did win a thousand dollars. Wouldn't you like to spend it on children less fortunate than yourself? Wouldn't you like to give some swings and trapezes to the orphanage? Wouldn't you like to buy poor Rufus Johnson a new shoe?"

The boy began to back away from the bar. Then suddenly he leaped forward and hung with his mouth open over his plate. Sheppard groaned again. Everything came up, the cake, the peanut butter, the ketchup—a limp sweet batter. He hung over it gagging, more came, and he waited with his mouth open over the plate as if he expected his heart to come up next.

1. The relationship between Norton and Sheppard can best be described as

   (A) loving and open
   (B) aggressive and violent
   (C) uncommunicative and disjointed
   (D) sickening and unnatural
   (E) friendly and supportive

2. The author's tone is intended to make the reader feel how about Norton?

   (A) Sympathetic
   (B) Angry
   (C) Protective
   (D) Cynical
   (E) Disgusted

3. The author's tone is intended to make the reader feel how about Sheppard?

   (A) Cynical
   (B) Protective
   (C) Disgusted
   (D) Sympathetic
   (E) Angry

4. According to Sheppard, operating a small loan company would be

   (A) a sign of self-involvement
   (B) a lucrative career move
   (C) a fate similar to losing one's soul
   (D) an unlikelihood for Norton
   (E) a good job for Norton

5. How does the author intend the reader to interpret Sheppard's name?

   (A) Ironically
   (B) Symbolically
   (C) Humorously
   (D) Incorrectly
   (E) No interpretation (if you're considering this, read the passage again)

6. Why does the author keep referring to the character as "the child" instead of "Norton"?

   (A) To make the reader dislike him
   (B) Because Sheppard dislikes him
   (C) To establish distance between the two characters
   (D) To establish distance between Norton and the reader
   (E) To distinguish between Rufus and Norton

7. What did Norton have for breakfast?

   (A) cake and cereal
   (B) cake, cereal, and peanut butter
   (C) cereal, cake batter, peanut butter and ketchup
   (D) cereal, ketchup, and batter
   (E) cake, peanut butter, and ketchup

8. According to Sheppard, what's the least desirable fault someone can have?

   (A) A violent temper
   (B) Selfishness
   (C) A tendency to lie
   (D) Putting ketchup on cake
   (E) Operating a loan company

9. What does Sheppard do for a living?

(A) Reform counselor
(B) Baby sitter
(C) City Recreational Director
(D) Norton's dad
(E) Operator of a loan company

10. The relationship between Rufus and Norton can be expected to be

(A) unnatural
(B) filial
(C) subharmonic
(D) halcyon
(E) antagonistic

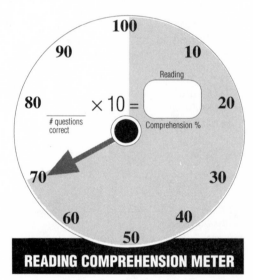

READING COMPREHENSION METER

Calculate your comprehension rate using the following formula. Multiply the number of questions you answered correctly by 10. That is your comprehension percentage. You want to keep your percentage above 70 percent for any type of reading. Below that, you start losing important information presented in the passages.

CHAPTER 8

Tricks
and
Traps

Rapid Reading: This course will increase reading speed a little each day until the end of the term, by which time the student will be required to read The Brothers Karamazov in fifteen minutes. The method is to scan the page and eliminate everything except pronouns from one's field of vision. Soon the pronouns are eliminated. Gradually the student is encouraged to nap.

—Woody Allen

Picture this—it's three o'clock in the morning, you've got a freshly made pot of coffee, you've got three different novels you have to read in front of you (their spines are all stiffer than yesterday's bubble-gum, because you haven't opened them since you bought them), and your exam is at eight that morning. If you had to theme mark, to map the argument, to keep track of symbols, you'd maybe get one-half of one novel done by the time your professor said "O.K. No Talking. Begin."

When you don't have much time (even though your fixations and saccades—remember those? If not, go back to chapter three and read *carefully* this time— are triple their normal rate) and you have to read a book, you should employ an important strategy called **skimming**. We're sure you've heard about skimming in various forms, and in practice, you probably already skim unconsciously. *Skimming is always a second-best alternative to reading carefully and efficiently* —believe us, though, we understand that people don't always have enough time to do things the right way. Have you ever eaten at McDonalds? Well, that's skim-eating. Have you ever watched a sports-highlight show—that's skim-viewing. Even though we're forced into all this "skimming" in daily life, you should really only skim when you have to.

Let's Go Surfing Now

TEXTBOOK SKIMMING

First, recognize that of all types of skimming, this is going to be the hardest to pull off. You don't have a plot to grab on to, the book is usually condensed stuff, so almost everything is important, and if its a science text, you've got concepts and equations to get under your belt. Should you give up hope, quit reading altogether and only pay attention to that sacred box of moving pictures in your living room?

Of course not. We'll break up the textbook skimming into types: social science texts and hard science texts.

SOCIAL SCIENCE TEXTS

Read the chapter headings and the bolded section headings. Use those to make a quick outline of each chapter. If a section heading is not clear to you translate it into something meaningful. For example, if you have a section heading in a book on the French Revolution which says "Mme Guillotine Collects Her Bill" you want to read that section and translate it into something, perhaps, that reads "After the revolution, the Jacobins started beheading everyone." Not as pretty, but much more useful on a test.

The point is to only read if you don't understand what that section refers to. If you have to read a section, try reading the first sentence of each paragraph. If you haven't reached the main point of that paragraph, keep reading until you do. Read no further—you don't have time to see everything.

SEE THE OUTLINES, MAKE AN OUTLINE

Outlining a textbook should take you a couple of hours—but then you start to see how everything relates to everything else. Pick one or two concrete examples to memorize, and pray that your teacher asks about them. Try to pick concepts that you remember the teacher discussing in class (no matter what your teacher says, they all like to see their own words repeated to them). A general concept which it helps to remember is that seeing the overriding idea of a course or a book is more important than memorizing every date and name. A teacher teaches to an overarching concept, not a specific. Even if he is teaching about the French Revolution, every book has an idea about the French Revolution (It wasn't a revolution, it was brought about by radicals, it was funded by the Americans, it was supported by the clergy, etc.) it tries to support. Use that idea to seek out a few points on what would be an interesting essay.

HARD SCIENCE TEXTS

Most people play the gamble game—they choose one topic, learn it well, cross their fingers and walk through the doors of the exam knowing that they will be at best only partially skewered by the exam. Skimming would save them not only heartache, but also their GPA.

Scientific texts usually have a summary section in the back that lists the important formulas. If it doesn't, go through each chapter looking for formulas. Find the section heading that relates to that formula. Write them down on an equation sheet. A typical entry from a chemistry textbook might look like "Heat, Temp, Size Relationship — $PV = nRT$ — P = Pressure, V = Volume, n = constant, R =

Moles of Gas, T = Temperature." If your test is going to be mainly quantitative, then work from this sheet. If your test is going to be conceptual, focus more on the chapter introductions and summaries. Those are the best ways to get a feel for what concepts are being examined, and how, in a chapter.

Read the summaries, the introductions, and the equations. Although some of the boxes with interesting information on subjects and pictures and graphs may appear fascinating, don't get sucked in. They are tangential to the main point, otherwise they would be referred to in the text. If they are, make sure you can recognize them and reproduce a few of them.

SKIMMING THROUGH JOURNALISTIC READING

Luckily, the way to skim-read journalistic reading is just how you learned to read journalism in the first place. Pre-read, read only what you need, and map the argument if it gets confusing.

Know the important people, countries or industries, what the issue is, and some differing points of view on the subject. You are going to do less reading with your pen, which will hurt your comprehension, but if you have very little time and a lot of reading, you can't do everything.

If you must skim journalistic reading, try to picture a larger context before you begin. Let's say you had to read a nonfiction collection of articles written during the Watergate conspiracy the night before your exam. It would be helpful to remember that the *Washington Post* broke the scandal—so you want to pay attention to any articles from them. You want to quickly identify who was protecting Nixon, and who was attacking Nixon. What examples did each type of author use to support his position? One way to picture the larger context is to divide the reading into groups, or categories. Use any category division that makes it easy to read and remember quickly. Choose one detail or one image which, for you, identifies the main point of the passage. Then, come exam day, you'll do just fine.

SPEEDING THROUGH FICTION

It's a fine last resort (as last resorts go) to skim fiction. But because fiction doesn't adhere to the "just-the-facts" method that journalism does, it's much harder to skim. The best way to skim fiction seems strange—but it works. Again, I want to emphasize that if your speed has increased, and you have a chance to read the book efficiently, do it. Skimming entails missing things.

1. First, you're not going to look for plot right away. Knowing too much hurts you. **Read the first and the last chapters in their entirety.** Don't worry too much about what has gone on. You are looking for how the story begins and how it ends. What is the tone at the beginning? What is the tone at the end? Can you see any kind of progression or movement? Does the first chapter start off as hopeful and the last one end in unhappiness? Try to see larger movements.

2. Second, **go on a plot-hunt.** Skim the book looking only for what happens. At this point, nothing else should interest you. Jump to the beginning of each chapter and see where the characters are and what they are doing. Skip long dialogue or descriptive passages. Skip anything which doesn't further the plot. Try to see the plot as developing the progression you saw from the first chapter to the last chapter.

3. Finally, **look for images** that populate the first chapter and skim the text a second time only looking for those images. Read carefully around where they appear. See if you can determine their meaning. Usually, you can make some guesses about specific images are employed. If a bird is circling overhead at the beginning of the book, and every time something bad happens that same stupid bird comes back, you can start to make some guesses as to what that bird represents. Be careful to avoid images which are common and meaningless. Because the sun comes up every morning and sets every evening, that doesn't mean that the author necessarily wants to impress on us the endless repitition of life. Don't see meaning in everything, just things which come back and are not so ordinary.

A note here on those "skim-books," which theoretically outline and explain a book. While they may summarize the plot clearly (and they don't always do that), they are not very useful as a substitute for reading the text. Those books contain only the most elemental, and not necessarily correct, ideas about a text. What if you say something on a final exam that your teacher disagrees with? Are you going to say, "But the Hill's Notes said that bluebirds were symbolic of peace?" Your teacher will set your exam book on fire. If you must use these synopses (you can guess by now we don't recommend them) use them only for plot. After that, skim for images and themes on your own.

Skimming is useful in very specific circumstances. Some people prefer to skim everything they read so they can be semi-informed on a number of topics. Some people feel more comfortable not having very high retention levels. It is very seductive to rely on skimming rather than reading; in the end, your understanding and your memory of what you have read will suffer. And what's the point of reading if you are not going to remember what you've read two months later? If you're going to read, and you have the chance, read smart.

THE TELEGRAM

How do people communicate most efficiently? Where it costs money for each word. In a telegram. A telegram drops everything but the nouns and the verbs important to get the message across. Would a telegram read:

> I am so dreadfully sorry, but I seem to have misplaced my wallet (at that lovely French restaurant, Bouley, where I met Inez that night after the play). If you could be a dear and send me some much needed money, I would be your loving servant. I promise to pay you back when I next see you. I hope your golf game is going well. Ta Ta—Nigel

Since the writer pays by word, this telegram would easily use up the money he requests! A more realistic telegram reads:

> Send money. Will reimburse. Nigel.

You see how much flavor is lost, but the same information gets across. It takes you much less time to read the second than the first.

The best skim-readers translate passages into telegram-like information when they are really pressed for time. The secondary information and words just drop out of their sight. They stop reading articles, prepositions, all those "filler words" which just slow you down.

Exercise # 19

Read the following paragraphs, translating them into telegrams in the margin. Try to read them as telegrams, skipping the unnecessary words.

1. Charles, that violent kung-fu expert, who appeared on *Geraldo* last week, kicked his wall, the one with the dull brown paint, so hard, that the entire support beam shook like a scared child. He was about to kick the wall again when the roof, that rickety, thatched, poorly constructed makeshift one, fell inward, filling the air with dust and smoke. By the time those hunky, strong ambulance workers arrived on the scene, it was too late. Charles, who had lived by violence, was dead.

2. Melanie walked determinedly across the carpet into Don's waiting arms. As she touched his chiseled features lightly with her fingertips, he let out an angelic sigh, which lifted from his lips like a prayer. Melanie whispered into his ear, "If you get top billing in the next film, I'm leaving you," as she raised her perfect and voluptuous knee into his unsuspecting groin.

3. Stan Lee, the creator of Marvel Comics, unleashed a powerful concept even he did not imagine when he created the lovable, angry, comedic and powerful character of Iron Man. Although he intended a man of steel and technology, empowered by sophisticated weaponry and computer strategy, he did not anticipate (even in his wildest dreams) that the heart ailment he gave the main character would make the indefatigable Iron Man a hero to all those physically challenged individuals to whom crossing the street is an act of unspeakable bravery.

4. Clawing at the striped tie which surrounded his collared shirt, Ethan presented to his friends the image of a man gone mad. Fires burned in his eyes like the infernos of Hades, and his fingers were twisted and contorted with claw-like grips on his silk cravat. He pawed the carpet like an animal, and dashed, not knocking over any of the furniture, not bumping into any guests, but sidestepping them, panther-like, from the ballroom.

5. No one knew how Uncle Walvis had won the election. His campaign slogan, "Uuurk Ooogh Maaghen Nooob," was not understood by a single person, not even his campaign manager. People were certain that the photos of his wife and Michael Jackson frolicking in the surf would hurt his chances, but they didn't. Even the curses he spouted at the debate were taken as signs of his "colorful nature." Despite all the problems and the pitfalls, Uncle Walvis was on his way to Washington, after, of course, he had few drinks at the Waloon Saloon on Tenth Street.

By the final passage, did you start to read these in a telegram style? When you're pushing your fixation rate as fast as it can go, and your eyes burn across the page, you should start reading in this choppy, driven way. I hope you read the passages for fun as well, not skimming them, because when you skim, you lose the feel of the language, a couple of precise adjectives or adverbs, and some imagery. But if you must read quickly, why not read the important stuff only? Turning prose into a telegram eliminates the unnecessary and increases your speed and retention.

The Way to Set Reading Goals

Have you ever said to yourself, "I'm just going to read until three o'clock, then I can go out and do some fun stuff." At two, you take a break, get some food, watch some television. At two-thirty, you sit in your chair, with your book in your hand, daydreaming, thinking about what you're going to do at three. Then, at two-forty-five, you start making phone calls, and admit that really, you're done reading. What can you get done in fifteen minutes?

Don't be embarrassed. That's the kind of stuff people do all the time. And it doesn't make them bad readers. But it stops them from being the best readers they could be. Instead of setting time limit goals, set reading goals. Sounds like a little thing, huh? But people tend to finish books much faster when they set page-number goals than time goals.

If you have a page-number goal, it doesn't matter if you daydream, take a break, or talk on the telephone. You still will not be any closer to going out and doing something fun. The point is you can waste time. You can't fake reading (unless you skim when you don't have to—and that's a huge waste of energy). By setting realistic reading goals every day, you guarantee that you can't even undermine yourself subconsciously. You simply have to do it. And once you start doing it , you work it into your daily schedule and it ceases to be any kind of burden whatsoever.

Get away from time goals—you'll find a way to fill the time with everything but reading.

WIDEN YOUR VOCABULARY

Something that keeps people from reading as fast as they otherwise could is a limited vocabulary. The best readers have a large vocabulary—primarily because they read and learn these new words, either in context or through explanations. The more you read, then, the more your vocabulary will be stretched.

If you want to jump a level in terms of speed and understanding, you have to work on your vocabulary outside of reading. We haven't asked you to do any pushups or situps in this book, we haven't asked you to do any outside research or to learn a foreign language. Working on your vocabulary is a lifelong task. No one knows every word. But the more you know the less likely you are to stare at a passage and say "what the heck is he talking about?"

Get a vocabulary book (personally, we recommend *Word Smart*—and no, the author of this book doesn't get any royalties for that). It should not only teach you specific words, but also roots and stems. Keep a list of new words you learn. Again, writing things down produces the highest retention levels.

Working on your vocabulary is one of those things which is a pain in the butt for the first couple of weeks, but rapidly becomes much easier. Just keep in mind that the smartest person in the United

States probably only knows two to three thousand more words than you. That's what separates the smartest person from the average person in terms of vocabulary. By learning five hundred new words, you jump to the top twenty percent of the country. This is the kind of learning that rewards hard work.

READING RACETRACK #11

Skim-read the following passage and answer the questions at the bottom. Try to summarize and make the passage into a telegram as you read it. Really push yourself—imagine that you have six minutes to read the passage and to answer the questions (we're so mean).

Las Vegas is a good restaurant town. It's not New York or San Francisco, but it offers respectable culinary and ethnic diversity, served dependably. Las Vegas hotel dining is relatively homogeneous in style and cuisine, while proprietary restaurants try hard to be different. The restaurant business in Las Vegas is as much a psychological as a culinary art, an exercise in perceived versus real value. In Las Vegas you can have the same meal in an astounding variety of environments for an unbelievable range of prices.

Left to its own devices, Las Vegas would be a meat and potatoes town. Owing to the expectations of its many visitors, however, Las Vegas restaurants put on the dog. There are dozens of designer restaurants, gourmet rooms as they are known locally, where the pampered and the curious can pretend they are dining in an exclusive French or Continental restaurant while enjoying the food they like most: meat and potatoes. It is a town full of Ponderosas masquerading as Lutèce or The Four Seasons.

What has saved the day for discriminating diners is the increased presence of foreign visitors, particularly Asians. The needs of these visitors in conjunction with their economic clout have precipitated great growth and improvement among proprietary ethnic restaurants, which in turn have forced improvement among the more staid hotel/casino dining rooms. While many of the hotel gourmet rooms continue to be gastronomic and stylistic carbon copies, Las Vegas's proprietary restaurants have established distinct identities based on their creativity in the kitchen.

There are two kinds of restaurants in Las Vegas: restaurants which are an integral part of a hotel/casino operation, and restaurants which must make it entirely on the merits of their food. Gourmet rooms in the hotels are usually associated with the casinos. Their mission is to pamper customers who are giving the house a lot of gambling action. At any given time, most of the folks in a hotel gourmet room are dining as guests of the casino. If you are a paying customer in the same restaurant, the astronomical prices you are charged help subsidize the feeding of all these comped guests. Every time you buy a meal in a gourmet room, you are helping to pay the tab of the strangers sitting at the next table. This is not to say the gourmet rooms do not serve excellent food. On the contrary, some of the best chefs in the country cook for hotel/casino gourmet rooms. The bottom line, however, if you are a paying guest, is that you are taking up space intended for high rollers, and the house is going to charge you a lot of rent.

Restaurants independent of casinos work at a considerable disadvantage. First, they do not have a captive audience of gamblers or convention-goers. Second, their operation is not subsidized by gaming, and third, they are not located where you will just stumble upon them. Finally, they not only compete with the casino gourmet rooms, but also go head-to-head with the numerous buffets and bulk-loading meal deals which casinos offer as loss-leaders to attract the less affluent gambler.

Successful proprietary restaurants in Las Vegas must offer something very distinct, very different, and very good at a competitive price, and must somehow communicate to you that they are offering it. Furthermore, their offer must be compelling enough to induce you to travel to their location, forsaking the convenience of dining in your hotel. Not easy.

All of this works to the consumer's advantage, of course. High rollers get comped in the gourmet rooms. Folks of more modest means can select from among the amazing steak, lobster, and prime rib deals offered by the casinos, or enjoy exceptional food at bargain prices at independent restaurants. People with hardly any money at all can gorge themselves on loss-leader buffets.

In many ways, Las Vegas restaurants are the culinary version of free-market economy. The casinos siphon off the customers who are willing to pay big bucks for food and feed them for free. This alters the target market for the independents and serves to keep a lid on their prices. Independents providing exceptional quality for such reasonable charges ensure in turn that buffets and meal deals stay cheap. Ah, America, what a country!

1. According to the passage, proprietary restaurants in Las Vegas are

    (A) all extremely similar
    (B) run by the casinos
    (C) inordinately expensive
    (D) crowded and scattered
    (E) creative and individual

2. The phrase "put on the dog," as used in the passage, means

    (A) serve meat and potatoes
    (B) become more fancy
    (C) keep things simple
    (D) cater to tourist needs
    (E) lower prices

3. According to the author, casino restaurants have an advantage over independent restaurants because

    (A) they offer room deals which include food at a considerable discount
    (B) their operations are subsidized by gambling revenues
    (C) they attract a more wealthy client
    (D) without rent, they are able to charge lower prices
    (E) All of the above

4. According to the author, food in Las Vegas can be generally described as

    (A) expensive and unpleasant
    (B) traditional American cuisine
    (C) scattered across the Strip and difficult to get to
    (D) competitive and differentiated
    (E) usually very inexpensive

5. According to the passage, the gourmet rooms

    (A) serve food to high rollers only
    (B) are priced high, but reasonably for the food
    (C) serve French and Continental cuisine only
    (D) are staffed by some of the best chefs in the country
    (E) pay no rent, and are therefore anti-competitive

6. An adjective used in the passage to describe the overall diversity and quality of the dining experience in Las Vegas is

    (A) pricey
    (B) compelling
    (C) gourmet
    (D) free-market
    (E) respectable

7. The Las Vegas term "gourmet room" means

    (A) an expensive restaurant
    (B) a supper club for local highrollers
    (C) a buffet room, subsidized by the casino
    (D) a restaurant which serves French or Continental cuisine
    (E) a designer restaurant

8. According to the author, dining in Las Vegas would be less palatable without

    (A) competitive pricing
    (B) the increase in foreign visitors
    (C) locally grown food supplies
    (D) a variety of price-range options
    (E) the overseeing arm of the price-control commission

9. What does the author mean by a "proprietary restaurant?"

    (A) Privately owned
    (B) Buffet style
    (C) Expensive
    (D) Exotic
    (E) Affiliated with a casino

10. Which of the following, if true, would most undermine the author's experience of dining in Las Vegas?

    (A) He contracted botulism from a bowl of soup at the Sands casino.
    (B) He couldn't get a reservation at Wolfgang Puck's cafe.
    (C) There is no Eskimo food in Las Vegas.
    (D) Las Vegas charges a minimum food tax of 73%.
    (E) The average restaurant in Las Vegas closes after three months of operation.

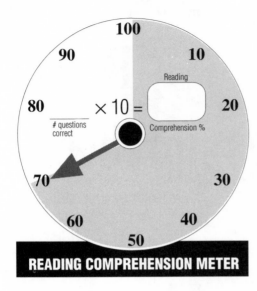

READING COMPREHENSION METER

Calculate your comprehension rate using the following formula. Multiply the number of questions you answered correctly by 10. That is your comprehension percentage. You want to keep your percentage above 70 percent for any type of reading. Below that, you start losing important information presented in the passages.

CHAPTER 9

Reading
Comprehension

"As far as I'm consciously aware, I forget everything I read at once, including my own stuff."

—Henry Green

If you skipped right to this section, stop for a minute. The terms and techniques that'll be used in this chapter will make no sense if you haven't read the book up to this point. At bare minimum, read the first four chapters and the textbook section. Then you'll at least have a fighting chance.

WHY EVER DO IT?

A reading comprehension test is something everyone who takes a multiple choice test, who takes the SATs, who takes the GREs (graduate school), the GMATs (business school), the LSATs (shark school) or any other major standardized test, has done. There are long, dry passages with poorly phrased ambiguous questions, and sometimes, it seems there is no right answer possible. And anyone who is not a zip zip zippy reader gets crushed under the wheels of that monster truck, TIME. There are ways to make this troubling situation easier, and to do better on these tests, but keep in mind that these techniques should *not* be used for normal reading. This method of reading is designed to help you get the questions at the end right—not to help you remember anything about the passage.

WAKE UP!

Doesn't it seem testwriters go out of their way to find the most boring, sleep-inducing passages? They find stuff like the history of some French viscomte who researched the pupa stage of insects, or the difference between a gust of wind and a gale, passages which really have no effect on your life whatsoever. Are testwriters just a bunch of creepy people with strange reading habits? No, they choose these passages for a different reason (although they may still be a bunch of creepy people—we'll never know).

They choose strange passages to avoid skewing the test in favor of one person or another. For example, what if a testwriter chose a passage on auto mechanics? Every kid who didn't know a bunch about cars would be at a huge disadvantage. What about a passage on baseball? Everyone who wasn't a fan would do much worse than the other people. Would it be a good idea to choose a passage on how to find the right guy? While many relationships would improve, many scores would drop considerably. By choosing a strange topic, attached to no specific group, and unusual enough that few people will know it anyway, they guarantee that most people are at the same disadvantage—it mystifies everyone equally. However, if you yourself are a strange person who knows the fluctuations of the jet-stream backwards and forwards and researches obscure facts for pleasure, you might just hit the jackpot! Don't count on it, though.

You're not supposed to be familiar with the information in a passage—so remain calm. Anyone who is driven to jitters by a standardized test is cheating themselves out of points. The reading comprehension questions are intended to make you want to tear you hair out, so when you see a passage on the migration pattern of the Crested Wallabee or the rate of plaque buildup on a dog's teeth, you should have one reaction—big fat deal. You should yawn and be very bored, because you expected this. Everyone around you will be banging their heads against their desks, trying to get excused from the test, looking to cheat off the smartest kid in the class. You don't have to. You're about to learn how to "read smart."

FACTS VS. THEMES

Before you read any passage, **pre-read the questions**. There are two types of questions on reading passages—*fact* questions and *theme* questions. A fact question is "In what year did Eli Whitney invent the cotton gin?" or "Martha's husband was named _____." A fact question tells you what to look for.

Theme questions are "The main point of the passage is" or "Which, if true, most undermines the author's argument." Fact questions can be quickly and easily searched out in the passage. Theme questions cannot. When you first go through the questions, don't worry about the specific information. Just look for whether it is a *fact* question or a *theme* question. Mark an "F" next to fact questions and a "T" next to theme questions. You're going to deal with each of these types of questions differently.

FIRST THE FACTS . . .

Go after *every* fact question. It's rare that we tell you to do everything, but you should answer every one of them, because the answers are all right in the passage. Scan the passage looking for words that quickly tell you where the answer is. These kind of words are called **stop signs**, because they show you where you should stop and look for the answer.

For example, here's the Eli Whitney question again: "In what year did Eli Whitney invent the cotton gin?" Why not look for Whitney, cotton gin, or all the dates in the passage? **Don't even read the sentences.** Just look for key words. If they don't tell you the answer, move on to the next stop sign. Fact questions are free points on a test—they are straightforward and easily handled. Use the stop signs to answer them efficiently and rake in the points.

...THEN THE THEMES

Once you've answered all the fact questions, go back and read the passage. Keep in mind the type of theme questions you're going to need to answer. Are you going to need to know the main point of the passage? How about reasons which lead to the conclusion of the passage? You are still going to be looking for information, but, unfortunately, it won't be as easy as looking for simple facts.

Are you going to read the whole passage? Nope. Read only the first paragraph and the first sentence of each subsequent paragraph. Usually, the first sentence will clearly tell you about what is going to follow. If the paragraphs are long, read the last sentence as well. If you still don't get the main idea, then keep reading until you do. Last, read the entire final paragraph. Don't pay attention to details, names and dates when theme reading—pay attention to ideas, arguments, and direction. Finding out the author's argument is critical to answering theme questions.

READING RACETRACK #12

Read the following passage and answer the questions after it to find your speed and comprehension levels. Time yourself on a watch with a second hand. Time only the reading portion of the exercise, not the question portion. Then calculate your reading speed and comprehension level, using the formulas at the end of the questions.

> The crucial years of the Depression, as they are brought into historical focus, increasingly emerge as the decisive decade for American art, if not for American culture in general. For it was during this decade that many of the conflicts which had blocked the progress of American art in the past came to a head and sometimes boiled over. Janus-faced, the thirties look backward, sometimes as far as the Renaissance; and

at the same time forward, as far as the present and beyond. It was the moment when artists, like Thomas Hart Benton, who wished to turn back the clock to regain the virtues of simpler times came into direct conflict with others, like Stuart Davis and Frank Lloyd Wright, who were ready to come to terms with the Machine Age and to deal with its consequences.

America in the thirties was changing rapidly. In many areas the past was giving way to the present, although not without a struggle. A predominately rural and small town society was being replaced by the giant complexes of the big cities; power was becoming increasingly centralized in the federal government and in large corporations. As a result, traditional American types such as the independent farmer and the small businessman were being replaced by the executive and the bureaucrat. Many Americans, deeply attached to the old way of life, felt disinherited. At the same time, as immigration decreased and the population became more homogeneous, the need arose in art and literature to commemorate the ethnic and regional differences that were fast disappearing. The incursions of government controls on the laissez-faire system, acting to erode the Calvinist ethic of hard work and personal sacrifice on which both the economy and public morality had rested, called forth a similar reaction. Thus, paradoxically, the conviction that art, at least, should serve some purpose or carry some message of moral uplift grew stronger as the Puritan ethos lost its contemporary reality. Often this elevating message was a sermon in favor of just those traditional American virtues which were now threatened with obsolescence in a changed social and political context.

In this new context, the appeal of the paintings by the Regionalists and the American Scene painters often lay in their ability to recreate an atmosphere that glorified the traditional American values—self-reliance tempered with good-neighborliness, independence modified by a sense of community, hard work rewarded by a sense of order and purpose. Given the actual temper of the times, these themes were strangely anachronistic, just as the rhetoric supporting political isolationism was equally inappropriate in an international situation soon to involve America in a second world war. Such themes gained popularity because they filled a genuine need for a comfortable collective fantasy of a God-fearing, white-picket-fence America, which in retrospect took on the nostalgic appeal of a lost Golden Age.

In this light, an autonomous art-for-art's sake was viewed as a foreign invader liable to subvert the native American desire for a purposeful art. Abstract art was assigned the role of the villainous alien; realism was to personify the genuine American means of expression. The argument drew favor in many camps: among the artists, because most were realists; among the politically oriented intellectuals, because abstract art was apolitical; and among museum officials, because they were surfeited with mediocre imitations of European modernism and were convinced that American art must develop its own distinct identity. To help along this road to self-definition, the museums were prepared to set up an artificial double standard, one for American art, and another for European art. In 1934, Ralph Flint wrote in *Art News*, "We have today in our midst a greater array of what may be called second-, third-, and fourth-string artists than any other country. Our big annuals are marvelous outpourings of intelligence and skill; they have all the diversity and animation of a five-ring circus."

The most commanding attraction in this circus was surely that of the American Scene painters, a category that may be broadened to accommodate both the urban realists, like Reginald Marsh, Isabel Bishop, Alexander Brook, and the brothers Isaac, Moses and Raphael Soyer, and the Regionalists, like Thomas Hart Benton, John Steuart Curry, and Grant Wood. American Scene painting was, to a degree, a continuation of the tradition of Henri and the New York realists, which had by no means died out. Its stronghold was the Art Students League, where John Sloan was elected director in 1931, and Kenneth Hays Miller and Yasui Kuniyoshi, also former Henri students, perpetuated Henri's approach. Here, too, Thomas Hart Benton preached the gospel of Regionalism.

1. According to the passage, one painter from the "urban realist" school was

   (A) Grant Wood
   (B) Thomas Hart Benton
   (C) Joan Sloan
   (D) Isaac Soyer
   (E) Isabel Bishop

2. According to the passage, in the 1930s, abstract art was seen as

   (A) uniquely American
   (B) uniquely European
   (C) relevant to post-war traumaticism
   (D) imitative of European modernism
   (E) counter to American regionalism

3. American Scene painters were characterized by

    (A) landscape painting
    (B) abstract painting
    (C) representing American values.
    (D) exploring an atmosphere of internationalism
    (E) depicting religious sentiment

4. In 1931, the director of the Art Students League was

    (A) Ralph Flint
    (B) Kenneth Hayes Miller
    (C) Thomas Hart Benton
    (D) John Sloan
    (E) John Steuart Curry

5. The "artificial double standard" mentioned in the passage refers to

    (A) the difference between standards of judgment for European art and American art
    (B) the difference between standards of judgment for Realism and Abstract art
    (C) the difference between museum officials and the common American perception
    (D) the distinction between art's movement toward Puritanism and America's movement toward hedonism
    (E) the difference between standards of judgment for politically oriented intellectuals and museum officials

6. According to the passage, one artist who advocated a return to earlier values was

    (A) John Steuart Curry
    (B) Thomas Hart Benton
    (C) John Calvin
    (D) Raphael Soyer
    (E) Ralph Flint

7. The best word to describe America in the 1930s would be

    (A) reactionary
    (B) consistent
    (C) dynamic
    (D) stolid
    (E) melancholic

8. According to the passage, one response to industrialization was

(A) abstract art
(B) a conservative movement in art
(C) a movement toward mobile art
(D) an abandonment of art
(E) a removal from European influences

9. According to the passage, Stuart Davis was a representative of

(A) regionalism responding in art
(B) dadaism as the future of art
(C) modernism as included in art
(D) futurism as expressed through art
(E) industrialization accepted by art

10. The best choice for title of the above passage would be

(A) The Thirties in Art: Reaction and Rebellion
(B) America in the Thirties: A Changing Time
(C) Thomas Hart Benton and Regionalism
(D) Art, Politics, and Growth in America
(E) The Art Students League: A History

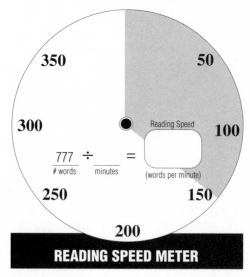

Calculate your reading speed using the following formula. First, mark down how long it took you, in minutes, to read the passage (if it took you 2 minutes, 15 seconds, then it took you 2.25 minutes). Divide the number of words in the passage by that number. This is your reading speed in words per minute. For example, there are 777 words in this passage. If it took you 6.5 minutes to read the entire selection, then divide 777 by 6.5. This would result in a reading speed of 120 w.p.m.

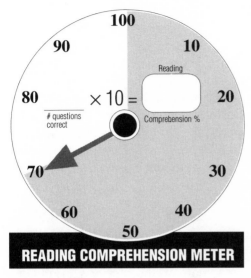

READING COMPREHENSION METER

Calculate your comprehension rate using the following formula. Multiply the number of questions you answered correctly by 10. That is your comprehension percentage. You want to keep your percentage above 70 percent for any type of reading. Below that, you start losing important information presented in the passages.

Did your pre-reading help you get through the passage faster? Without pre-reading, you would have read the passage and when you came to fact questions, you would have had to look them up anyway. The point is, burying yourself in a passage without knowing what you are going to need it for is a useless exercise. It's like reading anything. You have to know why you are reading it. Theme questions are more difficult to pin down, but by knowing them before you read, you can look for them and let them guide you through the piece.

PICK AND CHOOSE

Most passages contain a whole bunch of useless information (by that, we mean information which you don't need to answer the questions at the end). Reading the questions first is a great way to get around this worthless information. Also, avoid reading whole lists of anything, whether they are names, dates, groups, or countries. Another thing to look out for is the interesting stuff in the passage because it is usually *not* what you will be tested on. If there is a hilariously funny description of Burt Reynolds covered in chocolate and feathers, you can be certain that the questions will ask only about what he studied in college. Be careful not to get drawn in by any interesting, but secondary, information. Don't be fooled—test writers were not put on this earth to entertain you.

Watch That Turn

Remember when we told you how facts become stop signs that tell you to read that particular section? Well, there are **turn signs** as well. Look out for words which indicate a change in opinion, or a reversal of direction. Words like **although, however, but** and **in spite of** (anything which indicates a change of opinion) tell you that whatever the main point was in the previous section, a different point will take place in succeeding paragraphs. Circling these turn sign words will help you keep the argument's direction in mind.

Mini-Mapping

These turn sign words are crucial to our final reading technique called **mini-mapping**. You learned mapping from the discussion of journalism in chapter five—drawing a map of the author's argument. Mini-mapping does the same thing but is less specific and detailed.

Read the first paragraph. From the first paragraph you should be able to figure out the thesis for the entire passage. Summarize the thesis of the passage in the margin. For each subsequent paragraph, write next to it what job that paragraph does, keeping in mind it can only do a few things:

(1) It can **support the thesis**
(2) It can **provide an example** of the thesis
(3) It can **attack the thesis**
(4) It can **provide a different opinion** from the thesis.

Everything else the paragraph may do is not useful for theme questions, so, if a paragraph doesn't do any of these things, ignore it. Mini-mapping quickly tells you where to go to answer theme questions. Think of it this way: the difference between mapping and mini-mapping is like the difference between a big, beautiful Rand-McNally map and a map you Xeroxed from a McDonald's placemat. Although they may both cover the same geographical region, one is much more specific and detailed than the other. One is more useful for planning a long trip, the other is more useful for getting a general idea of the landscape. Mini-mapping also gives you a quick snapshot of the extent to which the passage supports or attacks an argument.

READING RACETRACK #13

Read the following passage and answer the questions after it to find your speed and comprehension levels Time yourself on a watch with a second hand. Time only the reading portion of the exercise, not the question portion. Then calculate your reading speed and comprehension level, using the formulas at the end of the questions.

Breach of Faith

In June, 1972, the District of Columbia police took into custody five burglars who had broken into the offices of the Democratic National Committee at the fashionable Watergate complex in Washington, apparently to plant a listening device. A trail of clues led incredibly from the perpetrators—three Cuban émigrés and two native-born Americans, all with CIA connections—to E. Howard Hunt, an administration consultant who a dozen years earlier had helped plan the Bay of Pigs invasion, and to G. Gordon Liddy, a Republican campaign official. All seven men were indicted. The head of the Nixon campaign committee, the president's close friend, former Attorney General John Mitchell, denied prior knowledge but resigned all the same.

As the Watergate Seven awaited trial that fall, the Democrats attempted unsuccessfully to make an issue of the episode. The American electorate, apparently unwilling to face the prospect of a McGovern presidency, behaved almost as a willing conspirator in the increasingly dubious pretense that the break-in had been the work of a few overzealous underlings. In fact, Nixon himself had secretly allowed his top domestic aide, H.R. Haldeman, to dissuade the FBI from a serious investigation that would have demonstrated otherwise.

Throughout 1973 and into 1974, the cover-up slowly came apart, partly because of pressure from a determined opposition, partly because Nixon and those around him displayed monumental ineptitude and inexplicable irresolution in dealing with a matter of political life and death. The events are well known: the conviction of the original Watergate burglars; the decision of their leader to implicate hitherto untouched administration figures; an investigation conducted by a special Senate committee headed by Sam Ervin of North Carolina; indictments of more administration figures; the resignations of FBI director L. Patrick Gray and Attorney General Richard Kleindienst; the appointment of Archibald Cox as special prosecutor; the discovery that the president had taped most of his confidential conversations; the inexorable push to make the tapes public; the Saturday Night Massacre firing of Cox and others in October, 1973; the conviction of various administration officials on charges such as perjury and obstruction of justice; continued pressure from a new special prosecutor, Leon Jaworski; the issuance of some "sanitized" transcripts; court orders mandating full release of the tapes. Along the way, there also occurred the forced resignation of Vice-President Agnew under charges of taking illegal payoffs, an Internal Revenue Service assessment against the president for back taxes, and the revelation that some of the Watergate burglars had been part of a White House "plumbers" unit that had engaged in other illegal activities. During the last week of July 1974, the House Judiciary Committee recommended impeachment. A few days later, Nixon was forced by his own angry lawyers to release the "smoking gun" transcript of June 23, 1972, proving conclusively that the president long had known about cover-up efforts. On August 8, 1974, he became the first chief executive in American history to resign from office.

As with any series of events played out on the level of epic human drama, Watergate was utterly fascinating in itself—for its human interest, its complexity, and its alteration of the course of American history. Beyond the public view of powerful men parading from the Senate committee rooms to the courtrooms and thence to public disgrace, however, there remain compelling questions. How could Watergate have happened in the first place? And how could a trivial surreptitious entry about which a president almost certainly had no advance knowledge be allowed to become a national obsession for nearly a year and a half? And how could this obsession bring down a leader who had been elected by overwhelming majorities? The answers appear to reside within Richard Nixon—in his own insecure, meanspirited personality and the responses it aroused.

1. According to the passage, the action initially responsible for the downfall of President Nixon was

   (A) the Bay of Pigs
   (B) the Watergate break-in
   (C) the taping of confidential conversations
   (D) the hiring of E. Howard Hunt
   (E) the firing of the independent prosecutor

2. The term "smoking gun," as used in the passage, implies

(A) information which led to discovery of the break-in
(B) information which led to resignation of the FBI director
(C) the weapon used by Nixon to kill himself
(D) information which proved Nixon's culpability
(E) information which implicated Nixon's participation in the break-in

3. The name of the *second* special prosecutor was

(A) Leon Jaworski
(B) L. Patrick Gray
(C) Archibald Cox
(D) Sam Ervin
(E) Spiro Agnew

4. The purpose of the initial break-in at the Watergate Hotel was to

(A) spy on the Democrats
(B) plant an agent at the Democratic National Convention
(C) steal documentation outlining the Democrats plans for the upcoming election
(D) assassinate George McGovern, the Democratic candidate
(E) plant listening devices

5. The special senate committee was headed by

(A) Archibald Cox
(B) Sam Ervin
(C) G. Gordon Liddy
(D) L. Patrick Gray
(E) Richard Kleindienst

6. Which of the following, if true, most supports the author's position?

(A) The FBI was later cleared of any complicity in covering up the break-in.
(B) President Gerald Ford subsequently pardoned Richard Nixon.
(C) Richard Nixon grew up insecure and unsure of his position in life.
(D) Pat Nixon, Richard's wife, was a Rhodes scholar.
(E) Archibald Cox later suggested that he was fired because he was discovering the truth.

7. Who, according to the passage, was most responsible for the downfall of President Nixon?

   (A) E. Howard Hunt
   (B) G. Gordon Liddy
   (C) John Mitchell
   (D) Spiro Agnew
   (E) Richard Nixon

8. Which member of the Nixon advisers was integral in the planning of the Bay of Pigs invasion?

   (A) Richard Kleindienst
   (B) G. Gordon Liddy
   (C) Sam Ervin
   (D) E. Howard Hunt
   (E) L. Patrick Gray

9. The title *Breach of Faith* refers to

   (A) the disregard of the President for the electorate
   (B) the disregard of the prosecutors for the President
   (C) the disregard of members of the cabinet for the President
   (D) the disregard of the Republican party for the Democratic party
   (E) All of the above

10. The "Saturday Night Massacre" mentioned in the passage refers to

   (A) the resignation of major cabinet officials in the face of potential prosecution
   (B) the firing of major cabinet officials in the face of potential prosecution
   (C) the firing of Archibald Cox and the special prosecutors
   (D) the firing of Leon Jaworski and the special prosecutors
   (E) the resignation of L. Patrick Gray and Richard Kleindienst in the face of potential prosecution

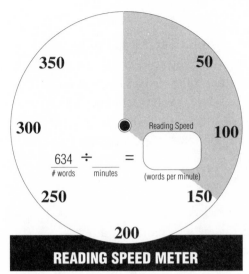

Calculate your reading speed using the following formula. First, mark down how long it took you, in minutes, to read the passage (if it took you 2 minutes, 15 seconds, then it took you 2.25 minutes). Divide the number of words in the passage by that number. This is your reading speed in words per minute. For example, there are 634 words in this passage. If it took you 3 minutes to read the entire selection, then divide 634 by 3. This would result in a reading speed of 211 w.p.m.

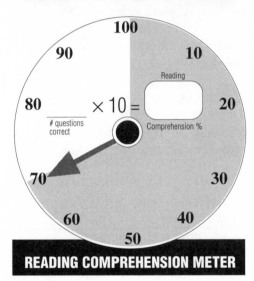

Calculate your comprehension rate using the following formula. Multiply the number of questions you answered correctly by 10. That is your comprehension percentage. You want to keep your percentage above 70 percent for any type of reading. Below that, you start losing important information presented in the passages.

KEEP YOUR COOL

A final note on reading comprehension. The reason most people
do poorly on reading passages has nothing to do with their reading
speed. It has to do with the way they take tests. They panic,
reread things, jump around the passage, sweat, and concentrate on
the feeling that they are getting beat up on a test. We have some
good advice for people who panic on tests, especially on tests with
reading passages: DON'T DO IT.

THINGS TO TAKE WITH YOU

1. It's not one thought that makes you panic on a test—
    it's an uncontrolled rush of many thoughts. If you
    find yourself starting to think about panicking, find
    some easy, common thing to take your mind off the
    problem. It's worth the ten seconds it takes to count
    the number of fingers on your hand, take a deep breath,
    and come back to the passage.

2. If you find a couple of questions you can't answer
    in a row, don't panic. That happens to everyone.
    Move on to other questions and come back to them
    later. The passage isn't going to change. Be careful
    and accurate.

3. If the passage is so dull you can't bear to look at
    it, take heart. It's like that for everyone. By pre-
    reading and mini-mapping, you have a huge advantage
    over everyone else in the room. That should make
    you happy, not panicked.

4. If all else fails, stab yourself in the leg with your
    pencil. Blame the person who always gets the highest
    grades—you'll go to the hospital, but she'll go to
    the principal's office and get a zero on the test.
    Everyone else will thank you, although it'll hurt like
    hell [This is merely a joke—self mutilation will never
    help you read faster or more efficiently, nor will it
    make you cooler or impress your friends].

Reading Racetrack #14

Read the following passage and answer the questions after it to find your speed and comprehension levels. Time yourself on a watch with a second hand. Time only the reading portion of the exercise, not the question portion. Then calculate your reading speed and comprehension level, using the formulas at the end of the questions.

October 31

A week ago I laughed myself silly over Macy's "Elf Wanted" ad; this afternoon I sat in the SantaLand office and was told, "Congratulations, Mr. Sedaris, you're an elf."

In order to become an elf I had to fill out ten pages of forms, take a multiple-choice personality test, undergo two interviews, and submit urine for a drug test. The first interview was general, designed to eliminate the obvious sociopaths. During the second interview we were asked why we wanted to be elves, which, when you think about it, is a fairly tough question. When the woman next to me, a former waitress in her late twenties, answered, she put question marks after everything she said. "I really want to be an elf? Because I think it's really about acting? And before this I worked in a restaurant? Which was owned by this really wonderful woman who had a dream to open a restaurant? And it made me think that it's like, really, really important? To have a dream?"

I told the interviewers that I wanted to be an elf because it was the most ridiculous thing I had ever heard of. I figured that for once in my life I would be completely honest and see how far it got me. I also failed the drug test. But they hired me anyway. Honesty had nothing to do with it. They hired me because I am five feet five inches tall.

November 19

Today we began our elf training. We learned the name of the various elf positions. You can be, for example, an "Oh, my God!" elf and stand at the corner near the escalator. People arrive, see the long line around the corner, and say, "Oh, my God!"; your job is to tell them that it won't take more than an hour to see Santa.

You can be an Entrance Elf, a Watercooler Elf, a Bridge Elf, Train Elf, Maze Elf, Island Elf, Magic-Window Elf, Emergency-Exit Elf, Counter Elf, Magic-Tree Elf, Pointer Elf, Santa Elf, Photo Elf, Usher Elf, Cash-Register Elf, or Exit Elf. We were given a demonstration of the various positions, acted out by returning elves who were so "on stage"

and goofy that it made me a little sick to my stomach. I
didn't know that I could look anyone in the eye and exclaim,
"Oh, my goodness, I think I see Santa!" or, "Can you close
your eyes and make a very special Christmas wish!" It makes
one's mouth hurt to speak with such forced merriment. It
embarrasses me to hear people talk this way. I prefer being
frank with children. I'm more likely to say, "You must be
exhausted" or, "I know a lot of people who would kill for
that little waistline of yours."

I am afraid I won't be able to provide the enthusiasm
Santa is asking for. I think I'll be a low-key sort of elf.

November 21
My costume is green. I wear green velvet knickers, a yellow
turtleneck, a forest-green velvet smock, and a perky little
hat decorated with spangles. This is my work uniform.

Today was elf dress rehearsal. I worked as a Santa Elf
for house number two. A Santa Elf greets children at the
Magic Tree and leads them to Santa's house. When you work
as a Santa Elf you have to go by your elf name. My elf
name is Crumpet. The other Santa Elves have names like
Jingle and Frosty. They take the children by the hand and
squeal with forced delight. They sing and prance and behave
like cartoon characters come to life. They frighten me.

1. The tone of the author is best described as

   (A) jocular
   (B) ironic
   (C) desperate
   (D) angry
   (E) pedantic

2. The author's "elf name" is

   (A) Creamy
   (B) Dreamboat
   (C) Strumpet
   (D) Trumpet
   (E) Crumpet

3. According to the passage, what was the author's reason for wanting to be an elf?

   (A) The health benefits.
   (B) He wanted to open a restaurant.
   (C) He still believed in Santa.
   (D) He needed the money.
   (E) He thought it the most ridiculous job in the
       world.

4. According to the passage, why was he chosen to be an elf by management?

   (A) He was honest.
   (B) He loved Christmas.
   (C) He passed the drug test.
   (D) He was the right physical type.
   (E) His had the shoes already.

5. All of the following are elf positions at Macy's EXCEPT

   (A) Escalator Elf
   (B) Emergency-Exit Elf
   (C) Watercooler Elf
   (D) Cash Register Elf
   (E) Train Elf

6. The job the author received was

   (A) Magic-Window Elf
   (B) Santa Elf
   (C) Maze Elf
   (D) Island Elf
   (E) Pointer Elf

7. The author's knickers were made out of

   (A) forest green
   (B) velvet yellow
   (C) velvet green
   (D) red and green
   (E) spangled green

8. The author can best be described as

   (A) a spunky elf
   (B) a low-key elf
   (C) an enthusiastic elf
   (D) an unenthusiastic elf
   (E) a frightened elf

9. Why did the woman next to the author at his second interview want to be an elf?

(A) She loved children.
(B) She loved Christmas.
(C) She was a flake.
(D) She was fired from her restaurant.
(E) She never really answered the question.

10. This piece would most likely be found in

(A) a diary
(B) a newspaper article
(C) a textbook
(D) a gossip column
(E) a novel

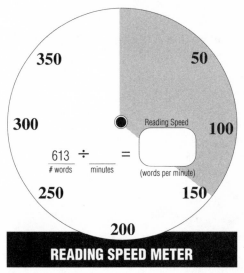

Calculate your reading speed using the following formula. First, mark down how long it took you, in minutes, to read the passage (if it took you 2 minutes, 15 seconds, then it took you 2.25 minutes). Divide the number of words in the passage by that number. This is your reading speed in words per minute. For example, there are 613 words in this passage. If it took you 3 minutes to read the entire selection, then divide 613 by 3. This would result in a reading speed of 204 w.p.m.

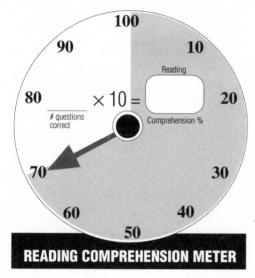

Calculate your comprehension rate using the following formula. Multiply the number of questions you answered correctly by 10. That is your comprehension percentage. You want to keep your percentage above 70 percent for any type of reading. Below that, you start losing important information presented in the passages.

CHAPTER 10

Poetry, Plays and Point-of-View

"I've written some poetry I don't understand myself."

—Carl Sandburg

I t's not easy to make stories of love, betrayal, violence, sex and greed uninteresting, but it can be done. When it happens, you feel like you've been had. That's the way most people feel about poetry and plays. They pick up a collection of poetry or a volume of Shakespeare and think "Hey, words on a page, how difficult can it be?" An hour later, that same book slaps up against the wall, thrown in frustration. Poetry and drama can be very *very* difficult. Unless you know a few ways to make them more accessible, these books can end up propping up that table with the uneven legs rather than on your bookshelf.

Why Is This Stuff So Strange?

Poetry and plays are literary forms in which people manipulate language to achieve a desired effect. People choose what form their writing takes and use the form that best fits what they are trying to say. Think of it like this: when a painter comes up with an image, he can do a bunch of things with it:

> He can paint it on a canvas.
> He can paint it on a billboard.
> He can paint it on his fingernails.
> He can design it on a computer.
> He can tattoo it across his chest.
> He can tattoo it across another person's chest.
> He can sketch it with charcoal.
> He can draw it on a sandy beach with his finger.
> He can shave it into his head.
> He can come to your house and spray-paint it on your sister.
> And so on...

The point is that the artist will achieve very different responses from people depending on how he chooses to present his image. Prose (writing in narrative form, usually in paragraphs and sentences) is the most common form of writing, just as canvas is the most common material on which to paint. It is safe, familiar and recognizable. Other means yield different results.

WHY POETRY?

Why would someone choose poetry? Because her concept, her idea, is best expressed through that form. You can tell a story, show characters, explain a conflict, do anything you can also do in prose, and then some. There are three additional things that you can use when you write a poem.

> **One**—*the words can take a shape.* In prose, you can tell the same thing in many different ways, but when someone looks at it on the page, they can't get an image, like words in the shape of a "V," or words which trail off like a person running out of words. This does not mean that all poetry uses its shape on a page to convey an idea. This just means that you should be aware and take a look. Some poetry is inherently visual.

> **Two**—*poetry is inherently oral.* It is a spoken medium. The *sounds* which emerge are sometimes as important as the exact words themselves. This doesn't mean just rhyme, although that can be a big part of it. Meter, rhythm, pauses, and timing all contribute to the feelings a poem can evoke. This does not mean you need to know what a caesura is, or what iambic pentameter specifically means. You just have to be aware of the cadence and the sound of the language. If you think you have no ear for sound and meaning, think of a song you like. The lyrics and the way they go together are just another form of poetry. Jon Bon Jovi may not win the Nobel Prize for literature, but it's the same idea.

> **Three**—*poetry removes much of the excess language of prose.* Poetry is a condensed form. Every phrase, every word, every syllable, and every punctuation mark is intentional, with meaning and a relationship to those around it. They are there for a reason. Though you might not guess it from the personality of most poets, poetry is all business, and anything that doesn't work for the poem is discarded. If something jumps

out at you as unusual, or a strange way of writing or punctuating, stop and ask yourself, "What is this doing? Why is this here?" Poetry is concentrated meaning. Everything in it contributes.

Now that you know all of this, reading poetry becomes a snap. If people write poems with these three things in mind, you should read poems with these three things in mind. Ask yourself "What does it look like? Is there a shape on the page? Or has the person decided to use an old form, referring to some earlier time?" Next, read the poem out loud. What does it sound like? How do the words run together? Where are there pauses? What effect do they have? Finally, look at the precise meaning of all the words. Much in the way that we theme-marked earlier, look for repeated or similar words. They usually spell out an underlying theme of the poem.

The following is a poem by e.e. cummings (no, that is not a typo—he didn't capitalize his initials). He was a complicated and brilliant poet who is frequently misread and misunderstood. His poems appear (at first) strange and inaccessible. But by asking questions about his poem, you'll find that it's not so difficult after all. We'll take this one apart for you, so don't tax your brain too much yet. Just see how we dissect it.

into the strenuous briefness
Life:
handorgans and April
darkness, friends

i charge laughing.
Into the hair-thin tints
of yellow dawn,
into the women-colored twilight

i smilingly
glide.   I
into the big vermilion departure
swim, sayingly;

(Do you think?) the
i do, world
is probably made
of roses & hello:

(of solongs and, ashes)

QUESTION 1: WHAT DOES IT LOOK LIKE ON THE PAGE?

There are four paragraphs, and it ends in a single line in a parentheses. It starts with April (spring) and life, and it ends with ashes (death). What famous thing are there four of? How about the four seasons, about the movement from spring to winter? It doesn't have to be certain—it just has to make sense.

QUESTION 2: WHAT DOES IT SOUND LIKE?

It sounds like someone reminiscing about their life. The parenthetical statements are to be read like private thoughts.   The middle passages contain colors, and are sensual descriptions, even the words he uses to describe abandon and sensuality. Those vowel sounds are used to slip you from one word to the next, just in the way the seasons slip from one to the next with no clear ending or beginning. cummings is using language and sound to move you through an experience.

QUESTION 3: HOW IS THE LANGUAGE AND STRUCTURE DIFFERENT FROM NORMAL PROSE?

By asking the third question, you begin to wonder about cummings' strange fourth paragraph (actually, they call each block of words a stanza, but we don't want to get into *Poetry Smart*). Look, you're confused, it doesn't seem to make any sense. Grammatically, it doesn't. Apply your new knowledge to break cummings' code.

Break up what he says into clauses. One clause should read 'Do you think the world is probably made of roses and hello'— meaning, do you think life is about love and beginnings (roses and hello)? His answer is 'i do,' but why isn't 'i do' at the end of the poem? Because there is one end which follows his beliefs, and that is the inevitability "(of solongs and, ashes)"—of death.

Now, only e.e. cummings really knew for sure what he meant here, and even then, maybe not. But you should use everything given to you and believe everything is meaningful. Don't be afraid to take your best guess. You may be off, but that's certainly not a crime, as long as you back it up. All interpretation of poetry is a "best guess." There is no shame in voicing your ideas without certainty. This is not to say that every interpretation is entirely accurate. If we said the above poem was about aliens from the planet Zeldar, we would most likely be wrong. If we said it was about World War II, we would be wrong in a different way. If we said it was about courage and love in the face of inevitable demise, we would probably be right. But, within all the possible arguments, there is no single right interpretation. Just make sure that the language, the sound, the punctuation, and, if applicable, the shape all lead to your conclusion.

EXERCISE #20

Here's a poem for you to take apart on your own. There are no questions afterwards, mainly because there are no right answers (but we did include a brief analysis in Appendix B that you can compare to your own). A little background on the author, Sylvia Plath: she was emotionally troubled, exceptional with language, married to another famous poet, and, after years of psychological turmoil, she committed suicide.

> **Words**
> Axes
> After whose stroke the wood rings,
> And the echoes!
> Echoes traveling.
> Off from the center like horses.
>
> The sap
> Wells like tears, like the
> Water striving
> To re-establish its mirror
> Over the rock
>
> That drops and turns,
> A white skull,
> Eaten by wheaty greens.
> Years later I
> Encounter them on the road—
>
> Words dry and riderless,
> The indefatigable hoof-taps
> While
> From the bottom of the pool, fixed stars
> Govern a life.

THE PLAY'S THE THING

What is a play meant to be? It is meant to be performed, just as a score of music isn't meant to be read, but performed. It relies on people to bring it to life. So if you're reading a play, and it seems tough to follow, tough to read, that's O.K. Try reading it out loud. Sure, your roommates or your parents will think you're a lunatic. But who cares? You'll understand the play better than they will, and who knows, maybe you are destined for stardom, like Burt Reynolds or Adriane Barbeau. Remember that this method will take longer, and that you may lose your voice and have to buy some throat lozenges. We recommend Luden's, cherry-flavored if they have it. Otherwise, honey-lemon will do.

WHY PLAYS?

A playwright writes for actors. Keeping this in mind, each character should be a real, fleshed-out person. Try to picture what you think each character looks like, where they are, and what they wear. This may help you get beyond some dialogue you don't particularly like.

If you can find out the basic plot of the play before you pick it up, do that. Plays are about language and character. If you're studying a play, the plot is the skeleton that allows development of character and use of language. Even in a play like *Deathtrap*, which relies on suprises and trickery, the state of mind of each character is more important than the plot. Or how about the classics? Let's look at *Hamlet*. A kid sees his father's ghost claim he was murdered by his mother's new husband. The kid drives them nuts so they pay for their action, and he's nuts too. Or maybe not. And that's the point. Oh, and he's the prince of Denmark. That's it. Is that why this play is a classic? Absolutely not. It's because of the language, and the extremes to which this situation drives the characters.

If you have the opportunity to see a play in addition to reading it (even if you have to rent the Mel Gibson version) see it. Keep in mind that Hollywood and your local theater *always* change at least one important thing, so you shouldn't rely solely on seeing a play to get all you can out of it. The reason you should see a play is because it makes the words come alive. They move from the page to a character's mouth. Even if you go see Shakespeare performed in French, you miss a lot of the language, but you can still pick out the characters and understand the action.

"Read the book!" "See the movie!"

Drawing by Levin; © 1993 The New Yorker Magazine, Inc.

THE ARC OF TRIUMPH

Plays generally (but not always—particularly from 1950 on) progress in an arc. What do we mean by arc? Basically, plays begin with a given situation, and end with a modified situation. The play is about how they got from beginning to end, about what caused the change. The arc of the play, then, is that movement, from beginning, through conflict or change, to the end. If you're reading a book and you're pressed for time, you can read the first and last chapters to see this kind of change, and figure out the rest. In a play, its the change itself that is the important thing. So you must understand the specifics. Why did things occur? How did the change occur? Who was for it? Who was against it? Who is affected by it?

A good way to look at a play is to identify the following parts (don't worry if every play doesn't contain all these parts—they will have some of them):

The Prologue—this is what is considered "normal life" for the characters. It is intended give you a snapshot of each character and quickly identify who they are and what their situation is.

The Conflict—this is what is going to change the normal life of the characters presented. It can be the arrival of another character, the death of a character, an inheritance, a lawsuit, a robbery, even a ghost— almost anything that affects their way of life.

The Climax—this is where the conflict is resolved in one way or another. Climax doesn't have to be the most dramatic moment in the play—it just has to be the moment after which nothing is the same again. In smash-up movies, the climax is usually the big car-chase at the end. In plays, the climax can be anytime the world is changed. In *King Lear*, for example, the climax comes right at the beginning when he divides his kingdom. The rest is all. . .

The Epilogue—this is the new state of the world after the climax. It could be disastrous. It could be a change for the better (but not usually). The primary message of a play is usually found in comparing the epilogue to the prologue. Is the world better? Is the world worse? And do the characters have a future or not?

When you're reading a play, you should go through the text and find these spots. These sections are your most useful signposts. Use them to make the text more understandable and to enjoy the language more.

DON'T LET IT GET TO YOU

What if the play still bores you to tears? Find a way in through the characters. In a normal book, the author usually tries to present to you one character in as much full and imagined detail as possible. When the author tries to show you more characters, and develop them fully, the book can become overcrowded. A playwright, on the other hand, takes on every character in the play and tries to make each one as real and fully imagined as possible. Otherwise, the actors would have no idea how to perform each part. If the action doesn't compel you, the characters might.

One thing to keep in mind—because a playwright can't use lengthy descriptions and techniques of fiction, the playwright makes the language do all the work. Shakespeare doesn't have any stage directions, but it's crystal clear what everyone is supposed to be doing—his language makes it that way. By paying attention to the language, specifically what is said and how it is said, you can figure out most anything about a play.

Narrative Point of View

When you're arguing with someone, and you have different opinions, you might say: "Well, that's just your point of view." Literally, point of view is "from where you see." This is an issue in real life (as your parents will attest) and in literature.

Narrative point of view is the answer to the question "whose eyes are we seeing through?" Often, this is a clue to how much you can trust the work, and how close you are supposed to be to the work. Point of view allows you to look past what people say to how they say it.

Exercise #21

Read the following two statements, and decide which character is more trustworthy.

> I lie all the time. I cheat on my taxes. I call in sick all the time. I pretend to throw my dog sticks, just to see him start dashing to chase them. I just want a moment's peace, and I want a little fairness. The government takes all my money away, so I cheat them. My boss pays me slave wages, so I lie to him. My dog barks all night, so I give him a little grief. I take care of my house, my kids, my car. I don't rob anyone, I don't hurt anyone. I'm just an average Joe, trying to make a life.

or

> John believed himself to be an honest man. He never lied
> to his wife; she just never asked him if he was having an
> affair. After all, he thought, he worked hard, and provided
> well. So what if he dabbled a little in extramarital bliss?
> It's not like he didn't love his wife. He just had grown
> bored with her. He felt he was only being honest with himself
> by admitting he needed another. And besides, how was it
> hurting her? She didn't know.

Both of these characters show themselves to be liars. But which
one do you trust (and like) more? The first character is forthcoming
with his faults, is more honest with himself, and gives you a chance
to identify with him. The second character is presented more distantly,
shows rampant hypocrisy, and makes you want to smack him. Here,
point of view is working to establish trust and distrust.

Point of view determines the relationship between the narrator
(the tone and voice of the character the story is about) and the reader
(you). It is important to notice the point of view of every narrator.
Here is a quick list of the most common points of view and their
characteristics:

> **First Person**—This point of view can be identified
> by the use of the first person pronoun, "I." It is
> used to bring you close to a narrator, to let you into
> his or her thoughts, and to identify you with the
> narrator. It doesn't mean they are always telling you
> the truth, though. It just tells you how close you
> are going to be to them throughout the book.

> **Second Person**—This point of view is identified by
> its use of the second person pronoun, "you." It works
> like the first person narration, because it sounds like
> someone is telling you a story about yourself, but
> it is a way of distancing, like when a person tells
> a really painful story about themselves. They can't
> admit that they are talking about themselves.

> **Third Person**—This is characterized by the pronouns
> "he" and "she," with no "I" or "you." This lends
> some objectivity to a story, to make it appear that
> the story is not on anyone's side or from anyone's
> point of view. Don't be fooled. A story always has
> a point of view.

Third Person Intimate—This is also characterized by the pronouns "he" and "she," with no "I" or "you," but it also allows you to hear the thoughts and the feelings of one of the characters. It is meant to combine the attempted objectivity of normal third person with the closeness of first person. Sometimes it works. Sometimes it doesn't. But be aware of what the author is trying to do, if she or he uses it.

Omniscient Narrator—All rules are off. The narrator knows everyone's thoughts, everyone's feelings and can dip into anyone's head at any time. Stephen Crane's "The Open Boat" starts off with the line "None of them knew the color of the sky." This tells you that the narrator can see into everyone's head, and even know things that they themselves do not know. It makes the narrator very apparent and active in the story. Often, it is done poorly (not by Stephen Crane, though).

Don't confuse the author with the narrator! They are two separate people. Sometimes the narrator will claim to be the author, like the character Humbert Humbert in *Lolita*. Don't trust them. The real author of *Lolita*, Vladimir Nabokov, lies behind everything Humbert Humbert writes. It's like saying you love the actor Patrick Swayze because the *character* he played in *Ghost* was so darn intelligent! A writer made that character. And Patrick, in real life, might be quite a different fellow indeed. Who knows? The point is, a character and an author (or actor) should be seen as independent of each other. To read as smart as you can, you should be sure to have that distinction clear in your mind.

CHAPTER 11

Everything You Wanted to Know About Reading

(but Were Afraid to Ask)

"The greatest masterpiece in literature is only a dictionary out of order."

—Jean Cocteau

This chapter will answer some commonly-asked questions about reading. It will also answer some not-so-common, but important questions; the kind of things you felt you shouldn't ask your teachers because you'd be embarrassed. Some of the answers, too, are things your teacher or your boss will never tell you.

Q: **What should I do if a book is really dull? I mean absolute snooze-central boring. I mean this book is so boring it would put a hyperactive coffee addict to sleep.**

A: Read it. As tough as any book is, there has to be a reason for reading it and a way into it. To make it more interesting, try to find out some stuff about the author, or learn some facts about the literary movement this book fits into. If it's a textbook, try to figure some common-sense examples which will help you visualize it. If it tells a story, try and find some part of the story you can relate to your own life. Another good technique is to pick a fight with the author. Looking for flaws in an argument can be interesting and engrossing, and it can keep your eyes on the page long after your friends are deep asleep.

Q: **What about books that are translated? Are all copies the same?**

A: Nope. If one translation seems to suck, or be lacking something, try to find another translator. Often a beautiful work of art will be made into hamburger helper by a lazy translator. A good way to determine the quality of your translation is to look at the back of the book. Most good translations will put rave quotations on the back not about the original author, but about the translation itself. If the back blurbs only talk about a guy who has been dead for fourhundred years, then the translation is probably not much to speak of. Another thing to keep in mind is that if your translation is from over fifty years ago, the translated language may be just as inaccessible to you as a lousy translation. You may need a more recent translation.

Q: **What if after reading carefully, I don't get something. Should I spend even more time on it or should I move on?**

A: The general rule is, try to find a way for it to make sense to you. If you can't, and you want to throw the book into the trash compactor, just mark the section and continue reading. Whether it's a textbook, a business plan, or an article that interests you, don't let lack of comprehension of one part discourage you from reading the other parts. Don't stop reading, but make a list, and then, the next day, when you are around other people who have read the same thing, ask a friend to explain to you the section you didn't get, or look up the words. There is a popular misconception that asking questions means you're not smart, or that you didn't do your work carefully. Teachers, managers, and other people who used to be in your position know better: people who ask smart questions, who ask about what they don't understand, and learn it, will make better managers, students, and leaders. Think about it: if your doctor didn't understand much about the heart, would you rather she asked about it while in school, or just skipped by, hoping that it wouldn't be on the final? Asking questions is vitally important to real learning.

Q: **I get headaches when I read too much. Is there anything I can do about it?**

A: There is a lot you can do to help yourself. First, check your lighting and your seating. You may find that you're sitting in an uncomfortable position anyway. Often, dim lighting makes your eyes work harder and read sections over. Also, back and neck pain can result in a headache. Would you work out and lift heavy weights for more than a few hours? So why do you think that it would be okay to do that with reading? Your eyes are guided by muscles, smaller and more precise than the ones you work out with. Don't overuse them—they'll be sore the next day. On the other hand, the more reading you do, the more "ripped" your eye muscles will be. And believe me, there's nothing more attractive than muscular eyes.

Q: **I hear about these speed-reading courses. Are they worth spending money on?**

A: It depends. They spend most of their time increasing the speed of your fixations and saccades—similar to the way the first few chapters of this book has. You've already improved most of your fixation and saccade speed, but with intensive training, most people can improve a bit more. These courses should have all sorts of machines and workbooks and reading passages. And when you're done, your speed should be up. But there's a downside—your comprehension will go down. There's no way around that relationship. The faster you read, the less detail you notice. The slower you read, the more detail you notice. In the end, it pays more to read smarter than to read faster.

Q: **I want to read more. What books should I buy? There are umpteen zillion books in a bookstore these days.**

A: Yes, there a lot of books. But you can use a few strategies to make sure you're not throwing money away. First, see if there is any author you like, and if they have any books you haven't read. Second, ask your friends. Try not to rely on the bookstore salesperson. A salesperson's job could be to get you to buy many expensive books, not one good one. And besides, the salesperson's taste might be different from yours. Third, read the back cover of any book you are interested in. You can't judge positively about a book by its cover, but you can certainly rule against it. If the book describes itself as "a slow passage through the molasses of memory of a tenth-century pheasant plucker, with many references in Latin and Greek to horticulture," you may want to pass. If, on the other hand, this kind of thing appeals to you, then you don't need *Reading Smart*. You need serious, professional help.

Q: **What about the "classics," like Shakespeare? Why do people love them so when they are so difficult to get through?**

A: Because they refer to some idea or some conflict which is timeless and important. Often the language, the references, the characters and the situations are far removed from what we are used to. Don't get all bothered by it. Whenever you read a classic, try to translate its story into modern terms. Take *Macbeth*, a play by this guy Bill Shakespeare. What's it about? It's about a guy who kills his boss so he can be the boss, except that once he kills the boss, everything that can go wrong goes wrong—he goes nuts, his power-hungry wife goes crazy from guilt, and he gets killed. Look at each of the characters and see how what each one says lets you know about him. Once you don't have to worry about plot, then the stuff doesn't seem so confusing anymore.

(One hint for getting through Shakespeare specifically is to read it quickly. Don't stop at every word. Don't read the word translations at the bottom of the page. Remember that it was meant to be spoken, and try to maintain that rhythm while reading it.)

Q: **I'm reading a textbook, and every other word is a mystery to me. I'm trying not to stop, but I'm just not sure what everything means.**

A: This happens to everyone. If the reading is for a field of study in which you don't plan to take any more courses, try and get the concepts down and at least be able to recognize the terms, even if you not sure exactly what they all mean. If you plan to study more in this field, make a vocabulary list. Improving vocabulary is a lifelong endeavor.

Q: **What if I can't tell the various types of reading apart?**

A: Use your best judgment. Most reading isn't going to scream "I'm journalistic!" or "I'm textbook-style!" You know what each technique is designed to do, so just ask yourself "would this technique work on this passage?" If you're still having problems, try all the combinations of techniques until you find the ones that work best. Don't lose your common sense—if you're reading a novel, but it begins to feel like journalism, it's O.K. to read it like a journalistic piece. Remember that authors use other styles all the time to illustrate their point.

Q: **What should I do if my eyes still stop on every word—if my fixation rate is roughly the same as when I started?**

A: Practice is the key here. Mark up a passage as we did in the opening chapters. Another good way to start seeing clusters of words is to take three different color highlighters and mark up a third of a line in one color, the middle of the line in a second color, and the end of the line in the third color. Your eye should start taking in each color in one sweep. A final way to train your eyes is to draw a heavy line where your fixation should be. Try and focus only on that line. Gradually, the words around that line should come into focus. As a last resort, read the passage first to get the meaning. Then work on clustering without worrying about comprehension or speed. Sometimes overthinking leads to overfixation.

CHAPTER 12

A Day at the Races

"'The time has come,' the Walrus said,
'To talk of many things.'"

—Lewis Carroll

I n this section, there will be five exercises on improving your fixations and saccades, and ten practice reading passages. Use these to reinforce everything that you've learned. If you find yourself reverting to your old habits, stop! It's not worth it! You'll get discouraged and your rates will drop. Adjust your speed to each passage, and keep your eyes fixed on the page. **Don't do all of these at once**. Use them periodically. The real test of how much improvement you can expect from this should become apparent in real life. Use your new skills on all your reading, from newspapers to business plans, from poetry to pulp fiction.

You understand what you read by identifying it with something you already know. So the best readers are those who know a lot of things. By reading, they learn more, and then reading becomes easier still for them. By improving the way you read, you make reading easier for yourself.

I. Exercise #22: Fixations

Move your eyes from dot to dot, using your peripheral vision to gather clusters of words with each fixation. If you find your eyes moving from word to word, you're not focusing on the dot. Stop and restart yourself at the beginning. At first, it should feel a bit awkward. As you get more practice, begin pushing yourself to a greater and greater speed.

When • Helen

he was • not

conversation • since

spices and • shoved me

to forgive • and forget

would be • no further

Uncle Bob • came over

have known • right there

suspect • his intentions.

I noticed his • other hand

smiling • the whole time

measuring • my waist to

he had in • store for me

sister's • forehead with

asked • about

my • favorite

the time • he

into the • hot oven.

so long as • she would

repeat episodes • of his

wearing his • cooking

that he • hadn't changed

As he shook • hands with

sprinkling a • pinch of salt

asking me • how much

see if I was • too big for

before dinner. • I objected

butter and • sprigs of

Uncle • Bob

subject • of

covered • me with

But I was • willing

promise • that there

earlier • problems.

apron and • I should

and that I • should

me to • apologize

above me. • He was

fat I had put • on and

a special • "suprise"

as he • basted my

parsely but it • was clear

he enjoyed • the preparation so I • nearly broke down and • cried with delight. I suggested we • broil her and this made • him so happy he did a • little jig in the middle of • the kitchen. How gleeful • he looked! It was • a difficult decision I • had to make. He had to • be sent away as soon • as possible. After I called the police, • I told my sister to • shower off the butter • (he had used too much) and • then I called the pizza • place. I reminded • them "no anchovies."

II. Exercise #23: Fixations

Move your eyes from dot to dot, using your peripheral vision to gather clusters of words with each fixation. If you find your eyes moving from word to word, you're not focusing on the dot. Stop and restart yourself at the beginning. At first, it should feel a bit awkward. As you get more practice, begin pushing yourself to a greater and greater speed.

Chester • Alexander   invented • the   left- • handed

crescent • wrench.   Some • might   say • that

a wrench • of any   type • can be   used by • any

person, • left-handed   right- • handed,   or • ambidextrous.

They • would be   correct. • There is   a history • of people

inventing • items which   are less • useful   than the • inventor

would have • thought.   Sara • Bleikoff, a   noted • pincushion

maker • invented the   pin • extractor, a   tweezer- • like item

that was • used to take   pins out • of pincushions without • using the

fingers. • People, it turned out, liked • to use their fingers • to take

pins out • of pincushions.   David Lumsby • invented   a moon • burn salve

to protect • against the harsh rays of the • full moon.   Needless to • say, there

were few • takers for his unusual • and unecessary product. • Have you heard of

a person getting • burned by the rays • of the moon?   Feeling • warm under the

moon?   Let's • mince words no more. • These people are lunatics. • Completely

insane. This is • not to discourage any • potential inventors out • there. On the

contrary, you • should be encouraged • that these people • were able to   find

funding for • their projects. But think • out your projects before • you proceed.

You will • save youself, and • others, years of needless • heartache.

III. Exercise #24: Fixations

Move your eyes from dot to dot, using your peripheral vision to gather clusters of words with each fixation. If you find your eyes moving from word to word, you're not focusing on the dot. Stop and restart yourself at the beginning. At first, it should feel a bit awkward. As you get more practice, begin pushing yourself to a greater and greater speed.

When • cooking	Italian • food	it is • important
to act • as	much • like	an Italian • as
you can. • You	should • first	have lots • of wine
handy; • although	the French • are	known • more for
their • wine, it	doesn't • matter.	Wine is • wonderful
with any • meal.	Second, you • should	read many • books
in Latin • while cooking.	Whereas • this may	not improve • your
cooking, you • will have	a greater • appreciation	of Italian • history and
Italian culture. • Third	you should • find some	good Italian • music,
preferrably • from after	the sixteenth • century	(those mandolins • always
give me a • headache).	If possible, • have a native	Italian in • the kitchen with
you. Ask • them about	where they • are from,	their family, • their friends.
The more • you know	of them • the closer	to • their cooking

you will be. • Ask them if they would • like to cook. As a matter • of fact, tell

them it is • an honor to be invited • to cook at another's house • in yourcountry.

Tell them it • will be a grave insult if • they don't start cooking • right away. Then

sit down, • pour yourself a big glass of • wine, put on some Italian • music, and

read your book • on Italy. You are now • enmeshed in the entire • Italian

experience. • Bon appetit!

IV. Exercise #25: Fixations

Move your eyes from dot to dot, using your peripheral vision to gather clusters of words with each fixation. If you find your eyes moving from word to word, you're not focusing on the dot. Stop and restart yourself at the beginning. At first, it should feel a bit awkward. As you get more practice, begin pushing yourself to a greater and greater speed.

Bank • robbery is not • the best • summer job a kid • can get but• it was the • only one my • uncle Rocco would • help me procure. • He introduced me to • Larry "Blue Eyes" • Dean, Stephen "Lefty" • Tubbs, and • Morris "the Accountant" • Kelger (Morris kept • track of how many • of us there were). • We watched the bank • for three days, carefully • noting when the bank • guards would be on break • and where to get the • best donuts. The police • asked us to move our • folding chairs from in • front of the bank on the • third day, because we • blocked people from • going in or out. The • next day we made our • move. Larry, unfortunately, • slept through his • alarm, and Steven thought • we were holding up the • donut store, so he went to • the wrong place. My Uncle • Rocco checked with Morris • to make sure there were • only two of us, but Morris • had gone on vacation. Rocco • also had forgotten our • weapons; I had a water • pistol and he brandished a • roll of Mentos menacingly. • We walked to the • bank, masks on, ready to tussle, • grab the loot then split, • but when we got • there, the doors were locked. • Apparently, my Uncle • was working off an • ancient calendar from the • tenth century—it was • Saturday. The bank was • closed. In disgust, Rocco walked • to the donut shop to get • some coffee where • he was promply robbed by • Stephen.

V. Exercise #26 : Fixations

Move your eyes from dot to dot, using your peripheral vision to gather clusters of words with each fixation. If you find your eyes moving from word to word, you're not focusing on the dot. Stop and restart yourself at the beginning. At first, it should feel a bit awkward. As you get more practice, begin pushing yourself to a greater and greater speed.

Learning • to   play • an   instrument • at

a young • age   can • increase   a • youngster's

self- • confidence,   sense • of pride,   and give • the youth

a feeling • of   accomplishment. • The   important • thing to

remember • is that   not every • instrument   is as • supportive and

nurturing, • for either   parent or • child. Imagine   your child, • enthusiastic

about your • choice of   a drum set • for him or   her. Imagine • that child

wanting to • practice at   three, four • or five in the   morning, • whenever the

inspiration • strikes. If   you want to • avoid   throttling • your teenager

or breaking • the electric guitar over • his head, choose a • quiet, personal

instrument which • will represent his • individuality. I recommend • purchasing

the triangle because • it can never get too • loud. Or a guitar with • no strings. At

last resort, buy • your child a box of • cotton balls and tell your • child the cotton

ball is the • instrument of the future—it • has to be blown on just • right to make

it sound wonderful. • Hopefully, your child • will hyperventilate and • pass out,

obviating the • need for any other instrument. • If not and your • child trades her

triangle for • a set of bongos, you can • wad the cotton balls • and stuff them in

your ears. • Even though your child • must grow, it doesn't • mean you must

grow • deaf.

READING RACETRACK DIRECTIONS

Read the following Reading Racetrack passages and answer the questions after them to find your speed and comprehension levels. Time yourself on a watch with a second hand. Time only the reading portion of the exercise, not the question portion. Then calculate your reading speed and comprehension level, using the following formulas:

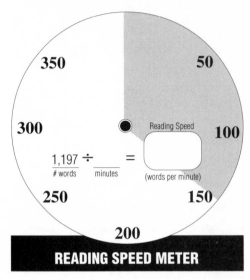

Calculate your reading speed using the following formula. First, mark down how long it took you, in minutes, to read the passage (if it took you 2 minutes, 15 seconds, then it took you 2.25 minutes). Divide the number of words in the passage by that number. This is your reading speed in words per minute. For example, there are 1,197 words in this passage. If it took you 8.5 minutes to read the entire selection, then divide 1,197 by 8.5. This would result in a reading speed of 141 w.p.m.

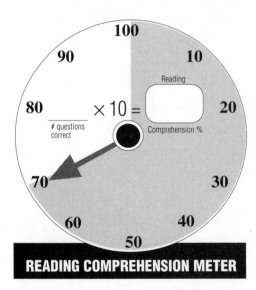

Calculate your comprehension rate using the following formula. Multiply the number of questions you answered correctly by 10. That is your comprehension percentage. You want to keep your percentage above 70 percent for any type of reading. Below that, you start losing important information presented in the passages.

READING RACETRACK #15

Don't Think: Write!

When we write, for whom do we write? Or as we would be more likely to ask, who do we write for?

It sounds like an easy question to answer, and in some ways it is. But when it is applied to the matter of fiction, the logical answer—that we write for a specific audience—does not work. At least not for me.

Each year I teach at one or more writers' workshops. I enjoy them for many reasons, not the least of which is the opportunity to meet other workshop leaders, often writers whose work I have long admired. Writing is a solitary profession, and a writers' conference gives us a chance to get together. Another reason I enjoy the workshops is that I am forced to articulate what I have learned about the techniques of the craft of fiction writing; it is easy to get forgetful and sloppy. Having to explain imagery, simile, metaphor, point of view, is a way to continue to teach myself as well as the people who have come to the workshop.

At one workshop, I talked, as usual, about all the hard work that precedes the writing of fiction. Often there is research to be done. For my Time Trilogy I had to immerse myself in the new physics: first, Einstein's theories of relativity and Planck's quantum theory for *A Wrinkle in Time;* then cellular biology and particle physics for *A Wind in the Door;* and astrophysics and non-linear theories of time for *A Swiftly Tilting Planet.* For *The Love Letters* I had to learn a great deal more about seventeenth-century Portuguese history than I needed or wanted to know, so that the small amount needed for the book would be accurate. Before, during, and after research, the writer needs to be thinking constantly about the characters, and the direction in which the novel seems to be moving.

Does the story have the Aristotelian beginning, middle and end? How do the events of the novel relate to me, personally, in my own journey through life? What are my own particular concerns at the time of writing, and how should they affect—or not affect—the story? When I actually sit down to write, I stop thinking. While I am writing, I am listening to the story; I am not listening to myself.

"But," a young woman in the class said in a horrified tone of voice, "my creative writing teacher says that we must keep the audience in mind at all times."

That is undoubtedly true for the scientists writing an article that is expected to be understood by people who have little or no scientific background. The writer will have to keep simplifying scientific language, explaining technical terms.

Keeping the audience in mind is probably valuable for reporting in newspapers and magazines. The reporter is writing for the average reader; language should be neither so bland as to be insulting, nor so technical as to demand special knowledge.

As for lawyers, I assume they have each other in mind at all times as they write. Certainly they don't have most of us in mind. Their grandiosity appalls me. In a movie contract, I was asked to grant the rights to my book to the producers, in perpetuity, throughout the universe. When I wrote in, "With the exception of Sagittarius and the Andromeda galaxy," it was accepted. Evidently the lawyers, who are writing to avoid litigation in a litigious world, did not anticipate a lawsuit from Sagittarius.

Of course I am being grossly unfair to many lawyers; I come from a family of fine lawyers. But the language used in a will or a contract is indeed a special language, and it is not aimed at the reader who enjoys stories, the reader of fiction.

Whom, then, does the writer of fiction write for? It is only a partial truth to say that I write for myself, out of my own need, asking, whether I realize it or not, the questions I am asking in my own life.

A truer answer is that I write for the book.

"But why do you write for children?" I am often asked.

And I answer truthfully that I don't. I haven't been a child for a long time, and if what I write doesn't appeal to me, at my age, it isn't likely to appeal to a child. I hope I will never lose the child within me, who has not lost her sense of wonder, of awe, of laughter. But I am not a child; I am a grown woman, learning about maturity as I move on in chronology.

A teacher, in introducing me to a class of seventh graders, said, "Miss L'Engle has made it in the children's field, and she is now trying to break into the adult market."

I felt that I had better not explain to this teacher that I had no desire to break into the adult market and see my fiction in "adult bookstores." I am not interested in writing pornography. I did explain that my first several books were regular trade novels, which means that they were marketed for a general audience, not for children. And I explained that when I have a book that I think will be too difficult for a general audience, then we will market it as a juvenile book. It is a great mistake to think that children are not capable of understanding difficult concepts in science or philosophy.

A book that has a young protagonist will likely be marketed as a children's book, regardless of content. Since adolescents are usually more willing than their elders to ask difficult questions, and to accept the fact that the questions don't have nice, tidy answers but lead on to more difficult questions, approximately half of my books have young protagonists. But while I am writing, I am not thinking of any audience at all. I am not even thinking about myself. I am thinking about the book.

This does not imply anything esoteric. I do not pick up the pen and expect it to guide my hand, or put my fingers on the keyboard of the typewriter and expect the work to be done automatically. It is work. But it is focused work, and the focus is on the story, not on anything else.

An example of the kind of focus I mean is a good doctor. The good doctor listens to the patient, truly listens, to what the patient says, does not say, is afraid to say, to body language, to everything that may give a clue as to what is wrong. The good doctor is so fully focused on the patient that personal self-consciousness has vanished. Such focused listening does not make the doctor—or any of the rest of us—less ourselves. In fact, such focused listening makes us more ourselves.

The same thing is true in listening to a story as we write it. It does not make us any less writers, this strange fact that we do not think about writing as we are writing; it makes us more writers.

1. What profession does the author of the passage liken to being a good writer?

    (A) Lawyer
    (B) Astronaut
    (C) Therapist
    (D) Doctor
    (E) Physicist

2. Which of the following adjectives does the author use to characterize the profession of writing?

    (A) Rigid
    (B) Solitary
    (C) Childish
    (D) Noble
    (E) Sloppy

3. A book written by the author of the above passage is called

   (A) *A Wrinkle in Space*
   (B) *The Wind in Time*
   (C) *A Door in Time*
   (D) *A Swiftly Tilting Universe*
   (E) *The Love Letters*

4. A "trade novel," as defined in the passage above, is

   (A) one specifically written for children
   (B) one written for a specific trade
   (C) one marketed for children
   (D) one marketed for a specific trade.
   (E) one marketed for a general audience.

5. According to the passage, all of the following are things the author explains to her creative writing classes EXCEPT

   (A) simile
   (B) metaphor
   (C) imagery
   (D) resonance
   (E) point of view

6. The author has had to resist the label of being a(n)

   (A) children's author
   (B) adult author
   (C) trade author
   (D) popular author
   (E) esoteric author

7. The author would most likely DISAGREE with which of the following statements:

   (A) Writing should be performed with the work in mind, not the audience.
   (B) Teaching writing can be a valuable experience for the teacher.
   (C) Young protagonists are often mistakenly viewed as childish.
   (D) Difficult concepts should be written about with adults in mind, not children.
   (E) When one is writing well, the work will be focused.

8. Her annotation of the contract selling her rights, excluding those rights in Sagittarius and the Andromeda Galaxy, was meant to be

   (A) detached
   (B) ironic
   (C) angered
   (D) political
   (E) sophomoric

9. For whom does the author write?

   (A) The work
   (B) Her audience
   (C) Her protagonists
   (D) Her children
   (E) Children of all countries

10. Which of the following summarizes the main point of the passage?

    (A) Work which contains children should not be assumed to be juvenile literature.
    (B) Whereas certain types of writers write for an audience, the fiction writer should write for the work.
    (C) Whereas certain types of writers write for an audience, the journalistic writer should write for the work.
    (D) Whereas certain doctors who listen are good, so are certain writers who listen to the story in their heads.
    (E) To assume that writing is an easy task is false.

READING RACETRACK #15 METERS

For directions on how to fill out your meters, see page 198.

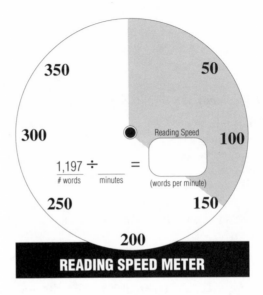

READING SPEED METER

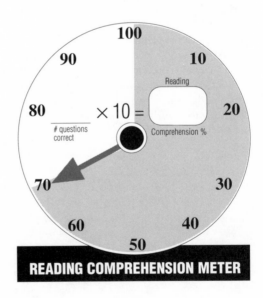

READING COMPREHENSION METER

Reading Racetrack #16

Read the following passage and answer the questions after it to find your speed and comprehension levels. Time yourself on a watch with a second hand. Time only the reading portion of the exercise, not the question portion. Then calculate your reading speed and comprehension level, using the formulas at the end of the questions.

To the red country and part of the gray country of Oklahoma, the last rains came gently, and they did not cut the scarred earth. The plows crossed and recrossed the rivulet marks. The last rains lifted the corn quickly and scattered weed colonies and grass along the sides of the roads so that the gray country and the dark red country began to disappear under a green cover. In the last part of May the sky grew pale and the clouds that had hung in high puffs for so long in the spring were dissipated. The sun flared down on the growing corn day after day until a line of brown spread along the edge of each green bayonet. The clouds appeared, and went away, and in a while they did not try any more. The weeds grew darker green to protect themselves, and they did not spread anymore. The surface of the earth crusted, a thin hard crust, and as the sky became pale, so the earth became pale, pink in the red country and white in the gray country.

In the water-cut gullies the earth dusted down in dry little streams. Gophers and ant lions started small avalanches. And as the sharp sun struck day after day, the leaves of the young corn became less stiff and erect; they bent in a curve at first, and then, as the central ribs of strength grew weak, each leaf tilted downward. Then it was June, and the sun shone more fiercely. The brown lines on the corn leaves widened and moved in on the central ribs. The weeds frayed and edged back toward their roots. The air was thin and the sky more pale; and every day the earth paled.

In the roads where the teams moved, where the wheels milled the ground and the hooves of the horses beat the ground, the dirt crust broke and the dust formed. Every moving thing lifted the dust into the air; a walking man lifted a thin layer as high as his waist, and a wagon lifted the dust as high as the fence tops, and an automobile boiled a cloud behind it. The dust was long in settling back again.

When June was half gone, the big clouds moved up out of Texas and the Gulf, high heavy clouds, rainheads. The men in the fields looked up at the clouds and sniffed at them and half wet fingers up to sense the wind. And the horses were nervous while the clouds were up. The rainheads dropped a little spattering and hurried on up to some other country. Behind them the sky was pale again and the sun flared. In the dust there were drop craters where the rain had fallen, and there were clean splashes on the corn, and that was all.

A gentle wind followed the rain clouds, driving them on northward, a wind that softly clashed the drying corn. A day went by and the wind increased, steady, unbroken by gusts. The dust from the roads fluffed up and spread out and fell on the weeds beside the fields, and fell into the fields a little way. Now the wind grew strong and hard and it worked at the rain crust in the corn fields. Little by little the sky was darkened by the mixing dust, and the wind felt over the earth, loosened the dust and carried it away. The wind grew stronger. The rain crust broke and the dust lifted up out of the fields and drove gray plumes into the air like sluggish smoke. The corn threshed the wind and made a dry, rushing sound. The finest dust did not settle back to earth now, but disappeared into the darkening sky.

The wind grew stronger, whisked under stones, carried up straws and old leaves, and even little clods, marking its course as it sailed across the fields. The air and the sky darkened and through them the sun shone redly, and there was a raw sting in the air. During a night the wind raced faster over the land, dug cunningly among the rootlets of the corn, and the corn fought the wind with its weakened leaves until the roots were freed by the prying wind and then each stalk settled wearily sideways toward the earth and pointed the direction of the wind.

The dawn came, but no day. In the gray sky a red sun appeared, a dim red circle that gave a little light, like dusk; and as that day advanced, the dusk slipped back toward darkness, and the wind cried and whimpered over the fallen corn.

Men and women huddled in their houses, and they tied handkerchiefs over their noses when they went out, and wore goggles to protect their eyes.

When the night came again it was black night, for the stars could not pierce the dust to get down, and the window lights could not even spread beyond their own yards. Now the dust was evenly mixed with the air, an emulsion of dust and air. Houses were shut tight, and cloth wedged around doors and windows, but the dust came in so thinly that it could not be seen in the air, and it settled like pollen on the chairs and tables, on the dishes. The people brushed it from their shoulders. Little lines of dust lay at the door sills.

In the middle of that night the wind passed on and left the land quiet. The dust-filled air muffled sound more completely than fog does. The people, lying in their beds, heard the wind stop. They awakened when the rushing wind was gone. They lay quietly and listened deep into the stillness. Then the roosters crowed, and their voices were muffled, and the people stirred restlessly in their beds and wanted the morning. They knew it would take a long time for the dust to settle out of the air. In the morning the dust hung like fog, and the sun was as red as ripe new blood. All day the dust sifted down from the sky, and the next day it sifted down. An even blanket covered the earth. It settled on the corn, piled up on the tops of the fence posts, piled up on the wires; it settled on roofs, blanketed the weeds and trees.

The people came out of their houses and smelled the hot stinging air and covered their noses from it. And the children came out of the houses, but they did not run or shout as they would have done after a rain. Men stood by their fences and looked at the ruined corn, drying fast now, only a little green showing through the film of dust. The men were silent and they did not move often. And the women came out of the houses to stand beside their men—to feel whether this time the men would break. The women studied the men's faces secretly, for the corn could go, as long as something else remained. The children stood near by, drawing figures in the dust with bare toes, and the children sent exploring senses out to see whether men and women would break. The children pecked at the faces of the men and women, and then drew careful lines in the dust with their toes. Horses came to the watering troughs and nuzzled the water to clear the surface dust. After a while the faces of the watching men lost their bemused perplexity and became hard and angry and resistant. Then the women knew that they were safe and there was no break. Then they asked, What'll we do? And the men replied, I don't know. But it was all right. The women knew it was all right, and the watching children knew it was all right. Women and children knew deep in themselves that no misfortune was too great to bear if their men were whole. The women went into the houses to their work and the children began to play, but cautiously at first. As the day went forward the sun became less red. It flared down on the dust-blanketed land. The men sat in the doorways of their houses; their hands were busy with sticks and little rocks. The men sat still—thinking—figuring.

1. The characters in the above passage are concerned with what natural phenomenon?

   (A) Storms
   (B) Drought
   (C) Animal death
   (D) Poverty
   (E) Eclipse

2. An image or images which appear(s) throughout the passage are

   (A) dust
   (B) redness
   (C) clouds
   (D) wind
   (E) all of the above

3. The tone of the passage is

   (A) journalistic
   (B) textbook-like
   (C) novelistic
   (D) biblical
   (E) ominous

4. The attitude of the passage is

   (A) optomistic
   (B) pessimistic
   (C) neutral
   (D) concilliatory
   (E) hateful

5. The image of the men in the doorway at the end is most likely meant to inspire

   (A) hope
   (B) despair
   (C) ridicule
   (D) anger
   (E) love

6. The phrase "[t]he dawn came but no day" means

   (A) there was an eclipse
   (B) the sun rose but no light could be seen
   (C) the sun was clear in the morning, but became
        more clouded by noon
   (D) the day was blotted out by fog
   (E) the smoke from the fires covered up the sun

7. This passage would be most appropriate as

   (A) the opening to a novel
   (B) the closing of a novel
   (C) the opening of a short story
   (D) the closing of a short story
   (E) an entire short story

8. Which of the following is given human attributes
   throughout the passage?

   (A) The clouds
   (B) The corn
   (C) The weeds
   (D) The wind
   (E) All of the above

9. The term "rainheads" as used in the passage means

   (A) people who keep looking for signs of rain
   (B) Gulf weather
   (C) heavy clouds
   (D) light sprinkling
   (E) dust which settles before rain

10. The dust settling like "pollen" in the houses is meant to
    be

    (A) a painful and ironic reminder of the land's
         infertility
    (B) a promise of a more fruitful future when the dust
         will pass
    (C) a powerful symbol of the possibilities of life in
         the house, but not out of the house
    (D) a brutal, killing gesture destroying all hope for the
         future
    (E) All of the above

READING RACETRACK #16 METERS

For directions on how to fill out your meters, see page 198.

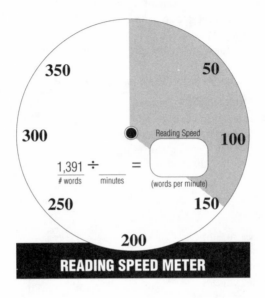

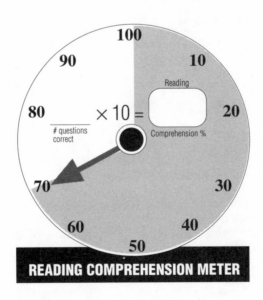

READING RACETRACK #17

Read the following passage and answer the questions after it to find your speed and comprehension levels. Time yourself on a watch with a second hand. Time only the reading portion of the exercise, not the question portion. Then calculate your reading speed and comprehension level, using the formulas at the end of the questions.

Kim Il Sung, the North Korean dictator—redeemer to his people, and madman with a bomb to almost everyone else— sits in isolation in his capital, Pyongyang, letting the world guess what he is thinking. He is eighty-one years old and affects the trappings of semiretirement. He wears Panama hats and color-coordinated outfits. He hunts wild boar from a safe distance, with rifles fitted with telescopic sights. He is said to have relinquished the everyday affairs of state to his son and heir, Kim Jong Il, who is fifty-one. All that is missing is a photograph with grandchildren. He is believed to have at least two.

The affectation is deceptive. Forty-eight years after Stalin set Kim IL Sung on his throne, he remains an object of fear, and perhaps never more so than now. This is a considerable achievement for a ruler whose economy is believed to be in such ruin that his people are encouraged to eat just two meals a day. Kim Il Sung inspires fear not only because he may possess one or two nuclear weapons but also because he has made the world believe he would not hesitate to use them. Through the fall and winter, the United States has been trying to get North Korea to allow inspections of seven sites where bombs may be being made. Negotiators have trod warily, first hunting at confrontation and then backing off, the better not to provoke him.

A deal may be near—one in which the North Koreans will allow International Atomic Energy Agency inspectors to visit those seven sites but not two additional sites where inspectors suspect they might find evidence of bomb pro- duction. Satellite surveillance has its limits; the I.A.E.A. is demanding on-site inspections. The North Koreans, in return for complying with terms that they had in fact agreed to in 1985, will win the suspension of the United States-South Korea war games known as Team Spirit, which usually begin in late winter. And, more important, the North Koreans will force the Americans, whom they blame and despise for splitting Korea at the end of the Second World War, to negotiate the future of diplomatic relations between North Korea and the United States directly, and not in tandem with the South Koreans whom the North Koreans dismiss as American puppets.

But those who have watched Kim Il Sung over the years don't expect the crisis to end here. This confrontation with the West, they feel, is just the beginning. There is a growing suspicion that after the North Koreans agree to inspections they will contrive to make the visits difficult, if not impossible. The North Koreans are considered capable of reversing themselves once the inspectors arrive, perhaps barring entry to some of the sites, or maintaining that they never agreed to inspections at the very places specified in the agreement. Kim Il Sung has been waiting a long time for the moment when his powerful enemies—the Americans, in particular— are compelled to accept him as the leader of a nation that matters.

For decades, Kim Il Sung endured as a journalistic chestnut: the lunatic who presided over the world's most bizarre and longest-lasting cult of personality. North Korea was an Orwellian nightmare—a source of stories of a robotic people wearing Kim Il Sung pins, chanting his name, holding up colored placards to generate his likeness along the length of Kim Il Sung Stadium, and extolling the manifold accomplishments of the Great Leader and his son, the Dear Leader. Then the North Koreans would hold the crew of a captured American spy ship for eleven months, as they did after seizing the U.S.S. Pueblo, in 1968; or blow up half the South Korean Cabinet, as they did in 1983, in Rangoon; or blow up a South Korean airliner, as they did in 1987. For a while, at least, the eye-rolling would stop, and people in Washington, Seoul, Tokyo, and every other capital who felt themselves threatened by the angry whims of Kim Il Sung would once again try to determine just who it was they were dealing with.

The task was not easy. Although North Korea has diplomatic relations with more than a hundred countries, it has effectively cut itself off from most of the world. Visitors find their tours and their access tightly limited and closely monitored. Diplomats who have spent years in Pyongyang tell of never visiting a North Korean home, or even having a candid conversation with a North Korean. The word that recurs when they speak of that posting is "irrational." I have never met Kim Il Sung. Though I have been to South Korea many times, I have never been granted permission to visit the North. American journalists visit North Korea on rare occasions; usually, the visit is arranged for a group and coincides with a showcase event, like Kim Il Sung's birthday. He almost never grants these visitors an interview. He spoke with the *New York Times* and the *Washington Post* for the first, and last, time in 1972.

It has been tempting, then, to see Kim Il Sung only in terms of threatening bombast, the vulgarity of his cult, the monuments he has ordered built to preserve his likeness for eternity. But to do that is to underestimate his cunning. Kim Il Sung has always known what he wanted for himself and for the nation he created in his own image. He wanted the powerful countries to come to him, and to treat him and his small nation as an equal. And, because he has been willing to take his nation time and again to the brink of disaster, to risk war with the United States, he has made his enemies dread him. Now, to the world's discomfort and chagrin, he is on the verge of realizing his vainglorious dream.

1. The picture of Kim Il Sung as an uninvolved, relaxed man is, according to the passage

   (A) exaggerated
   (B) accurate
   (C) difficult to belive
   (D) a complete lie
   (E) an enticing image

2. The annual military exercise between South Korea and the United States was known as

   (A) the I.A.E.A.
   (B) the Pyongyang Conflict
   (C) the Wargames
   (D) the Winter Games
   (E) the Team Spirit

3. According to the passage, all of the following are attributed to the North Koreans EXCEPT

   (A) seizing of the U.S.S. Pueblo
   (B) raiding the South Korean border for supplies
   (C) blowing up a South Korean Airliner
   (D) blowing up half the South Korean cabinet
   (E) holding American soldiers captive for eleven months

4. According to the passage, the economic state of affairs in North Korea is considered

(A) dire
(B) recovering
(C) booming
(D) pre-Industrial
(E) industrial

5. Kim Il Sung's attitude toward war can best be described as

(A) cavalier
(B) brinksmanship
(C) reluctance
(D) recalcitrance
(E) silent

6. The author would most likely DISAGREE with which of the following statements:

(A) Kim Il Sung remains a leader worth fearing.
(B) Kim Jong Il is not as powerful as Kim Il Sung.
(C) The on-site nuclear inspections will most likely, under the I.A.E.A., go smoothly.
(D) Kim Il Sung is unlikely to grant another western interview.
(E) Kim Il Sung is a smart, albeit difficult, man.

7. The North Koreans despise the Americans because of

(A) the war like posture the United States has held toward dictatorships
(B) the economic stability of the United States
(C) resentment over the splitting of Korea after WWII
(D) resentment over the colonization of Korea in the 1950s
(E) the growing suspicion over nuclear rearmament.

8. The term "journalistic chestnut," as described in the passage, means

(A) reporter's enigma
(B) investigative riddle
(C) reporter's comestibles
(D) investigative prize
(E) investigative power

9. The tone of the passage can best be described as

    (A) threatening
    (B) jocular
    (C) objective
    (D) warning
    (E) occluding

10. According to the passage, tours to North Korea can be
    best described as

    (A) difficult and unimpressive
    (B) akward and unenlightened
    (C) ignorant and ill-considered
    (D) limited and unrevealing
    (E) enlightening and frightening

READING RACETRACK #17 METERS

For directions on how to fill out your meters, see page 198.

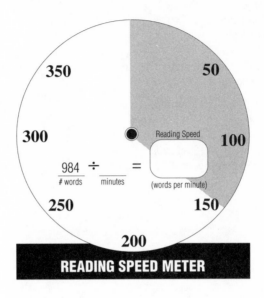

$$\frac{984}{\# \text{ words}} \div \frac{}{\text{minutes}} = \boxed{} \text{ (words per minute)}$$

READING SPEED METER

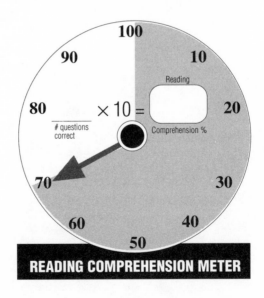

$$\frac{}{\substack{\# \text{ questions} \\ \text{correct}}} \times 10 = \boxed{} \text{ Comprehension \%}$$

READING COMPREHENSION METER

READING RACETRACK #18

Read the following passage and answer the questions after it to find
your   speed and comprehension levels. Time yourself on a watch
with a second hand. Time only the reading portion of the exercise,
not the question portion. Then calculate your reading speed and
comprehension level, using the formulas at the end of the questions.

Reflecting the developments in religion and philosophy, much
Hellenistic culture was cosmopolitan and urbane, although
some was individualistic and specialized. Above all, the
Hellenistic age was a time when Greek culture spread through
much of the inhabited world. It went to Asia, northern Africa,
and eventually to Italy and the West. So firmly did it take
root that it prevailed in Asia until the Arabs swept all before
them in the seventh and eighth centuries A.D. It retained
its dominance in the Byzantine Empire and much of it was
introduced by the Romans into the lands around the western
Mediterranean. There was some reciprocity in the process
because the Greeks learned from the people they conquered;
never, however, did the eastern cultures supplant the Greek.

Hellenistic culture was a modified continuation of the
Hellenic. Its chief characteristics were more individualism,
a greater emphasis on man and nature, less idealism, and
more realism. Knowledge became more specialized. Less
often did thinkers concern themselves with all knowledge,
as did Plato and Aristotle, but rather they concentrated on
some area of knowledge. The most enduring contributions
of Hellenistic culture were made in science, generally by
scientists patronized by the Hellenistic monarchs. In math-
ematics Euclid (c. 300 B.C.) developed geometry which he
explained in his book the *Elements*. Hipparchus (c. 150 B.C.)
invented trigonometry for his measurements of the earth and
his astronomical calculations. He supported the geocentric
theory which triumphed over the heliocentric theory of
Aristarchus of Samos (c. 275 B.C.). Eratosthenes (276-196
B.C.) projected a map of the earth with lines of longitude
and latitude and calculated the circumference of the world
to within two hundred miles of the exact figure. The gifted
Archimedes of Syracuse (287-212 B.C.) discovered specific
gravity, explained the movement of heavenly bodies, and
made marvelous mechanical inventions. He even did elementary calculus and solved the value of *pi*. Stimulated by the
vast conquests and the new lands and peoples they saw, other
thinkers did good work in geography and botany. The excellent achievements in medicine helped to relieve human

suffering, to improve medical care, and to prevent disease. Studying the human anatomy, Herophilus (c. 300 B.C.) identified the functions of the brain and nervous system and showed the role of the arteries in the circulation of blood. In this period the science of physiology began.

Scholarship flourished also in the humanities which were supported by the Hellenistic monarchies, especially the Ptolemaic at Alexandria. Since Greek was the universal language of the Hellenistic age, cultivated scholars studied its construction and wrote grammars on it. Others worked at literary criticism and rhetoric. Great libraries developed at Alexandria, Pergamum, Rhodes and Antioch. In the museum at Alexandria scholars were subsidized by the Ptolemies just to "do scholarship."

Although Hellenistic literature did not rival the excellence achieved in the fifth and fourth centuries B.C., it retained a vitality and the ability to develop new forms and themes for expressing the feeling of men whose sensibilities and tastes had been altered by the changes in politics, economics, science, philosophy, and religion. The poet Callimachus (c. 250 B.C.), for a time head of the library at Alexandria, popularized the short epic dealing with mythological themes not used previously by poets. He engaged in a bitter literary feud with Apollonius of Rhodes (c. 210 B.C.) who adhered to the style of the long Homeric epic and who composed the immensely popular *Argonautica* with its tale of Jason and his quest for the Golden Fleece. Callimachus, after reading this poem, made his famous comment: "A big book, a big evil." The *Argonautica*, however, is still a favorite whereas the short epics of Callimachus have not enjoyed such success. As a protest against the more complex urban life, Theocritus of Sicily (c. third century B.C.) wrote pastoral idylls praising the rural life with its shepherds, flocks, and natural, bucolic scenes. Unfortunately only one complete play and fragments of others by the playwright Menander (342-290 B.C.) are extant, but they show that he created a new form of comedy and was a worth continuator of Aristophanes. Menander portrayed life and its manners rather than some general incident or theme. His insights into ordinary people and his reflections on life are indicative of the realism and cynicism that, in contrast to the Hellenic period, pervaded the Hellenistic Age. His observations, "We live not as we will, but as we can," reveals the contemporary view of life. Menander became a model for later Roman comedy and inspired the comedies of Moliere in the seventeenth century.

There was no history in the Hellenistic age to equal that of Herodotus or Thucydides, but the *Histories* of Polybius (205-125 B.C.) who wrote about Rome from 266 to 146 B.C.

has been acknowledged in all ages as great history. Originally a Greek politician, Polybius became a prisoner of the Romans in 168 B.C. and was taken to Rome. There he soon became a friend of cultivated Romans, among them the general, Scipio Africanus. The perspective of Polybius was later widened by visits to lands overseas under Roman rule. He became an enthusiastic admirer of Rome and decided to write a history that would attempt to explain why the Romans became the masters of the Mediterranean world in fifty-three years. Like Thucydides, Polybius was not content merely to describe historical events; he wanted to know why events occurred. His analysis of why Rome was so successful in politics and military affairs is still largely accepted by historians. His theory that history moves in cycles has long influenced historians interested in the rise and decline of states and civilizations.

1. How does the passage characterize Hellenistic culture?

   (A) Individualistic and specialized
   (B) Cosmopolitan and urbane
   (C) Religious and philosphical
   (D) Pastoral and bucolic
   (E) Plebian and choleric

2. All of. the following are characteristic of Hellenistic culture EXCEPT

   (A) a lesser emphasis on man
   (B) a greater emphasis on nature
   (C) a greater degree of individualism
   (D) a lesser degree of idealism
   (E) an enhanced sense of realism

3. Who wrote the *Argonautica*?

   (A) Homer
   (B) Calimachus
   (C) Archimedes
   (D) Apollonius
   (E) Menander

4. According to the passage, all of the following were achievements of Archimedes EXCEPT

   (A) elementary calculus
   (B) advances in geometry
   (C) the discovery of specific gravity
   (D) the invention of mechanical devices
   (E) an explanation of the movement of heavenly
       bodies

5. One of the famous libraries of the Greek civilization was located in

   (A) Pergamum
   (B) Athens
   (C) Sparta
   (D) Luxandra
   (E) Antioch

6. According to the passage, Greek culture spread to all of the following places EXCEPT

   (A) Asia
   (B) the Middle East
   (C) Northern Africa
   (D) Western Europe
   (E) Italy

7. Who wrote the *Histories*?

   (A) Polybius
   (B) Herotodous
   (C) Thucydidies
   (D) Scipio Africanus
   (E) Aesop

8. According to the passage, which best describes the development of knowledge in the Hellenistic era?

   (A) More generalized
   (B) More specialized
   (C) More rational
   (D) More mystical
   (E) Less accurate

9. Which of the following in use today were developed during the Hellenistic era?

   (A) The idea of history as cyclical
   (B) The use of maps for navigation
   (C) The geocentric theory
   (D) All of the above
   (E) None of the above

10. All of the following were Hellenistic figures EXCEPT

   (A) Euclid
   (B) Hipparchus
   (C) Aristotle
   (D) Eratosthenes
   (E) Archimedes of Syracuse

READING RACETRACK #18 METERS

For directions on how to fill out your meters, see page 198.

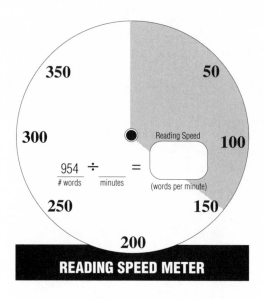

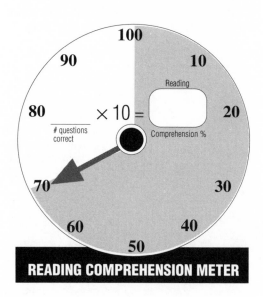

READING RACETRACK #19

Read the following passage and answer the questions after it to find your   speed and comprehension levels. Time yourself on a watch with a second hand. Time only the reading portion of the exercise, not the question portion. Then calculate your reading speed and comprehension level, using the formulas at the end of the questions.

My first evening in Hollywood. It was so typical that I almost thought it had been arranged for me. It was by sheer chance, however, that I found myself rolling up to the home of a millionaire in a handsome black Packard. I had been invited to dinner by a perfect stranger. I didn't even know my host's name. Nor do I know it now.

The first thing which struck me, on being introduced all around, was that I was in the presence of wealthy people, people who were bored to death and who were all, including the octogenarians, already three sheets to the wind. The host and hostess seemed to take pleasure in acting as bartenders. It was hard to follow the conversation because everybody was talking at cross purposes. The important thing was to get an edge on before sitting down to the table. One old geezer who had recently recovered from a horrible automobile accident was having his fifth old fashioned—he was proud of the fact, proud that he could swill it like a youngster even though he was partially crippled. Every one thought he was a marvel.

There wasn't an attractive woman about, except the one who had brought me to the place. The men looked like businessmen, except for one or two who looked like aged strike breakers. There was one fairly young couple, in their thirties, I should say. The husband was a typical go-getter, one of those ex-football players who go in for publicity or insurance or the stock market, some clean all-American pursuit in which you run no risk of soiling your hands. He was a graduate of some Eastern University and had the intelligence of a high-grade chimp.

That was the set-up. When every one had been properly soused dinner was announced. We seated ourselves at a long table, elegantly decorated, with three or four glasses beside each plate. The ice was abundant, of course. The service began, a dozen flunkies buzzing at your elbow like horse flies. There was a surfeit of everything: a poor man would have had sufficient with the hors-d'oeuvres alone. As they ate, they became more discursive, more argumentative. An elderly thug in a tuxedo who had the complexion of a boiled

lobster was railing against labor agitators. He had a religious
train, much to my amazement, but it was more like
Torquemada's than Christ's. President Roosevelt's name almost
gave him an apoplectic fit. Roosevelt, Bridges, Stalin, Hitler—
they were all in the same class to him. That is to say, they
were anathema. He had an extraordinary appetite which served,
it seemed, to stimulate his adrenal glands. By the time he
had reached the meat course he was talking about hanging
being too good for some people. The hostess, meanwhile,
who was seated at his elbow, was carrying on one of those
delightful inconsequential conversations with the person
opposite her. She had left some beautiful dachshunds in Biarritz,
or was it Sierra Leone, and to believe her, she was greatly
worried about them. In times like these, she was saying,
people forget about animals. People can be so cruel, especially
in time of war. Why, in Peking the servants had run away
and left her with forty trunks to pack—it was outrageous.
It was so good to be back in California. God's own country,
she called it. She hoped the war wouldn't spread to America.
Dear me, where was one to go now? You couldn't feel
safe anywhere, except in the desert perhaps.

The ex-football player was talking to someone at the
far end of the table in a loud voice. It happened to be an
Englishwoman and he was insulting her roundly and openly
for daring to arouse sympathy for the English in this country.
"Why don't you go back to England?" he shouted at the
top of his voice. "What are you doing here? You're a menace.
We're not fighting to hold the British Empire together. You're
a menace. You ought to be expelled from the country."

The woman was trying to say that she was not English
but Canadian, but she couldn't make herself heard above
the din. The octogenarian, who was now sampling the
champagne, was talking about the automobile accident. Nobody
was paying any attention to him. Automobile accidents were
too common—everyone at the table had been in a smash-
up at one time or another. One doesn't make a point about
such things unless one is feeble-minded.

The hostess was clapping her hands frantically—she
wanted to tell us a little story about an experience she had
in Africa once, on one of her safaris.

"Oh, can that!" shouted the football player. "I want to
find out why this great country of our, in the most crucial
moment . . ."

"Shut up!" screamed the hostess. "You're drunk."

"That makes no difference," came his booming voice.
"I want to know if we're all hundred percent Americans—
and if not why not. I suspect that we have some traitors
in our midst," and because I hadn't been taking part in any

of the conversation he gave me a fixed, drunken look which was intended to make me declare myself. All I could do was smile.

1. Who says "you couldn't feel safe anywhere, except in the desert perhaps"?

    (A) The author
    (B) The narrator
    (C) The host
    (D) The hostess
    (E) The football player

2. What is the narrator's tone?

    (A) Ironic
    (B) Objective
    (C) Impressed
    (D) Spiteful
    (E) Disapproving

3. When would be the appropriate era for this piece?

    (A) The Spanish Inquisition
    (B) World War II
    (C) Pre-World War II
    (D) Post-World War II
    (E) Vietnam

4. What was a subject of discussion prior to dinner?

    (A) America's entry into the war
    (B) The octagenarian's condition
    (C) Model trains
    (D) Anathema
    (E) The hostess's African safari

5. Why did the football player accuse the narrator of being a traitor?

    (A) The narrator supported Roosevelt.
    (B) The narrator did not support Roosevelt.
    (C) The narrator advocated support for the British.
    (D) The narrator remained silent.
    (E) The football player didn't accuse him.

6. To whom did the octogenarian tell the story of his accident?

(A) The old accident victim
(B) The football player
(C) The football player's wife
(D) The narrator
(E) No one at all

7. According to the passage, the hostess has never travelled to

(A) Biarritz
(B) Africa
(C) Germany
(D) Peking
(E) Sierra Leone

8. What topic "stimulated the adrenal glands" of one of the guests?

(A) Hitler and Stalin
(B) Roosevelt and Bridges
(C) The main course
(D) America's entry into the war
(E) Alcohol

9. How long had the author been in Hollywood on the evening discussed?

(A) He had lived there for over ten years.
(B) He was spending his first night in Hollywood.
(C) He was spending his third night in Hollywood.
(D) He had lived there for one year.
(E) He had lived there for three years.

10. Which of the following best describes the author's attitude toward the other guests?

(A) Comical
(B) Respectful
(C) Dislike
(D) Anathema
(E) Friendly

READING RACETRACK #19 METERS

For directions on how to fill out your meters, see page 198.

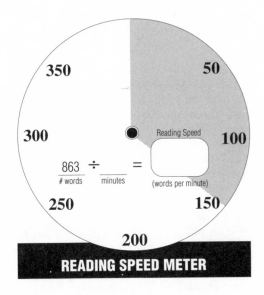

350

50

300

Reading Speed

100

$$\frac{863}{\text{\# words}} \div \underline{\hspace{1cm}} = \boxed{}$$
$$\text{minutes} \qquad \text{(words per minute)}$$

250

150

200

READING SPEED METER

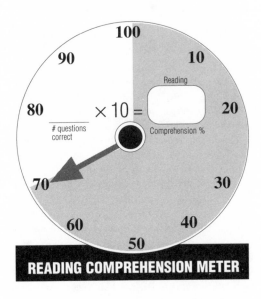

100

90

10

Reading

80

$\times 10 =$

20

questions correct

Comprehension %

70

30

60

40

50

READING COMPREHENSION METER

READING RACETRACK #20

Read the following passage and answer the questions after it to find your   speed and comprehension levels. Time yourself on a watch with a second hand. Time only the reading portion of the exercise, not the question portion. Then calculate your reading speed and comprehension level, using the formulas at the end of the questions.

In another age and time, Walter Mondale might have been a sure bet to win the presidency. The son of a minister and piano teacher, descendant of Norwegian stock, and the anointed heir of Hubert Humphrey, Mondale embodies the midwestern ethos of hard work, compassion, and public service. His political career represented a lifetime of preparation for the nation's highest office. A student leader at Macalester College, he became Humphrey's protégé as attorney general in Minnesota, then moved on to the U.S. Senate to carry forward the New Deal/New Frontier program of liberal democracy. Mondale was bright, he worked hard, and his colleagues respected him. After Jimmy Carter chose him as his running mate in 1976, Mondale became a full partner in the new administration, playing—with Carter's encouragement—an active and daily role in all major decisions. He knew the tensions, the ambiguities, the challenges of the Oval Office better than any person except the president himself. Mondale was ready.

In 1984 the Minnesotan also believed he could win—not easily, to be sure, but if Mondale could draw together the New Deal coalition, add a few allies, and appeal to America's sense of "fairness," maybe he could do it. After all, even Reagan's budget director, David Stockman, had admitted that the Reagan tax program was simply the old Herbert Hoover "trickle-down" theory revisited. If one gave enough to the rich, it would eventually have some impact on the poor. "I mean," Stockman told a reporter," [our proposals were] always a Trojan Horse to bring down the top tax rates." The result, Yale University economist James Tobin noted, was the redistribution of "income, wealth and power—from government to private enterprise, from workers to capitalist, from poor to rich." Mondale believed that the country would reject this "class struggle on behalf of the right."

With equal conviction, Mondale believed that voters favored a relaxation of world tensions. More than 70 percent of all Americans supported a nuclear freeze with the Soviet Union. Three-quarters of a million people had demonstrated in New York City on behalf of such a freeze. Reagan's arms build-up not only fueled out-of-control deficits, it also created the possibility of confrontation with the Soviet Union. As George Kennan wrote in 1983, Soviet-American relations were in a "dreadful and dangerous condition." Reagan's rhetoric, the father of containment wrote, was "childish, inexcusably childish, unworthy of a people charged with responsibility for conducting the affairs of a great power in an endangered world." Whether or not the average citizen would go that far, there seemed ample evidence from the polls that most Americans were deeply disturbed by the possibility of a new Vietnam in Central America and wished for a shift in Soviet-American relations from confrontations to cooperation.

With these concerns as a base, Mondale was convinced that he could put together a coalition that would successfully challenge the president. Political scientists had blamed Democratic failures in the 1970s on the party's inability to retain traditional Democratic constituencies. Now, Mondale sought out these constituencies, going to the AFL-CIO, the National Education Association, civil rights groups, and women's organizations for support. According to public opinion polls, the most significant new political phenomenon in America was the "gender gap." Women differed from men by 10 to 15 points when asked about war and peace, or social justice at home. If he could cultivate the support of groups like the National Organization for Women, go back to the trade unions, and sell his case on fairness at home and relaxation of tensions abroad—then, Mondale believed, he could line up the troops and begin a march to victory.

In this election year, however, even a good idea turned on itself. Critics charged that the former vice-president was *too* subservient to special interest groups. He seemed to *pander* to the unions, the teachers, the blacks. Moreover, he was dull, familiar, too predictable. And then there were the other pursuers of the prize—John Glenn, trying to be his party's answer to Reagan, an all-American hero whose life was about to be memorialized in a new movie; Gary Hart, the young, attractive senator who talked about new ideas, looked like John Kennedy, chopped his right hand like Kennedy, fingered his coat button like Kennedy; Alan Cranston, the nuclear freeze candidate; and Jesse Jackson, the charismatic disciple of Martin Luther King, Jr., who electrified the country with his message. "Our time has come," Jackson announced. "From freedom to equality, from charity to parity . . . from aid to trade, from welfare to our share, from slave ship to championship—our time has come." All these candidates—all preying on Mondale's weaknesses.

By the time the primaries ended and Mondale announced that he finally had enough delegates to guarantee his nomination, it was difficult to know how the "positives" could outrank the "negatives" of the Democratic battle. For a brief moment at the start of the convention, it appeared they might. Upbeat from the start, the convention witnessed a parade of eloquent orators. Mario Cuomo, the Italian-American governor of New York, started it off by celebrating the pride of immigrants who had risen from poverty to middle-class respectability. Jesse Jackson preached to the nation, pleading for love between brothers and sister of all races. Mondale himself rose to the occasion. Knowing he had to act boldly if his party was to have a chance, he chose Geraldine Ferraro to be the first woman ever nominated by a major party for the vice-presidency. The American people seemed to like what they saw. For the first time in more than a year, polls ranked Mondale even with Reagan.

Yet in retrospect, the very idea that anyone could have defeated Ronald Reagan seems bizarre. The economy was booming, inflation was down, America was strong again. In the summer of 1980, before Reagan was first elected, Americans had been held hostage in Iran. United States athletes had boycotted the Moscow Olympics, the economy was paralyzed, and American morale had sunk to its lowest level since the Great Depression. Now all that had changed. Americans swept the gold at the Los Angeles Olympics (helped no small amount by the nonparticipation of Soviet and Eastern European athletes), a new patriotism permeated the body politic, and America had demonstrated its strength—once and for all—in Grenada. Nothing seemed impossible any longer.

1. Which of the following was NOT a reason Mondale believed he could be elected?

   (A) He could use the gender gap to his advantage.
   (B) There was popular support for a nuclear freeze initiative.
   (C) There was a class struggle emerging on behalf of the right.
   (D) The economy was in a boom state.
   (E) He had a multifaceted coalition.

2. What was Mondale's relationship with Carter during the Carter presidency?

   (A) A full partner
   (B) Finessed by Carter
   (C) Involved in only domestic issues
   (D) Involved in only foreign issues
   (E) Informal and uninvolved

3. Which of the following contributed to Mondale's loss?

   (A) Mario Cuomo's electrifying keynote address at the Democratic National Convention
   (B) Jesse Jackson's speech galvanizing a multicultural coalition
   (C) Mondale's choice of Geraldine Ferraro as a running mate
   (D) Mondale's criticism of Reagan's tax policy
   (E) His relationship to special interest groups

4. From whom did Reagan adopt his "trickle-down" economic policy?

   (A) James Tobin
   (B) Herbert Hoover
   (C) George Kennan
   (D) Hubert Humphrey
   (E) Alan Cranston

5. All of the following happened in 1980 EXCEPT

   (A) the American hostages were trapped in Iran
   (B) the U.S. boycotted the Olympic games in Moscow
   (C) terrorists blew up the first British flight to Tel Aviv
   (D) the economy was paralyzed
   (E) American confidence had deteriorated

6. Walter Mondale attended which undergraduate institution?

   (A) Harvard
   (B) Yale
   (C) Stanford
   (D) University of Minnesota
   (E) Macalaster College

7. According to the passage, which of the following was a sign that the American public supported a nuclear freeze initiative?

   (A) Nuclear armaments accounted for 15% of America's annual budget.

   (B) Russia had made overtures to the American public about a nuclear freeze.

   (C) James Tobin, a Yale University economist, supported a nuclear freeze intitative.

   (D) More than forty percent of all Americans supported a nuclear freeze initiative.

   (E) Over 750,000 people protested for a nuclear freeze initiative in New York City.

8. According to the passage, there was significant reason to believe that most Americans were concerned with growing American military involvement in

   (A) the Soviet Union

   (B) Western Europe

   (C) Central America

   (D) South America

   (E) Vietnam

9. The Democratic candidate who "tried to be his party's answer to Reagan" was

   (A) Gary Hart

   (B) Walter Mondale

   (C) John Glenn

   (D) Jesse Jackson

   (E) Alan Cranston

10. Where had America demonstrated its military superiority during Ronald Reagan's first term?

   (A) Yugoslovia

   (B) Vietnam

   (C) The Falkland Islands

   (D) Moscow

   (E) Grenada

READING RACETRACK #20 METERS

For directions on how to fill out your meters, see page 198.

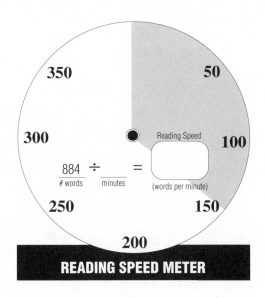

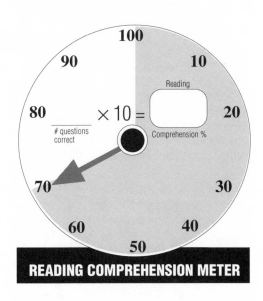

READING RACETRACK #21

Read the following passage and answer the questions after it to find your speed and comprehension levels. Time yourself on a watch with a second hand. Time only the reading portion of the exercise, not the question portion. Then calculate your reading speed and comprehension level, using the formulas at the end of the questions.

Log of the "Demeter"

Varna to Whitby.

Written 18 July, things so strange happening, that I shall keep accurate note henceforth till we land.

On 6 July we finished taking in cargo, silver sand and boxes of earth. At noon set sail. East wind, fresh. Crew, five hands . . . two mates, cook, and myself (captain).

On 12 July through Dardanelles. More Customs officers and flagboat of guarding squadron. Backsheesh again. Work of officers thorough, but quick. Want us off soon. At dark passed into Archipelago.

On 14 July was somewhat anxious about crew. Men all steady fellows, who sailed with me before. Mate could not make out what was wrong; they only told him there was *something*, and crossed themselves. Mate lost temper with one of them that day and struck him. Expected fierce quarrel, but all was quiet.

On 16 July, mate reported in the morning that one of crew, Petrofsky, was missing. Could not account for it. Took larboard watch either bells last night; was relieved by Abramoff, but did not go to bunk. Men more downcast than ever. All said they expected something of the kind, but would not say more than there was *something* aboard. Mate getting very impatient with them, fear some trouble ahead.

On 17 July, yesterday, one of the men, Olgaren, came to my cabin, and in an awestruck way confided to me that he thought there was a strange man aboard the ship. He said that in his watch he had been sheltering behind the deckhouse, as there was a rain-storm, when he saw a tall, thin man, who was not like any of the crew, come up the companion-way, and go along the deck forward, and disappear. He followed cautiously, but when he got to bows he found no one, and the hatchways were all closed. He was in a panic of superstitious fear, and I am afraid the panic may spread. Later in the day I got together the whole crew, and told them, as they evidently thought there was someone in the ship, we would search from stem to stern. First mate angry; said it was folly, and to yield to such foolish ideas would demoralise the men; said he would engage to keep them out of trouble with a handspike. I let him take the helm, while the rest began thorough search, all keeping abreast, with lanterns: we left no corner unsearched. As there were only the big wooden boxes, there were no odd corners where a man could hide. Men much relieved when search over, and went back to work cheerfully. First mate scowled, but said nothing.

22 July.—Rough weather last three days, and all hands busy with sails—no time to be frightened. Men seem to have forgotten their dread. Mate cheerful again, and all on good terms. Praised men for work in bad weather. Passed Gibraltar and out through Straits. All well.

24 July.—There seems some doom over this ship. Already a hand short, and entering on the Bay of Biscay with wild weather ahead, and yet last night another man lost— disappeared. Like the first, he came off his watch and was not seen again. Men all in a panic of fear; sent a round robin, asking to have double watch, as they fear to be alone. Mate angry. Fear there will be some trouble, as either he or the men will do some violence.

28 July.—Four days in hell, knocking about in a sort of maelstrom, and the wind of a tempest. No sleep for anyone. Men all worn out. Hardly know how to set a watch, since no one fit to go on. Second mate volunteered to steer and watch, and let men snatch a few hours' sleep. Wind abating; seas still terrific, but feel them less, as ship is steadier.

29 July.—Another tragedy. Had single watch to-night, as crew too tired to double. When morning watch came on deck could find no one but steersman. Raised outcry, and all came on deck. Thorough search, but no one found. Are now without second mate, and crew in a panic. Mate and I agree to go armed henceforth and wait for any sign of cause.

30 July.—Last night. Rejoiced we are nearing England. Weather fine, all sails set. Retired worn out; slept soundly; awakened by mate telling me that both man of watch and steersman missing. Only self and mate and two hands left to work ship.

1 August.—Two days of fog, and not a sail sighted. Had hoped when in the English Channel to be able to signal for help or get in somewhere. Not having power to work sails, had to run before wind. Dare not lower, as could not raise them again. We seem to be drifting to some terrible doom.

Mate now more demoralised than either of men. His stronger nature seems to have worked inwardly against himself. Men are beyond fear, working stolidly and patiently, with minds made up to worst. They are Russian, he Roumaninan.

3 August.—At midnight I went to relieve the man at the wheel and when I got to it found no one there. The wind was steady, and as we ran before it there was no yawing. I dared not leave it, so shouted for the mate. After a few seconds he rushed up on deck in his flannels. He looked wild-eyed and haggard, and I greatly fear his reason has given way. He came close to my ear, as though fearing the very air might hear: "It is here; I know it, now. On the watch last night I saw It, like a man, tall and thin, and ghastly pale. It was in the bows, and looking out. I crept behind It, and gave It my knife; but the knife went through It, empty as the air." And as he spoke he took his knife and drove it savagely into space. Then he went on: "But It is here, and I'll find It. It is in the hold, perhaps in one of those boxes. I'll unscrew them one by one and see. You work the helm." And, with a warning look and his finger on his lip, he went below. There was springing up a choppy wind, and I could not leave the helm. I saw him come out on deck again with a tool-chest and a lantern, and go down the forward hatchway. He is mad, stark, raving mad, and it's no use my trying to stop him. He can't hurt those big boxes: they are invoiced as "clay," and to pull them about is as harmless a thing as he can do.

It is nearly all over now. Just as I was beginning to hope that the mate would come out calmer—for I heard him knocking away at something in the hold, and work is good for him—there came up the hatchway a sudden, startled scream, which made my blood run cold, and up on the deck he came as if shot from a gun—a raging madman, with his eyes rolling and his face convulsed with fear. "Save me! save me!" he cried, and then looked around on the blanket of fog. His horror turned to despair, and in a steady voice he said: "You had better come too, captain, before it is too late. He is there. I know the secret now. The sea will save me from Him, and it is all that is left!" Before I could say a word, or move forward to seize him, he sprang on the bulwark and deliberately threw himself into the sea. I suppose I know the secret too, now. It was this madman who had got rid of the men one by one, and now he has followed them himself. God help me! How am I to account for all these horrors when I get to port? When I get to port! Will that ever be?

1. The Captain's attitude toward his crew's fears can be described as

   (A) contemptuous
   (B) concerned
   (C) uncaring
   (D) haughty
   (E) amused

2. By the end of the passage, the Captain

   (A) believes in the vampire
   (B) believes the whole crew has committed suicide
   (C) believes the First Mate has murdered the crew
   (D) believes he himself has murdered the crew while he was in a trance
   (E) no longer believes there is a God

3. The name of the ship was

   (A) the Dardanelle
   (B) the Olgaren
   (C) the Mayflower
   (D) the Demeter
   (E) the Persephone

4. Initially, the number of sailors on the ship is

   (A) 4
   (B) 5
   (C) 7
   (D) 9
   (E) 11

5. The first crew member to disappear was

   (A) Olgaren
   (B) Petrofsky
   (C) Biscay
   (D) Demeter
   (E) Dracula

6. The First Mate implies that he knows the creature is supernatural because

(A) he tried to touch it but his hand went right
through it
(B) he tried to shoot it but the bullet went through it
(C) he chased it and it flew away
(D) he tried to stab it but the knife went through it
(E) he saw lightning strike it with no effect

7. The use of capitalization in the First Mate's description of the intruder is used to

(A) indicate the creature is powerful
(B) indicate the creature is foreign
(C) indicate the creature is supernatural
(D) indicate formal respect for the creature
(E) indicate bad grammar skills

8. The "maelstrom" referred to in the entry for July 28th most likely means

(A) calm seas
(B) ship with three masts
(C) fight between two deck hands
(D) nautical graveyard
(E) large open water storm

9. During the course of the passage, the worsening weather and fog can be considered

(A) normal for the route taken by the Demeter
(B) incidental to the events of the passage
(C) common to stories that take place at sea
(D) a metaphor for impending doom
(E) the actual cause of many of the disappearances

10. The passage states that while the rest of the crew is Russian, the First Mate is

(A) English
(B) German
(C) Bulgarian
(D) Roumanian
(E) Transylvanian

READING RACETRACK #21 METERS

For directions on how to fill out your meters, see page 198.

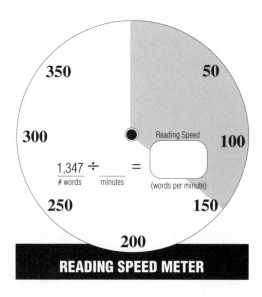

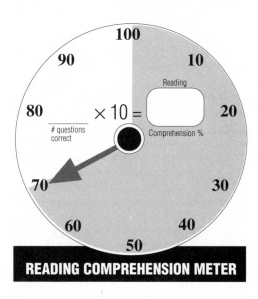

READING RACETRACK #22

Read the following passage and answer the questions after it to find your speed and comprehension levels. Time yourself on a watch with a second hand. Time only the reading portion of the exercise, not the question portion. Then calculate your reading speed and comprehension level, using the formulas at the end of the questions.

Across town the little boy in the sailor suit was suddenly restless and began to measure the length of the porch. He trod with his toe upon the runner of the cane-backed rocking chair. He had reached that age of knowledge and wisdom in a child when it is not expected by the adults around him and consequently goes unrecognized. He read the newspaper daily and was currently following the dispute between the professional baseballers and a scientist who claimed that the curve ball was an optical illusion. He felt that the circumstances of his family's life operated against his need to see things and to go places. For instance he had conceived an enormous interest in the works and career of Harry Houdini, the escape artist. But he had not been taken to a performance. Houdini was a headliner in the top vaudeville circuits. His audiences were poor people—carriers, peddlers, policemen, children. His life was absurd. He went all over the world accepting all kinds of bondage and escaping. He was roped to a chair. He escaped. He was chained to a ladder. He escaped. He was handcuffed, his legs were put in irons, he was tied up in a straight jacket and put in a locked cabinet. He escaped. He escaped from bank vaults, nailed-up barrels, sewn mailbags; he escaped from a zinc-lined Knabe piano case, a giant football, a galvanized iron boiler, a rolltop desk, a sausage skin. His escapes were mystifying because he never damaged or appeared to unlock what he escaped from. The screen was pulled away and there he stood disheveled but triumphant beside the inviolate container that was supposed to have contained him. He waved to the crowd. He escaped from a Siberian exile van. From a Chinese torture crucifix. From a Hamburg penitentiary. From an English prison ship. From a Boston jail. He was chained to automobile tires, water wheels, cannon and he escaped. He dove manacled from a bridge into the Mississippi, the Seine, the Mersey, and came up waving. He hung upside down and straight-jacketed from cranes, biplanes and the tops of buildings. He was dropped into the ocean padlocked in a diving suit fully weighted and not connected to an air supply, and he escaped. He was buried alive in a grave and could not escape, and had to be rescued. Hurriedly, they dug him out. The earth is too heavy, he said gasping. His nails bled. Soil fell from his eyes. He was drained of color and couldn't stand. His assistant threw up. Houdini wheezed and sputtered. He coughed blood. They cleaned him off and took him back to the hotel. Today, nearly fifty years since his death, the audience for escapes is even larger.

The little boy stood at the end of the porch and fixed his gaze on a bluebottle fly traversing the screen in a way that made it appear to be coming up the hill from North Avenue. The fly flew off. An automobile was coming up the hill from North Avenue. As it drew closer he saw it was a black 45-horsepower Pope-Toledo Runabout. He ran along the porch and stood at the top of the steps. The car came past his house, made a loud noise and swerved into the telephone pole. The little boy ran inside and called upstairs to his mother and father. Grandfather woke with a start. The boy ran back to the porch. The driver and the passenger were standing in the street looking at the car: it had big wheels with pneumatic tires and lamps in front of the radiator and brass sidelamps over the fenders. It had tufted upholstery and double side entrances. It did not appear to be damaged. The driver was in livery. He folded back the hood and a geyser of white steam shot up with a hiss.

A number of people looked on from their front yards. But Father, adjusting the chain on his vest, went down to the sidewalk to see if there was something he could do. The car's owner was Harry Houdini, the famous escape artist. He was spending the day driving through Westchester. He was thinking of buying some property. He was invited into the house while the radiator cooled. He surprised them with his modest, almost colorless demeanor. He seemed depressed. His success had brought into vaudeville a host of competitors. Consequently he had to think of more and more dangerous escapes. He was a short, powerfully built man, an athlete obviously, with strong hands and with back and arm muscles that suggested themselves through the cut of his rumpled tweed suit which, though well tailored, was worn this day inappropriately. The thermometer read in the high eighties. Houdini had unruly stiff hair parted in the middle and clear blue eyes, which did not stop moving. He was very respectful to Mother and Father and spoke of his profession with diffidence. This struck them as appropriate. The little boy stared at him. Mother had drank it gratefully. The room was kept cool by the awnings on the windows. The windows themselves were shut to keep out the heat. Houdini wanted to undo his collar. He felt trapped by the heavy square furnishings, the drapes and dark rugs, the chaise with a zebra rug. Noticing Houdini's gaze Father mentioned that he had shot that zebra on a hunting trip in Africa. Father was an amateur explorer of considerable reputation. He was past president of the New York Explorers Club to which he made an annual disbursement. In fact in just a few days he would be leaving to carry the Club's standard on the third Peary expedition to the Arctic. You mean, Houdini said, you're going with Peary to the Pole? God willing, Father replied. He sat back in his chair and lit a cigar. Houdini became voluble. He paced back and forth. He spoke of his own travels, his tours of Europe. But the Pole! he said. Now that's something. You must be pretty good to get picked for that. He turned his eyes on Mother. And keeping the home fires burning ain't so easy either, he said. He was not without charm. He smiled and Mother, a large blond woman, lowered her eyes. Houdini then spent a few minutes doing small deft tricks with objects at hand for the little boy. When he took his leave the entire family saw him to the door. Father and Grandfather shook his hand. Houdini walked down the path that ran under the big maple tree and then descended the stone steps that led to the street. The chauffeur was waiting, the car was parked correctly. Houdini climbed in the seat next to the driver and waved. People stood looking on from their yards. The little boy had followed the magician to the street and now stood at the front of the Pope-Toledo gazing at the distorted macrocephalic image of himself in the shiny brass fitting of the headlight. Houdini thought the boy comely, fair like his mother, and tow-headed, but a little soft-looking. He leaned over the side door. Goodbye, Sonny, he said holding out his hand. Warn the Duke, the little boy said. Then he ran off.

1. The tone of the passage is

    (A) fatalistic
    (B) optimistic
    (C) poetic
    (D) novelistic
    (E) journalistic

2. Houdini's manner in the little boy's house can best be described as

   (A) manic
   (B) forgetful
   (C) joyous
   (D) pleasant
   (E) mean

3. According to the passage, Houdini escaped from all of the following EXCEPT

   (A) a piano case
   (B) a milk can
   (C) a mail bag
   (D) a bank vault
   (E) a giant football

4. According to the passage, why were Houdini's escapes so mystifying?

   (A) He chose one more dangerous stunt after another.
   (B) He escaped from situations previously thought inescapable.
   (C) He never damaged the thing he escaped from.
   (D) He was muscular and clumsy.
   (E) His asthma should have prevented him from pursuing escapology as a career.

5. The dispute the boy follows in the newspaper is primarily one of

   (A) sports
   (B) fashion
   (C) history
   (D) current events
   (E) entertainment

6. The passage intends to link the image of the boy with the image of

   (A) his grandfather
   (B) his father
   (C) Harry Houdini
   (D) his mother
   (E) None of the above

7. Upon entering their home, Houdini's mood is

   (A) entertaining
   (B) jovial
   (C) somber
   (D) sinister
   (E) relaxed

8. Which of the following, if true, would most alter the portrait of Houdini presented in the passage?

   (A) Houdini died as a result of injuries sustained during a dangerous escape.
   (B) Houdini gave generously of his money to charities and old age homes.
   (C) Houdini took long vacations by himself to write his autobiography.
   (D) Houdini performed a special escape for the orphanage of St. Jude.
   (E) Houdini went with Peary on a fourth expedition to the North Pole the following year.

9. What detail or details impresses on the reader the idea that the child wants to leave home?

   (A) The child wears a sailor suit.
   (B) The child is fascinated by Houdini.
   (C) The child is interested in the newspaper.
   (D) The child stares at the fly which leaves the house.
   (E) All of the above

10. Why does the author use the word "inappropriate" to describe Houdini's suit?

   (A) Because tweed was unfashionable at that time in that place.
   (B) Because tweed is heavy and the weather is hot.
   (C) Because tweed is associated with professors, and Houdini is an entertainer.
   (D) Because tweed was not worn before dinner.
   (E) Because his suit did not fit properly.

READING RACETRACK #22 METERS

For directions on how to fill out your meters, see page 198.

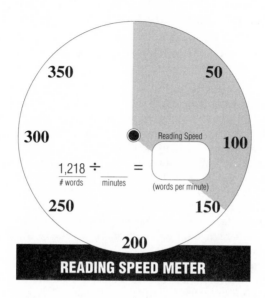

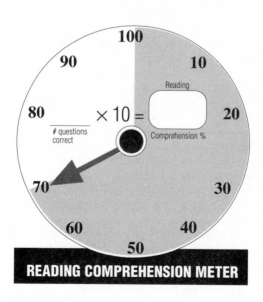

READING RACETRACK #23

Read the following passage and answer the questions after it to find your speed and comprehension levels. Time yourself on a watch with a second hand. Time only the reading portion of the exercise, not the question portion. Then calculate your reading speed and comprehension level, using the formulas at the end of the questions.

Joaquín Hinostroza Bellmont, who was destined to bring stadium crowds to their feet, not by making goals or blocking penalty kicks but by making memorable decisions as a referee at soccer matches, and whose thirst for alcohol was to leave traces and debts in many a Lima bar, was born in one of those residences that mandarins had built for them thirty years ago, in La Perla, with the aim of turning that vast empty tract of land into the Copacabana of Lima (an aim that miscarried due to the dampness, which—punishment of the camel that stubbornly insists on passing through the eye of the needle—ravaged the throats and bronchia of the Peruvian aristocracy).

Joaquín was the only son of a family that, in addition to being wealthy, had ties (a dense forest of trees whose intertwining branches are titles and coats of arms) with the blue bloods of Spain and France. But the father of the future referee and drunkard had put patents of nobility aside and devoted his life to the modern ideal of multiplying his fortune many times over, in business enterprises that ranged from the manufacture of fine woolen textiles to the introduction of the cultivation of hot peppers as a cash crop in the Amazon region. The mother, a lymphatic madonna, a self-abnegating spouse, had spent her life paying out the money her husband made to doctors and healers (for she suffered from a number of diseases common to the upper class of society). The two of them had had Joaquín rather late in life, after having long prayed to God to give them an heir. His birth brought indescribable happiness to his parents, who, from his cradle days, dreamed of a future for him as a prince of industry, a king of agriculture, a magus of diplomacy, or a Lucifer of politics.

Was it out of rebellion, a stubborn refusal to accept this radiant social and charmatistic glory to which he was destined, that the child became a soccer referee, or was it due to some psychological shortcoming? No, it was the result of genuine vocation. From his last baby bottle to the first fuzz on his upper lip he had, naturally, any number of governesses, imported from foreign countries: France, England. And teachers at the best private schools in Lima were recruited to teach him numbers and his ABC's. One after the other, all of them ended up giving their fat salary, demoralized and hysterical in the face of the little boy's ontological indifference toward any sort of knowledge. At the age of eight he hadn't yet learned to add, and, as for the alphabet, was still learning, with the greatest difficulty, to recite the vowels. He spoke only in monosyllables, was a quiet child who never misbehaved, and wandered from one room to the other of the mansion in La Perla, amid the countless toys imported from every corner of the globe to amuse him—German Meccano sets, Japanese trains, Chinese puzzles, Austrian tin soldiers, North American tricycles—looking as though he were bored to death. The one thing that seemed to bring him out of his Brahmanic torpor from time to time were the little cards with pictures of soccer players that came with boxes of Mar del Sur chocolates; he would paste them in fancy albums and spent hours on end looking at them with great interest.

Terrified at the idea that they had brought into this world an offspring who was the product of too rigid inbreeding, a hemophiliac and mentally defective, doomed to become a public laughingstock, the parents sought the aid of science. A series of illustrious disciples of Aesculapius were summoned to La Perla.

It was the city's number-one pediatrician, Dr. Alberto de Quinteros, the star of his profession, who shed the dazzling light of his knowledge on the boy's case and opened his tormented parents' eyes. "He is suffering from what I call the hothouse malady," he explained. "Plants that don't grow outside in a garden, amid flowers and insects, become sickly and produce blossoms whose scent is nauseating. This child's gilded cage is making an imbecile of him. All his governesses and tutors should be dismissed and he should be enrolled in a school where he can associate with boys his own age. He'll be normal the day one of his schoolmates punches him in the nose!"

Prepared to make any and every sacrifice to decretinize him, the haughty couple agreed to allow Joaquincito to plunge into the plebeian outside world. The school they chose for him was, naturally, the most expensive one in Lima, that of the Padres de Santa Maria, and in order not to destroy all hierarchical distinctions, they had a school uniform made for him in the regulation colors, but in velvet.

1. The main character's occupation (while living) was that of a(n)

   (A) tutor
   (B) author
   (C) teacher
   (D) psychiatrist
   (E) referee

2. The tone of the passage can be described as

   (A) overemotional and rageful
   (B) sympathetic and serious
   (C) comic and sarcastic
   (D) jocular and self-abnegating
   (E) magical and surreal

3. The main character's father was primarily

   (A) a nobleman
   (B) a politician
   (C) a referee
   (D) a businessman
   (E) a psychiatrist

4. It is implied that the illness of the mother is

   (A) infectious
   (B) fatal
   (C) rare and potentially life-threatening
   (D) imagined
   (E) chronic

5. The "Brahmanic torpor" referred to in the passage can best be described as

   (A) a zombie-like state
   (B) a hyperactive irreverence
   (C) a self-satisfied smugness
   (D) a childish eclecticness
   (E) a chemical deficiency

6. The physician who sheds light on the condition of young
   Joaquín is named

   (A) Dr. Perla
   (B) Dr. Hinostroza
   (C) Dr. Mar del Sur
   (D) Dr. Quinteros
   (E) Dr. Quinones

7. The main reason the character chooses the profession he
   chooses is because

   (A) his parents force him into it
   (B) to rebel against his parents
   (C) to be more like a common person
   (D) because it is his natural inclination
   (E) because it is the most unlikely occupation he
       could think of

8. Which detail is an indication of his parents' reluctance to
   allow him into the common world?

   (A) His parents hoped he would be a "Lucifer of
       politics."
   (B) His school uniform was made of velvet.
   (C) He was the only son of the family.
   (D) He was given foreign toys as a child.
   (E) He had not learned to read by the age of eight.

9. The country this piece takes place in is

   (A) Argentina
   (B) Peru
   (C) France
   (D) England
   (E) Spain

10. It is implied from the passage that the main character
    suffered from

    (A) kleptomania
    (B) dipsomania
    (C) agoraphobia
    (D) egomania
    (E) auriphobia

READING RACETRACK #23 METERS

For directions on how to fill out your meters, see page 198.

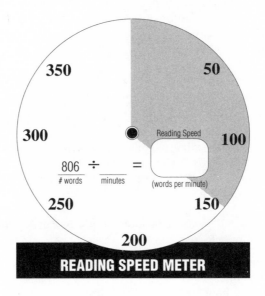

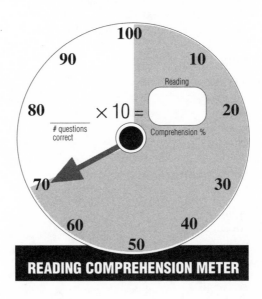

READING RACETRACK #24

Read the following passage and answer the questions after it to find your speed and comprehension levels. Time yourself on a watch with a second hand. Time only the reading portion of the exercise, not the question portion. Then calculate your reading speed and comprehension level, using the formulas at the end of the questions.

I define myself in this way: I am the son of Thomas Patrick McLean of Savannah, Georgia, a volatile brawling man who attended Benedictine High School and Carolina Military Institute, and as a Marine captain won a Navy Cross for his valor under fire during the invasion of Iwo Jima. He returned to Savannah as a wounded hero in 1944, went to work for Belk's department store, and married a girl from Dahlonega, Georgia, who worked in the perfume department after a brief stint in notions. I liked neither the Corps nor Belk's nor my father, but grew up worshipping the black-haired woman from the perfume department. My mother blamed my father's temper on Iwo Jima, but I entertained the heretical thought that he was a son of a bitch long before the Japanese invaded Pearl Harbor. When he was dying of cancer, he made me promise to attend and graduate from Carolina Military Institute, and through tears, I promised. He told me to stop crying and act like a man and I did. Then he made me promise I would be a pilot when I entered the service, that he didn't want any son of his getting killed on some godforsaken beach like Iwo Jima, especially a son he loved as much as he did me. Eight hours after he told me he loved me for the first time, he died of melanoma and left me a prisoner of his memory. At age fourteen, I was the man of the house.

My mother is a different case. As lovely a woman as I have ever seen, bred and nurtured like a gardenia, she has always seemed somehow odorless and sexless to me, yet viscerally seductive in the manner of Southern women, that taloned species who speak with restrained and self-effacing drawls, fill a room with elegance and vulnerability, move with the grace of wind-tilted cane, and rule their families with a secret pact of steel. The sweetness of Southern women often conceals the secret deadliness of snakes. It has helped them survive the impervious tyranny of Southern men more comfortable with a myth than a flesh-and-blood woman.

It took me years to spot the howitzers in my mother's eyes and many more to understand why they were there. Because of my father, my childhood was a long march of fear; my mother's dispassionate assent to his authority took me longer to discover. She won my everlasting love by wading fearlessly into battle with my father whenever he abused me. For years I looked at her uncritically. But I learned something in my long earnest study of my mother. The adversary who is truly formidable is the one who works within the fortress wall, singing pleasant songs while licking honey off knives. It was my mother who encouraged me to keep my promise to attend the Institute. It was my mother who made me stay. Because she was a Southern wife, my domination by things totalitarian did not end when my father died, weighing one hundred pounds less than he had in his prime. Her severity was soft, but severity nonetheless, for she was a product of the South as much as I was. My father's discipline was harsh and unmistakable; the discipline of my mother disguised itself in love and tenderness and often held far greater terrors. I am always writing revisionist histories of my mother. But because I needed to love her and love her deeply, her strafing runs against me brought on surrender almost immediately. I was all white flags and trembling fingers signing treaties and giving up territories to her. She, a Southern lady, had raised me to be a Southern gentleman, and that made us both foreigners in my father's house. In the lock step of my nineteenth year I entered Carolina Military Institute. I did it because of my mother. She and I agreed it was because of my father. A lifetime of practice had taught us to blame everything on him. My father had become the manager of Belk's, but he never could lure me from behind the perfume counter.

But in the end, the Institute was my choice and my responsibility. It, too, became part of my definition. My instincts were those of sheep, lemmings, and herring. I trundled along with the herd on the course of least resistance. My parents had trained me exquisitely in the fine art of obedience. Because I was Southern, the military school seemed like the place for a final honing, the polishing of the rough spots. I would emerge glossy and shiny from the Institute as a man to serve my country in any way I could, but with absolute devotion and forthrightness. A Southern man is incomplete without a tenure under military rule. I am not an incomplete Southern man. I am simply damaged goods, like all the rest of them.

At first, I thought I had wasted my college years, but I was wrong. The Institute was the most valuable experience I have ever had or will have. I believe it did bring me into manhood: The Institute taught me about the kind of man I did not want to be. Through rigorous harshness, I became soft and learned to trust that softness. Through the distorted vision of that long schizophrenia, I became clear-sighted. Under its system, a guerrilla was born inside me, and when the other boys rushed to embrace the cannons of the Institute, I took to the hills.

Whenever I look at photographs of myself in the cadet days, I stare into the immobile face of a stranger. His name is mine and his face seems distantly related, but I cannot reconcile the look of him. The frozen, unconvincing smile is an expression of almost incomprehensible melancholy. I feel compassion and unspeakable love for this thin, fearful ancestor. I honor the courage he did not know he possessed. For four years he was afraid. Yet he remained. A lifetime in a Southern family negated any possibility that he could resign from the school under any conditions other than unequivocal disgrace. Yet I know what he did and what he said, how he felt and how he survived. I relive his journey in dreams and nightmares and in returns to the city of Charleston. He haunts me and remains a stranger.

1. How does the narrator characterize his experience at the Institute?

   (A) Horrible and disastrous
   (B) Honest and true
   (C) Valuable and scarring
   (D) Familial and honest
   (E) Instructive and pleasant

2. The tone of the passage is

   (A) pained and recollective
   (B) timorous and nervous
   (C) confident and controlled
   (D) unhappy and lachrymose
   (E) military and precise

3. In the narrator's family, the most powerful member was

   (A) the father
   (B) the mother
   (C) the narrator
   (D) the sister
   (E) It is not mentioned in the passage

4. According to the passage, a Southern gentleman

    (A) wears traditional Southern attire
    (B) owns a plantation
    (C) goes to West Point
    (D) defers to women
    (E) drinks a lot of lemonade

5. The primary reason the narrator attended Carolina Military Institute was because of

    (A) his father's dying wish
    (B) his mother's insistence
    (C) his own desire to be a Southern gentleman
    (D) he was drafted into the army
    (E) he was the man of the house

6. What did the narrator's father die of?

    (A) Wounds from Iwo Jima
    (B) A fight in Dahlonega, Georgia
    (C) Wounds from pearl harbor
    (D) Melanoma
    (E) Perotinia

7. The narrator's reaction to his own photograph is best described as

    (A) hatred
    (B) unfamiliarity
    (C) fear
    (D) disgust
    (E) love

8. According to the passage, a Southern man is incomplete without

    (A) a taloned wife
    (B) a time in the military
    (C) a domineering father
    (D) a house in Savannah
    (E) love for your mother

9. The narrator chooses the animals to identify himself with because of their

   (A) ability to survive under harsh conditions
   (B) desire to take care of their own
   (C) willingness to blindly let others lead them
   (D) delicacy on the dinner table
   (E) longevity

10. According to the passage, the term "lock step" means

   (A) a time of rebellion
   (B) a time of obeisence
   (C) a time of obesity
   (D) a time of obscurity
   (E) a time of obliqueness

Reading Racetrack #24 Meters

For directions on how to fill out your meters, see page 198.

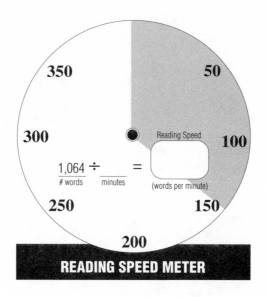

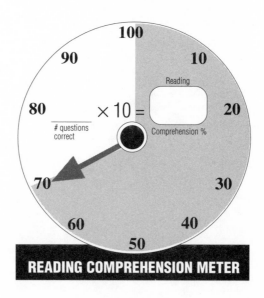

Reading Racetrack Answers

READING RACETRACK #1

1. D
2. D
3. C
4. E
5. A
6. D
7. E
8. C
9. E
10. A

READING RACETRACK #2

1. D
2. D
3. B
4. E
5. C
6. C
7. C
8. C
9. C
10. D

READING RACETRACK #3

1. D
2. A
3. A
4. E
5. B
6. D
7. A
8. B
9. E
10. E

READING RACETRACK #4

1. A
2. A
3. C
4. D
5. E
6. D
7. E
8. A
9. B
10. E

READING RACETRACK #5

1. E
2. A
3. E
4. D
5. B
6. E
7. E
8. A
9. E
10. D

READING RACETRACK #6

1. D
2. B
3. A
4. C
5. D
6. D
7. B
8. D
9. E
10. A

READING RACETRACK #7

1. D
2. D
3. B
4. D
5. D
6. A
7. A
8. B
9. D
10. D

READING RACETRACK #8

1. A
2. D
3. E
4. C
5. B
6. D
7. D
8. A
9. B
10. D

READING RACETRACK #9

1. D
2. A
3. D
4. E
5. A
6. A
7. C
8. C
9. E
10. D

READING RACETRACK #10

1. C
2. A
3. A
4. C
5. A
6. D
7. E
8. B
9. C
10. E

READING RACETRACK #11

1. E
2. B
3. B
4. D
5. D
6. E
7. ?
8. B
9. A
10. D

READING RACETRACK #12

1. E
2. E
3. C
4. D
5. A
6. B
7. A
8. B
9. E
10. A

READING RACETRACK #13

1. B
2. D
3. A
4. E
5. B
6. C
7. E
8. D
9. A
10. C

READING RACETRACK #14

1. A
2. E
3. E
4. D
5. A
6. B
7. C
8. D
9. E
10. A

READING RACETRACK #15

1. D
2. B
3. E
4. E
5. D
6. A
7. D
8. B
9. A
10. B

READING RACETRACK #16

1. B
2. E
3. D
4. B
5. B
6. B
7. A
8. E
9. D
10. A

READING RACETRACK #17

1. C
2. E
3. B
4. A
5. B
6. C
7. C
8. D
9. D
10. D

READING RACETRACK #18

1. B
2. A
3. D
4. B
5. E
6. B
7. A
8. B
9. D
10. C

READING RACETRACK #19

1. D
2. A
3. B
4. B
5. D
6. E
7. C
8. C
9. B
10. C

READING RACETRACK #20

1. D
2. A
3. E
4. B
5. C
6. E
7. E
8. C
9. C
10. E

READING RACETRACK #21

1. B
2. C
3. D
4. D
5. B
6. D
7. C
8. E
9. D
10. D

READING RACETRACK #22

1. D
2. D
3. B
4. C
5. A
6. E
7. C
8. C
9. E
10. B

READING RACETRACK #23

1. E
2. C
3. D
4. D
5. A
6. D
7. D
8. B
9. B
10. B

READING RACETRACK #24

1. C
2. A
3. B
4. E
5. B
6. D
7. B
8. B
9. C
10. B

Exercise Answers

EXERCISE #1

1. Fast
2. Medium
3. Fast
4. Medium
5. Slow
6. Fast
7. Slow
8. Medium
9. Fast
10. Slow
11. Medium
12. Slow
13. Medium
14. Fast
15. Medium

EXERCISE #6

1. The ball was / on the stairs.

2. My fingers, / stained with nicotine, pointed / to the west.

3. Vincent called / for his sister / after the storm.

4. Albert Einstein / married his cousin / on the sly.

5. Uncle Walvis plays bagpipe music / in the house / too loudy.

6. I like to read / *Catcher in the Rye* / over and over and over / and think about the President.

7. Marva wrapped tape / around her finger / until the digit / turned a delicate vermillion.

8. Vlad is quite / the man about town.

9. In a town like this, / you should go to your house / and stay there after dark.

10. Vampires feast / upon the blood / of the living.

11. Fogerty was / down on the corner, / then out in the street.

12. Uncle Walvis likes / to shout Gaelic curses / at the cars / as they pass.

13. No one believed me / about the alien pods / until it was too late.

14. They come / to your house / while you sleep.

15. The fiends / take over your mind / and teach you / about reading.

16. I liked the Stones in the sixties, / but their new stuff / is for the birds.

17. Dogs in the morning, / cats in the night—/ I like pets / if they don't bite.

18. A sunrise from space / is beautiful / above all things.

19. They bowl in the summer / and skate in the winter.

20. You light up my life / with halogen lamps.

21. Christine fell / down the stairs / but landed on her feet.

EXERCISE #7

Kathy left her address book | on the top | of the coffee maker.

After she noticed it | was missing, she retraced her steps.

Her path took her, | a vice president, | to the mailroom.

In a fit of anger, | she fired everyone.

She called the police | and reported they were all stealing.

Holding her phone, | she gripped the receiver | with claw-like hands.

The police told her | she couldn't prove anything.

They refused her request, | so she wrote the president.

After her anger subsided, | she rehired everyone | and | gave them raises.

It was a bad day | at the office | for Kathy to switch to decaf.

EXERCISE #8

	1	**2**	**3**
1.	intimate	slow	long time
2.	passing	fast	tomorrow
3.	casual	medium	tomorrow
4.	passing	fast	tomorrow
5.	intimate	slow	long time
6.	casual	medium	life
7.	passing	fast	tomorrow
8.	intimate	slow	long time
9.	intimate	med-slow	life
10.	casual	medium	tomorrow
11.	passing	fast	tomorrow
12.	intimate	fast	tomorrow

EXERCISE #9

1. a lock and key
2. a hemisphere
3. the Arctic
4. an atlas
5. kleptomania
6. an assembly line
7. friction
8. a pencil
9. the vocal cords
10. Elvis Presley

EXERCISE #10

1. reaction + heat = good
   reaction + HEAT = bad
   reaction + catalyst = great

2. <u>Nichiren</u>
   Buddhist revivalism

3.

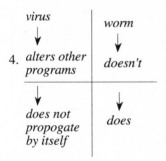

5.   (Tax Reporter)
   ACRS

<u>1</u>	<u>2</u>	<u>3</u>
devalue	*depreciate*	*ignore*
before	*quick if not*	*salvage*
it does	*building*	*value*

EXERCISE #11

Financial Accounting...	*No*
Vietnam...	*Yes*
From Fish to Man...	*Yes*
Russia's Quiet Threat	*Yes*
America the Beautiful	*Yes*
Society...	*No*
Myths of Gender	*Yes*
Why I Kill...	*Yes*
Parents and Children...	*Yes*
The Evolution of...	*No*
Zen and the Art....	*Yes*
Advanced Pascal	*No*
On Becoming a Novelist	*No*
Reading Smart	*No*
Information...	*No*

EXERCISE #12

Primary Facts:

1. Thirty thousand years ago Neanderthal man disappeared.

2. He was replaced by Cro-Magnon man.

3. Cro-Magnon man was physically different from Neanderthal man in his descended larynx, and was slimmer, more agile, and taller.

4. Cro-Magnon man was organizationally different from Neanderthal man in his variety of tasks, more cooperative system of living, and more complicated but sustainable lifestyle and language.

5. Neanderthal man and Cro-Magnon man coexisted for thirty-thousand years but there was no interbreeding.

Exercise #12 (con't)

Secondary Facts:

1. Other mammals have separate airways and esophagi. That is why we (Homo sapiens) are the only creature that can choke to death.

2. Sudden Infant Death Syndrome curiously occurs during the same time period as the descending of the larynx.

3. Neanderthal man was physically incapable of making the /ee/ sound as in "bee" or the /oo/ sound as in "boot."

4. Had Neanderthal man survived, we might have used him as a slave.

5. Basque may be the only surviving remnants of Neanderthal language, as it has no known relationship to other languages and because it also is found around the region of the first cave paintings.

Exercise #14

1. Democrat

2. Republicans

3. • The DNC chairman lives in Chicago and advises the mayor.
   • Mayor Daley's brother William helped Clinton pass the North American Free Trade Agreement.

4. • The Governor of Illinois is a Republican.
   • Chicago has historical significance for the Republicans (14 Republican conventions have been held there.)
   • Illinois will be a key state in the 1996 Presidential race.

5. Cooperative.

6. Money.

7. The fiasco of the 1968 Democratic convention.

Exercise #18

1. Plot

2. Character

3. Character

4. Character

5. Character

6. Character

7. Character

8. Plot

9. Character

10. Setting

Exercise #20

An analysis of *Words*, by Sylvia Plath.

Words are important and powerful ("Axes/After whose stroke the wood rings"), free and indeterminate ("traveling/Off from the center like horses"), but fate ("fixed stars") triumphs over mere words in the end.

Yet words write the poem. They guide us to the "fixed star" of fate.

Think about this poem in context of Sylvia Plath—her art and her life. Arguably the most beautiful language poet of her age—powerful, painful—she was haunted by her inner torment. While words were her whole life, they also weren't enough.

Grateful acknowledgment is made to the following for permission to reprint previously published material:

The Economist: Article from the January 8, 1994 issue of *The Economist*. Copyright © 1994 by The Economist Newspaper Group. Reprinted by permission.

Alfred A. Knopf, Inc.: Excerpt from "Where I'm Calling From" from *Cathedral* by Raymond Carver. Copyright © 1981, 1982, 1983 by Raymond Carver. Excerpt from *The Sportswriter* by Richard Ford © 1986 by Richard Ford. Reprinted by permission.

National Gallery of Art: Excerpt from *The Art of Paul Gaugin*. Reprinted by permission.

The New Yorker: Excerpt from "Kim's Ransom" by Michael Shapiro from the January 31, 1994 issue of *The New Yorker*. Copyright © 1994 by Michael Shapiro. Originally in *The New Yorker*. Excerpt from "Letter From Vietnam: Prisoners of the Past," by Neil Sheehan from the May 24, 1993 issue *of The New Yorker*. Copyright © 1993 by Neil Sheehan. Reprinted by permission.

Penguin Books USA, Inc.: Excerpt from Chapter 1 of *The Grapes of Wrath* by John Steinbeck. Copyright © 1939 and renewed 1967 by John Steinbeck. Reprinted by permission of *Viking Penguin*, a division of *Penguin Books USA Inc.*

Prentice Hall: Excerpt from *The Unofficial Guide to Las Vegas* by Bob Sehlinger. Copyright ©1993 by Bob Sehlinger. Reprinted with permission.

Simon and Schuster: Excerpt from *Wiseguy* by Nicholas Pileggi. Copyright © 1986 by Pileggi Literary Properties. Reprinted by permission of *Simon and Schuster, Inc.*

Van Nostrand Reinhold: Page 176 from *Information Systems Security* by Fites/Krantz. Reprinted by permission.

The Writer, Inc.: Excerpt from *The Writer's Handbook* by Madeleine L'Engle. Copyright © 1990 by Madeleine L'Engle. Reprinted by permission.

Liveright Publishing Corporation: Excerpt from *Complete Poems, 1904-1962* by e.e. cummings. Reprinted by permission.

Wylie, Aitken & Stone, Inc.: Pages 93-95 from *American Art Since 1900* by Barbara Rose. Copyright © 1967 by Frederick A. Praeger, Inc. and Copyright © 1975 by Barbara Stone. Reprinted by permission of *Wylie, Aitken & Stone, Inc.*

Dryden Press: Page 102 and page 375 from *Financial Accounting: An Introduction to Concepts, Methods and Uses, Fifth Edition* by Sidney Davidson, Clyde P. Stickney, and Roman L. Weil. Copyright © by the Dryden Press. Reprinted with permission of the publisher.

Avon Books: Excerpt from *Mother Tongue: English and How It Got That Way* by Bill Bryson. Reprinted by permission of *Avalon Books.*

MacMillan Publishing Company: Excerpt from *The Sun Also Rises* by Ernest Hemingway. Copyright © 1956 by Ernest Hemingway. Reprinted with permission of *MacMillan Publishing Company.*

About The Author

Nick Schaffzin graduated from Stanford in 1990 and is in the Writing Division at Columbia University. He has been teaching and writing for The Princeton Review since 1990.

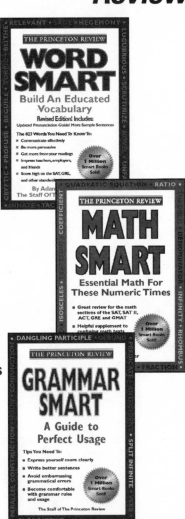